Television Studies

SHORT INTRODUCTIONS

Television Studies

Jonathan Gray and
Amanda D. Lotz

polity

First published in 2012 by Polity Press
Reprinted 2012, 2013, 2014, 2015, 2016, 2017

Polity Press
65 Bridge Street
Cambridge CB2 1UR, UK

Polity Press
350 Main Street
Malden, MA 02148, USA

ISBN-13: 978-0-7456-5098-2
ISBN-13: 978-0-7456-5099-9(pb)

A catalogue record for this book is available from the British Library.

Typeset in 10 on 12 pt Sabon
by Toppan Best-set Premedia Limited
Printed and bound by CPI Group (UK) Ltd, Croydon, CR0 4YY

For further information on Polity, visit our website: www.politybooks.com

Contents

Acknowledgments

In doling out thanks, it may seem odd to start by thanking those who have made the writing of this book all the *harder* a task, but we nevertheless wish to thank all of our many peers and forerunners for making television studies something that is so vibrant, interesting, challenging, diverse, and nuanced that putting it in a short book could never have been and never will be a simple task, for us or for others.

More specifically, we extend heartfelt thanks to some of the field's pioneers and shining lights who at various times walked us through moments in television studies history: Charlotte Brunsdon, John Fiske, Christine Geraghty, Bruce Gronbeck, John Hartley, Henry Jenkins, David Morley, Horace Newcomb, Paddy Scannell, Ellen Seiter, and Lynn Spigel.

Other colleagues and friends who pushed us in helpful directions with criticism and friendly advice include Rob Asen, David Bordwell, Joshua Green, Michele Hilmes, Aswin Punathambekar, and Serra Tinic. Many thanks, too, to Matt Hills and Polity's other reviewer for invaluable comments on the entire manuscript.

Finally, we'd like to thank those who played the biggest roles in introducing each of us to television studies: Horace Newcomb in the case of Amanda, and Nick Couldry and David Morley in the case of Jonathan. We're proud to call these gracious, warm, and brilliant teacher-scholars our mentors and friends. The field has gained so much from their work, but so have we as individuals. We dedicate the book to them, with thanks.

Introduction: Why Television Studies? Why Now?

By the mid 2000s, pronouncements of the death of television were all too common. If various magazine and newspaper stories were to be believed, we'd soon all bin the large square boxes around which we had organized our living rooms (despite having recently upgraded them to hi-def flat screens) and we'd reallocate the seven or so hours a day that we'd supposedly been spending with the box to texting, Tweeting, watching video online, and updating our Facebook status. Those of us who made our living studying television rolled our eyes at this all too familiar pronouncement about our object of study; for years we'd contended with explaining why it was important to study a popular medium such as television. Now that we'd finally convinced many of the significance of this technology that could be found in more US homes than telephones, we were being rhetorically supplanted by "new media" and rendered yet again unimportant.

Despite the dismal pronouncements about television's future, though, we feel fairly certain that, as you read this, streets across the country are not littered with flat black boxes, and it is unlikely that students will need to ask their parents or older siblings to explain what television was. It is certainly the case that this is a particularly dynamic moment in television history around the world. Nevertheless, television continues to be a crucial part of the media landscape in most societies, and it is only just arriving as a major cultural force in many others. Even as the Global

North supposedly whizzes past television to the exciting new possibilities offered by mobile telephony and the internet, usage statistics of such media from the United States to Finland, Australia to the UK, often serve as all too embarrassing a reminder of how many people remain excluded from a future sponsored by Google and Sony Ericsson even in the most wired of nations.

Television, meanwhile, hasn't gone anywhere. Granted, in years gone by, particular *programs* may have held greater sway, as when 82.6% of American television-owning households tuned to *The Ed Sullivan Show* in 1956 to watch Elvis, when 32.3 million Britons tuned in to watch England defeat Germany in the World Cup Final in 1966, or when the *M*A*S*H* finale played to 125 million Americans in 1983. But just as we could hardly announce that sports are dead simply because not everyone is playing football, so too does television remain a force to be reckoned with. Television can still regularly command a nightly broadcast viewing audience of over 100 million in the United States, and while ratings-topping shows such as *American Idol* in the US or *The X Factor* in the UK may "only" have garnered audiences of 20 million (6.5% of the US population) in 2010 and 13 million (20.1% of the UK population) in 2009 respectively, such numbers are still amazing, the populations of Canada, Uganda, or Iraq when the two audiences are combined. Thus, while patterns of use and the screens we use are changing, the need to understand the relationships of television as a business, cultural storyteller, and object of considerable popular interest remains as crucial as ever.

Television may be evolving and a new medium or application seems to catch fancy daily, but this is precisely why it is a good time for a book about television studies. For the most part, television became available in the aftermath of World War II in the late 1940s and early 1950s in the US and Britain (some television existed in Britain before the war). However, the study of television, particularly the specific approaches and norms that we categorize and explore here as *television studies*, is a much newer phenomenon. The next four chapters trace the development of television studies in various traditions from the 1960s through the 1990s – when television studies emerged as an identifiable entity – to the current day. So although television is far from a "new medium," an approach distinguishable as television studies is a fairly recent development.

It is also the case that, despite its name, as an approach for studying media, television studies has and continues to offer a lot to those interested in studying newer media and their role in society. After all, a great deal of content on YouTube is repurposed from television; an increasing amount of television is watched on DVD, streamed over the internet, or otherwise downloaded; Tweets, Facebook status updates, and some of the more active internet forums often respond to television; Facebook still asks all users about their favorite TV shows as one of its lone identity markers; and rather than see an exodus from the business of television by telecommunications companies, we see more attempting to *enter* the field, as when both Verizon and then AT&T recently challenged the regular pack of cable operators in many American markets by offering television service. Television is neither "beating" nor "losing" to new media in some cosmic clash of technology; rather, television is an intrinsic part of "new" media.

Because the boundaries of media are so slippery at the moment, we regard television studies not foremost as a *field* for the study of a singular medium; rather, we see television studies as an *approach* to studying media. The significance of that word choice may not stand out to some readers, but it is deliberate on our part. There remains significant discussion among those who study television about whether it is a "field" of study, although most agree it is not a "discipline," such as psychology or law. Others identify it as an "area of study" within the field of media studies or communication. For our purposes here, the precise term used to categorize television studies isn't all that important. What is significant for explaining what is and isn't included in this book is our supposition that an approach to studying television has been established. Although many books explore key ideas within this approach, few articulate a distinctive entity, even fewer explain how and why it has taken the form it has, and many impoverished and knee-jerk popular, mainstream accounts pontificate explanations of television oblivious to and ignorant of this established tradition of rigorous study. Knowing something about the formation and trajectory of television studies is a way to avoid replicating such accounts and promises a fast track to developing more sophisticated approaches over time. We argue that a particular way of studying television now exists – which we call television studies – and in the following pages we explore the various intellectual, institutional, and sociocultural forces that characterize its distinction.

What television studies?

Here's a bit of a mind-bender: someone can study television and not be doing "television studies," while someone else can also be studying something other than television (like YouTube) and be doing "television studies." In this book, we take the position that, regardless of whether you want to call it a field, in the last twenty years a set of methods and theories has come to be identified as television studies. Thus, television studies is not defined simply by studying television. Psychologists research television in studies that, for instance, examine the relationship between viewing certain content and engaging in violent behavior, and literary scholars examine television in analyses of the themes present in shows such as *The Sopranos*; however, neither typically engage with the range of methods and theories characteristic of television studies. This book does not provide an exhaustive list of the various ways television is studied; rather, it presents an in-depth look at how the approach of television studies developed and the primary areas it has examined. Throughout the book, we use the term "studies of television" to denote approaches outside of those that tend to characterize the mainstream of television studies.

The "mind-bender" of the last paragraph may have slightly overstated the case of television studies being applied to other media. While this does happen in practice, it is not likely the case that someone would describe his or her project as "taking a television studies approach to YouTube." More likely in that case, the researcher would describe the approach as "media studies." In some contexts, particularly outside of the United States, media studies and television studies tend to be used somewhat interchangeably in reference to a consistent approach to study. Thus, television studies seems to be a term that is more prominent in the United States, although it can be found in the work of scholars around the globe. Part of this speaks to the variable history of how the study of television has been institutionalized. Whereas English, psychology, or philosophy departments everywhere tend simply to be called English, psychology, or philosophy departments, television and media studies have grown from a variety of institutional seeds and consequently can be found in a wide array of institutional homes, from radio/television/film to theater and performance studies, and sociology to communication studies. In the United States, there has often been a more contentious relationship between film studies and that which we call television studies, whereas a greater degree of overlap between film and television studies in the UK and some other countries encouraged the use of a broader term, "media studies," even when that term is often conspicuously absent, or combined always with "communication," in the United States. We mention this by way of explaining our use of terms to all readers, and also of the roots from which some US "television studies" scholars have subsequently turned to the study of other media. But we also mention it by way of apologizing to those for whom it seems we are stuffing a bigger topic into the smaller jacket of "television studies."

As we talk of US–UK divides, we should also explain why these two countries and their television systems and scholars hold sway over this book. Part of the reason here is simply personal – we trained in the American (Lotz) and British (Gray) systems, and thus many of our more familiar points of reference are American or British. Another cause results from these countries' early endeavors in television and the fact that these national contexts offered more television to study early on. However, this book's focus on these two systems is also due to their considerable role in the development of television studies. Both countries have produced more scholarship on television from an earlier date than have others, and especially because the two countries' scholars began to cross-germinate ideas at an early stage, each reinforced the other's prominence in the literature. This is not to say that other countries have been absent from the tale of television studies: the Netherlands, the Nordic countries, and Australia in particular have often contributed significantly to the development of television studies, especially given the free flow of ideas and intellectuals between these areas and the US and especially the UK. And while the brand of media analysis conducted in other countries has at times worked in different veins, at other times it has greatly informed trends and paradigm shifts in American and British television studies. Linguistic barriers have limited the easy flow of ideas across other national borders, and have thus – as with many fields of inquiry – allowed Anglophones a position of centrality. Moreover, given the high reputations and funding enjoyed by certain American and British universities, many graduate students from around the world have come to them for training, and have either stayed to work within American–British television studies, or returned to their home countries with an American–British training and frame for their work and pedagogy. For a variety of reasons, then, the US and UK model has enjoyed a certain centrality, and has featured prominently in the history of television studies. That said, an increasing number of scholars are now turning their attention to global and diasporic television and media, exploring parts of the globe that have been absent from television scholarship for far too long. As we tell the story of television studies, therefore, we will be keen to examine ways in which it has of late dealt with its global frontiers.

Hopefully these paragraphs offer enough introduction of our key terms, but we have not yet offered much description of what television studies includes or entails. We continue to expand these ideas in the next section in which we delve into these issues in greater depth by providing an abbreviated history of the development of television studies. We now go back to the 1960s – which really isn't very long ago relative to other fields of study – to trace how and why television studies developed. As you'll see, television studies very much responded to its context,

particularly the sociohistorical milieu of the times and the existing dominant ways of studying and thinking about other media such as newspapers, radio, and film.

A brief genealogy of television studies

Despite attempts by many observers during its history to pin it down as
a single, knowable entity, television is many different things. The medium,
in other words, is not the message, as Marshall McLuhan famously suggested, since the medium is many things to different people, and its
messages are infinite.[1] As such, when scholars, activists, parents, policy-
makers, and watchers began to discuss television, these discussions took
a wide variety of forms and occurred in multiple sites. Here, we may
draw a parallel to "new media." Almost every department on the campus
of a good university will have someone wrestling with ideas of new
media: philosophers may ponder how they change our relationship to
reality or embodiment, women's studies professors may ask about how
gender works online, education departments may study how new media
can be used in classrooms or for other forms of learning, anthropologists
may study nascent forms of community, economists may study new
media regulation and commerce, and so forth. So too did the study of
television spring from multiple seeds, and, just as the current expansion
of new media into all realms of public and private life demands study
from a varied group of special interests, so was television's arrival into
public and private life in the 1940s and 1950s greeted by significant
interest and concern.

Television, like any new invention, entered societies that had established norms of social relations. It also entered societies that had experience with other media and art. Both of these realities figure prominently
in early conceptualizations of television and understanding how and why
television studies developed as it has. A first consideration is that as
television was introduced in the US and UK, it was presented as a popular
form of media that was meant for use in the home – meaning a device
that was supposed to be accessible to people of all ages and classes. This
led people first experiencing television to understand it as much more
like radio, somewhat like film (which targeted broad audiences, but
required one to leave the home), and less like art forms such as the
symphony or theater that are engaged out of the home and more likely
to be accessed by narrower populations of the economically privileged.
But television's positioning as a popular medium – a medium of the
people – was also crucial to how it was understood and studied (or not
studied). The fact that television was a popular medium contributed to

establishing many initial presumed biases against it as being unsophisticated, simplistic, and in the US, crassly commercial.

In addition to being compared with other existing forms of entertainment, leisure, and art, and assessed to be a popular form of media, television was also recognized as a media form with the ability to communicate ideas widely. Thus, understanding why television has been studied in various ways requires acknowledging the history of media study that predated television's arrival. Experience with radio events such as the *War of the Worlds* broadcast and particularly the media propaganda surrounding World War II gave rise to a research paradigm that was focused on investigating media effects. Significant work in this area predated television, and much of what was understood about media effects was quickly applied to television. Meanwhile, generations of humanities instruction in universities and secondary schools had conditioned people to see fiction and art as possibly offering keys to enlightenment, and had thus sought to draw distinctions between accepted, elite culture and the alleged mindlessness of popular narratives that circulated in pulp fiction, comic books, radio plays, and so forth. Yet as exhibited by the oft-cited examples of Shakespeare and Dickens – both popular in their day, yet later "rescued" as elite culture – the supposed hard and fast lines between elite and popular culture are in fact marked by considerable tension. Given television's popularity, the medium quickly became a key battleground for discussions of what constituted "culture."

Various approaches to studying television were heavily influenced by: (1) the cultural and political unrest of the 1960s, which led many to believe in the significance of media in inspiring broad social change or in offering more subtle and complicated, less overt impediments to such change; (2) the earliest ways of studying media, such as newspapers and radio, that focused on explaining the propagandistic dangers of media; and (3) attitudes of disdain toward television as mass culture that were shared by academics and the populace. The significance of the late 1960s cultural revolutions – particularly for the college-aged cohort which was the first that had grown up with television – was impressive enough to outweigh the latter two factors that had led to the previous tendency to disregard television viewing as important, or to believe that it had uniformly negative effects if it was deemed significant at all. As John Hartley notes, television was hated by many academics, and by many in upper middle-class society, even before it existed, as a long tradition of fearing any new popular medium's assault on high culture prefigured a common response to television. Without too much exaggeration, he writes that "the successful student was the one who could catalogue most extensively the supposed evils associated with television, although of course these evils only affected *other* people, possibly because the students were not encouraged to watch TV themselves, only to opine haughtily about it."[2] Thankfully, though, in the wake of the 1960s, a different type of student began to develop alongside the telephobes.

The immediate perception of television as a popular media form and its understanding relative to other preexisting media are contextual features that were largely established before anyone began considering the serious and systematic study of television. Throughout the remainder of this section, we trace how various early approaches to studying television influenced the formation of television studies, as well as the effect of the particular social, historical, and national contexts of these efforts to understand television. We organize the key intellectual influences on television studies broadly as social science approaches, humanities approaches, and cultural studies approaches. In addition to synthesizing their influences here, we return to the specific influences of each in subsequent chapters in discussing how they affected particular objects of television studies.

Social science approaches

The terminology of "social science approaches" is on one hand exceptionally broad; however, as is the case of the companion terminology of "humanities approaches," these monikers prove generally useful in organizing the realm of intellectual approaches to media that predate television. By social science approaches, we mean to indicate the empirical research done in psychology, sociology, and budding communication departments. Overwhelmingly, this research tradition focused on attempting to answer questions about the effects of media or their influence on audiences and societies. Early social science approaches saw television as *a medium of popular communication* in the tradition of radio and, somewhat, newspapers. Attitudes toward and expectations of such pretelevisual media prepared television's introduction; although, for reasons still unclear today, television was quickly regarded with even greater suspicion and disapprobation than its predecessors.

For the sake of brevity, we do not extend as far back historically as is perhaps possible in preparing the development of television studies. This story might begin in the 1930s with the studies of sociologists and psychologists who provide the precursors to the field of communication with their studies of the effects of radio and film.[3] The predominant social science research paradigm in the decades prior to television's arrival sought to prove radio, film, and newspaper to have strong persuasive power over those who used them. As television actually became available, however, the previous flurry of effects studies – much based around the work of Paul Lazarsfeld and Harold Lasswell – slowed as the outcomes of this research showed the media to work in far more complicated ways than early hypotheses assumed.[4] By the time television arrived in the 1950s, social science research moved toward models and theories that presumed media to be less powerful than earlier assumptions; as communication scholar Elihu Katz explains, researchers came to argue "that media content was filtered by interpersonal networks, by individual need, and by selectivity in exposure and perception."[5] Although this research went on both in the US and Britain, particularly with regard to wartime consequences of media, Katz describes this earliest social science research as "surely an American science."[6]

This shift, however, was fairly short-lived as the historical context of the times aided in the reassertion of models presuming more powerful effects.[7] Just as real world experience with the rise of the Nazi Party before World War II led to studies that supposed the powerful propaganda effects of media in the 1940s, the Cold War and context of social upheaval and questioning during the 1960s again led to suspicions that media must be responsible for shifting social attitudes. With regard to the American context, Katz explains, "The beginning of the revival of theory and research on mass communication came in the early 1960s when the black revolt, the youth revolt, women's liberation, the Vietnam War, and ultimately Watergate led to second-thoughts about television."[8] In the UK and Europe, many of these revolts were also under way, though added to them were numerous labor disputes, strikes, and clashes, and, as with the US, the role of television in mediating citizens' understandings of and reactions to such developments was a key concern for all parties. However, rather than focus on the wide range of identity issues at the core of much of this social examination, government funders particularly seized on concerns about the consequences of violence depicted on television. In the late 1960s, in the US, the Commission on the Causes and Prevention of Violence funded at least twenty-five studies with one million dollars, and as Katz explains, "there is no doubt that the pump-priming of the Committee gave new life to media research."[9] In the UK, as Philip Lodge recounts, Home Secretary R. A. Butler found himself under pressure to respond to complaints regarding television's effects on youth delinquency, and thus pushed for a Television Research Committee (TRC), through which the government funded numerous analyses of the medium. Though these studies would range in focus, and would in time reject the solitary interest in youth and crime, a clear trace of the nature of the government's initial concerns remained in the TRC being accountable to the Prison Department of the Home Office.[10]

Some of the most notable influences of this research tradition developed during the late 1960s and 1970s. In the US, George Gerbner became one of the leading social science voices and worked to construct an adequate methodology for examining the consequences of television violence. Founding the Cultural Indicators Research Project, Gerbner, who understood television's force as that of a storyteller, remains best known for his explanation of televised violence's effect as creating "mean world syndrome." Rather than looking for direct and immediate effects, Gerbner's concern was with how the steady diet of crime and violent television led viewers to imagine the world as a more fearful and scarier place, and what the consequences of those fears might be. Gerbner engaged in public discussion of his research and testified before Congress in 1981. Gerbner was particularly concerned about television because of its central role in cultural storytelling and his later work was critical of US television's emphasis on telling stories only of certain types of people and of the consequences of exclusion for others.

A similarly politically motivated research initiative began in the UK during this decade with the founding of the Glasgow University Media Project, which received its early funding from the Social Science Research Council. With their controversial publication of *Bad News* in 1976, a group of media scholars in Glasgow, including Brian Winston, John Eldridge, and Greg Philo among many others, took aim at analyzing television news with a particular focus on its coverage of industrial relations.[11] The question of bias in coverage of the trade unions was particularly controversial at this time, and the coverage by television news became a particular flashpoint because of the public funding of the BBC and its mandate to serve the citizenry. Similarly, commercial television at the time maintained that it offered an unbiased presentation of news, but the analysis of the Glasgow Group indicated the many ways that practices presumed to be standard and objective contributed to perceptions of information that were arguably quite biased. The analysis of the Glasgow Group led to intense debate between researchers and broadcasters that was important in drawing attention to the previously unexamined norms of television news, the constructed nature of "news," and the consequences of news provision that does not interrogate its process and norms.

The importance of the social science approach to studying media is arguably primarily as an influence that television studies responds *against*. Television studies does not take up the quantitative, positivist, and experimental research central in this early social science work, nor does it presume the negative effects of television that led to the government funding that has supported this tradition. Rather, many of television studies' earliest architects were suspicious of the cultural and artistic factors disregarded in this preliminary research and sought to counter the simple story about negative media effects that pontificating legislators and cultural commentators drew from often much more sophisticated and nuanced social science research. Just as television was perceived from its origins with suspicion because of its apparent mass appeal, television was also understood as a bad object because of the social science tradition that had spent years trying to explain media influence.

Nevertheless, one of the primary challenges faced by those who sought to seriously engage in the study of television was legitimating their object of study, and many of television studies' earliest voices have reflected on how helpful the tradition of social science approaches proved in establishing that television was culturally, socially, and politically relevant to the lives of viewers, even if it went about exploring this relevance through different methodological tools.[12] Social science approaches also contributed to the more sociological emphasis that has been far more central to television studies than cinema (although this influence also came from cultural studies), and contributes to the emphasis on a contextual understanding that remains a hallmark of television studies today.

Humanities approaches

Early efforts to understand television that developed from humanities traditions did so with limited interaction with the social sciences. There are arguably two main threads of early television study that emerged from humanities fields prior to television studies: literary studies and film studies. In his history of broadcast research written in the 1970s, Katz reflected that, in the 1960s, "humanities re-entered the field of popular culture via linguistics, and joined with the anthropologists and literary critics who were won over by the new semiology."[13] Such intellectual perspectives were well suited to the study of television – at least for those intrigued by the storytelling of the medium – although justifying critical engagement with a "popular" medium proved more challenging.

The humanistic study of television was also slow to generate, in large part because television was continually subjected to criticism as the "boob tube" or "idiot box." Arguably the most famous statement about television to this day was Federal Communications Commission chair Newton Minow's attack on 1960s American commercial television as "a vast wasteland," filled with mindless, cheap fare. Whereas the humanistic tradition of studying art and literature was deeply rooted in an interest in "the best that has been thought and said," in Matthew Arnold's formation, and in culture that would uplift and enlighten society through providing images of beauty, Minow's and many other critics' attacks on television suggested a medium devoid of anything worth studying as a complex expression.[14] This humanistic tradition held considerable sway over universities, but is all the more evident in high school English classes, wherein *Hamlet, Lord of the Flies, Brave New World*, or the like are examined in depth as important contributions to human thought and as reflections on the human condition. Few saw television's early programs as worthy of similar treatment. Instead, television often played the role of whipping post for humanists who would point to the medium as a sign of the supposed costs for society of abandoning the study of what they asserted as more noble fare: if we gave up teaching Shakespeare to youth, so went the argument, we'd risk wall-to-wall cheap entertainment and would, in Neil Postman's infamous words, "amuse ourselves to death."[15]

Such criticisms still exist today, all too easily trotted out occasionally, and a central reason why television criticism or media literacy are so rarely taught in schools. But their centrality within the humanistic study of art and literature was radically destabilized in the 1960s and 1970s by the rise of critical approaches that went beyond cataloguing or evaluating cultural products' "beauty" or inner truths, and instead focused on how they constructed and/or maintained ideology and ideas of "common sense," beauty, or truth in the first place. A wide range of theories and approaches to the study of culture was added to the humanistic tradition by Marxist critics, critical race and gender studies scholars, psychoanalysis, rhetoric and discourse theories, post-structuralism, and eventually postmodernism. All of these theories opened up new ways to explore television and other media, and new ways of finding deep structures of meaning, many of which were not predicated on an interest in the cultural product as a monument to enlightenment, and several of which explicitly challenged and sought to deconstruct the product's authoritative claims. *Hamlet* was no longer simply a monument to expression and beauty; it could be explored for its gender constructions, for a pronounced enactment of the Oedipal complex, as a resource for discussing attitudes towards madness and/or depression, and so forth. As critical theory transformed what could be done with art, literature, and media, it similarly shifted notions of what was appropriate or inappropriate to study. Television programs, in short, were now definitively open for analysis, and given their popular status, some critics regarded them as *especially* rich for study.

A certain brand of film studies and of "screen theory" was in part born in this moment. If the social sciences tradition risked focusing overmuch on the audience with its examination of media effects in a manner that disregarded the intricacies of the program under analysis, the humanistic tradition often risked fetishizing the program, forgetting contexts of production or reception. The humanistic tradition had long refused to discuss audiences and assumed that a powerful cultural product would have the desired effect – such as of uplift and enlightenment – on its audience. Screen theory – developed in film studies as a way of examining the ideological work of the film, and discussed further in chapter 1 – saw media as creating and disciplining their own audiences, placing the screen above the individuals watching it in significance. Production was also marginalized in importance within screen theory. And finally, screen theory was often fondest of film, whether because film was still a favored art form, and/or because its address to large groups in a darkened room served as a better breeding ground for theories of the screen constructing its own audience, leaving television still sidelined and of lesser importance.

The study of television also emerged within the humanities-based areas of communication, namely rhetorical studies and criticism. However, the classical discipline of rhetoric only truly shifted primary focus away from public address to include the analysis of popular culture in the 1970s, by which point television studies had begun developing in its own right. Thus, while rhetorical analysis certainly preceded television studies – by many hundreds of years – it was less a precursor to the founding of television studies than a contemporary.

Overall, the humanistic tradition developed in some key ways that diverged from what would become television studies by attending closely to art, literature, film, and other cultural products, but eschewing audiences, contexts, and conditions of production. However, television studies' interest in understanding how programs work, how they create meaning, and in developing a series of tools for analyzing everything from a program's words to its images, and from its more explicit meanings to its suggested and implied meanings, all stemmed directly from the humanistic tradition. Some of the early foundations of television studies were published in the mid through late 1970s. Horace Newcomb's *TV: The Most Popular Art* appeared in 1974, as did Raymond Williams's *Television: Technology and Cultural Form*, while John Fiske and John Hartley's *Reading Television* was published in 1978.[16] Many regard these books as the first scholarly monographs on television and as the first defining publications of television studies, although they were written in such a way that they could also reach non-academic audiences. All three examine how television tells its stories and the relationship of those stories to the society that produces and consumes them. Like several others trained in humanities disciplines such as literature and the then-nascent film studies, Newcomb, Williams, Fiske, and Hartley turned to television as an important object of study, and their serious treatment of television as storyteller and mythmaker with great cultural significance helped create a space to engage in intellectual consideration of television.

Cultural studies approaches

A third key seed from which television studies grew, one that Williams had helped nurture, and one that was in full bloom when Newcomb's and Fiske and Hartley's books were published, was planted at the University of Birmingham in England when then Professor of Modern English Literature Richard Hoggart founded the Centre for Contemporary Cultural Studies (CCCS) in 1964. A triumvirate of Hoggart's *Uses of Literacy: Changing Patterns in English Mass Culture* (1957), Raymond Williams's *Culture and Society* (1958), and E. P. Thompson's *The Making of the English Working Class* (1963) had boldly argued against the long-standing tradition of studying elite, "high" culture as the only culture worthy of analysis.[17] Instead, Hoggart founded the CCCS as a site for the examination of popular culture, arguing that culture and the creation of meaning were not restricted to the upper classes alone. As committed neo-Marxists, many within the CCCS shared a concern for the effects of the industrialization of cultural production, and they also showed considerable interest in the media as an apparatus of state control and of maintaining bourgeois, patriarchal culture. Hence, rather than study cultural products ("texts") as works of art from which we should glean as much enlightenment as possible, the CCCS approach sought to explore texts' varying roles within society, especially as purveyors of power. Moreover, the CCCS refused to regard texts as mere "conveyor belts" that unproblematically transferred ideas from producer to consumer, nor did they regard audiences as mere dupes; thus a great deal of their efforts were expended studying exactly how power and ideology worked at the level of the text.

The CCCS is most famous for its work in the 1970s, under the leadership of Stuart Hall, who took over from Hoggart when the latter departed in 1968. This decade was one of continued political crisis in Britain, with racial tensions leading to several prominent riots, with a clash between the government and the National Union of Mineworkers leading to wide-ranging results including a reduction of the working week to three days, and with the rise of numerous subcultures and civil rights groups. The heated battles of the decade were fought not only on the streets of Britain, but also in the media, and most prominently on television. Consequently, the Media Group at the CCCS was formed, largely to examine the media's representations of the multiple clashes, and to better understand the media's relationship to the state and to ideological change or stasis. Of particular interest, too, was how ideas of "common sense" were formed, and, while much of the group's early work examined "hard news" and factual television, it gradually shifted focus to look at the ideological role of popular media more generally, including both factual and fictional television entertainment.

The Media Group's methods were wide ranging, and something of a starting point for what would become television studies' methods. On one hand, continental European work on "semiotics" or "semiology" provided a significant influence with its ideas on how language and images were imbued with meanings that connoted power relations, or in the parlance, performed ideological work. Similarly, work from within film and screen studies influenced the Group's commitment to textual analysis. Yet the group rejected the determinism assumed by film studies, in which audiences, or "subjects," were mere projections from the text, not actual thinking beings. Raymond Williams had also convincingly attacked the notion, in *Television: Technology and Cultural Form*, that any technology could be understood free from the social context that gave it meaning. Hall famously wrote a paper, oft-revised and oft-republished, in which he wrote of "encoding" and "decoding" as two separate, yet equally important moments in the life of any cultural text.[18] After analyzing "encoding" primarily, and textual construction, a great deal of the CCCS's work turned to analyzing the politics of everyday life and moments of "decoding." Rejecting the survey- and number-based approach of social scientists, though, and working in tension against the Glasgow Group – driven by similar politics, yet objecting to Glasgow's methodology – CCCS's work became renowned for a more ethnographic, qualitative method. By 1978, the Media Group had already conducted work examining the text of a popular "soft" news program, *Nationwide*, and followed this with work exploring how audiences, and particularly the working classes, made sense of the show.[19] Charlotte Brunsdon and Dorothy Hobson would later explore the British soap *Crossroads*, also conducting audience analysis.[20] Notably, much of this early work was informed by feminist perspectives and thus, from its origins, television studies made gender and feminist criticism a core component of its analyses. Angela McRobbie examined young girls' understandings of magazines, and Dick Hebdige explored how punk culture refashioned mainstream culture in the production of a thriving subculture.[21] As this selection of topics should suggest, cultural studies scholars also examined the media's relation to nation, class, gender, youth, and race.

Cultural studies work thus came to represent a way to talk about markers of identity, power, and the media, but it also represented a move beyond the humanistic determinism that the text answered all relevant questions, the political economic determinism that the structure of the industry answered all relevant questions, and the reduction of audience behavior to quantifiable effects particularly evident in US social scientific approaches to television. Cultural studies' followers would later be heavily criticized for audience determinism, an accusation to which we will return in chapter 2, but such charges are without grounding if we examine its early days.

In the wake of the CCCS, and of its members' austere careers elsewhere, a particular way of looking at television was institutionalized in England and in other countries that followed suit. The Media Group never focused exclusively on television, though television was the centerpiece for much of their work, and consequently a particularly strong bond formed between cultural studies methodology and television as object of study. As David Morley has also subsequently noted, the impact of the CCCS may be obscured in retrospect precisely by its success:

> It now seems to almost "go without saying" that there is more to the media than questions of economics; that issues of culture, representation and signification are equally important; that we must pay attention not only to questions of class but also of "race," gender and sexuality; that low-status fictional media forms can play just as important a political role as high profile news and current affairs television; and that audiences are evidently not passive dupes or zombies. However, in the early 1970s none of this was widely accepted in the field. If it now seems no more than common sense, this is because cultural studies media work has, over the subsequent period, made it so.[22]

Though television studies is not just cultural studies, much of its method was born at this point.

An origins story

Despite the fact that a bookshelf can be filled with volumes taking *Television Studies* as their title, there are few, if any, coherent intellectual histories of television studies. Most of the received wisdom has been passed along to the graduate students of those who were part of early conferences. What we offer here is an attempt at something more systematic than we've found published to date. We've mined a rich array of articles and chapters that offer drips and drabs of events that retrospectively might be considered as the origins of television studies. The writings provide much of the substance for what we've pieced together, but we've also talked with some about their recollections. Developing an intellectual history of something that still exists uncertainly is a tricky enterprise. Our hope is to offer greater clarity through our synthesis, but we freely admit that this story is only partial and largely interpretive.

It is from the broad influences of the social sciences, humanities, and cultural studies that we find the origins of the distinctive approach we identify as television studies. Admittedly, the influence of the social sciences is primarily to establish an existing approach which television studies responds against. Importantly, this wasn't only about eschewing social science methods but also many of its presumptions of the research enterprise. US television studies scholar Lynn Spigel notes that:

> Perhaps the greatest difference between the traditional mass communications paradigm (through which television was first studied in the 1940s and 1950s) and television studies per se (as it developed in subsequent decades through encounters with literary and film theory, qualitative audience research, media sociology, video collectives such as Paper Tiger, and the advent of cultural studies) is the reflexive turn in which scholarship takes account of its own role in relation to the object and the people who watch TV.[23]

Thus, television studies takes on a specific television – particular shows and genres, not an abstract television, as in the "television" invoked in concerns that "television will rot your mind," and it also willingly implicates its researcher as someone who watches television. Though seemingly basic now, in the 1970s it was no simple task to convince academics that, in order to study television properly, they must watch it.

Reflecting on how television studies emerged, British television scholar Charlotte Brunsdon argues: "There have been two prerequisites for the development of the primarily Anglophone discipline of television studies. The first was that television as such be regarded as worthy of study. . . . The second prerequisite was that television be granted, conceptually, some autonomy and specificity as a medium."[24] As a first task in creating a space for television studies, scholars working within the nascent areas of film and cultural studies in the 1970s did the work of establishing television as an important object of analysis. Notably, in writings in the 1980s, both Newcomb and Fiske credit the tradition of social science research with being tremendously helpful in this task.[25] The decades of serious social science research on the effects of media aided in legitimating the object of study for these other approaches, despite the fact that their methods and assumptions differed significantly from those beginning to study television from humanities perspectives.

A key part of this second prerequisite occurred during the 1970s when a range of scholars began to think about television as having its own distinct attributes – as opposed to simply viewing it as a variation of a visual medium such as film or as a different type of popular medium such as radio or newspapers. Robert C. Allen identifies such a "new paradigm" for thinking about television emerging in the early 1970s.[26] Instead of the tradition of quantitative survey research or experiments examining media effects that had dominated the study of radio and newspapers, the new tradition was qualitative and interpretive. Instead of hypothesizing television use to have particular, often negative, effects, this new paradigm "focused on the pleasurability of the experience of television viewing"[27]; and, in contrast to previous approaches, this new approach was, "Interested in exploring the complexities of the fictional worlds created by television rather than comparing those worlds with the 'real' world outside television."[28]

This new paradigm was an important first step in the development of what we now identify as television studies, although we view it as the dawning of the formal pursuit of television *criticism* (as it was described at the time), rather than television studies. This is not to suggest there was no critical engagement with television until this point – as the work emerging from CCCS renders clear; rather, the emergence of what Allen terms a new paradigm led to a decade during which a more formalized pursuit of the study of television developed as an interdisciplinary enterprise supported by various institutions and foundations. Early conferences, such as those organized by the Aspen Program's Workshop on Television in 1974, funded by the National Endowment for the Humanities and the John and Mary Markle Foundation, brought together leading figures in the social scientific study of media, journalism, foundations, and industry to consider "Television as a Social Force" and then "Television as Cultural Force" in 1976.[29] Also, Newcomb published the first edition of his edited collection, *Television: The Critical View*, in 1976 as a repository of the best available writing on television.[30] The contents of the volume shifted considerably from journalists to academics over the first few editions, marking a path in the increasing possibility of serious thinking and writing about television. But prior to these works and meetings, the study of television had been much more haphazard and a key part of any writing about television was justifying the act of taking the medium seriously.

Although they did not endeavor from the outset to establish what we now reference as television studies, the work and teaching of those such as Newcomb, Fiske, Hartley, Morley and Brunsdon inspired a next generation of students to move farther from originating disciplines such as literature, film studies, and sociology toward the television-specific mode of study that Brunsdon argues was a second prerequisite of television studies. Many within this tradition may not claim the title of being "television studies scholars" themselves, in part because they examined television as part of a larger project, and hence wished to avoid the sense of limiting their work to a single medium and its essence. "Literary studies" and "film studies" had been known to these scholars as fields with such aims, and some theorists were similarly trying to study television as a specific, defined entity (as will be discussed in chapter 4). By contrast, television studies was less interested in understanding television in and of itself, and more dedicated to using television as a means to other ends – such as understanding how "common sense" is formed – thus making the term "television studies" deeply problematic to some scholars. Even if in retrospect we can now see television studies' foundational scholars as instrumental in establishing a field that took a starkly different approach to the study of a medium, paradoxically – if understandably – many were wary of the term.

By the mid 1980s, the efforts toward developing academic television criticism begun a decade earlier were yielding an increasingly coherent body of work, conferences for exchanging ideas, and what Newcomb identifies as a "new body of television criticism" emerged with the publication of books by US scholars such as Todd Gitlin, David Marc, Michael Intintoli, Hal Himmelstein, Robert C. Allen, and collections edited by E. Ann Kaplan, John E. O'Connor, Willard Rowland and Bruce Watkins, Jane Feuer, Paul Kerr, and Tise Vahamagi, and Patricia Mellencamp.[31] Likewise, a body of scholarship was emerging from British scholars including but not limited to Fiske and Hartley, Hobson, Roger Silverstone, Brunsdon and Morley, and David Buckingham.[32] The publication of these works allowed for more productive cross-fertilization of ideas among those based in different fields and different national contexts and truly prepared the arrival of television studies. Television studies also became a trans-Atlantic conversation at specialized conferences such as "Perspectives on Television and Video Art" at Rutgers University in 1981, which led to Kaplan's *Regarding TV* collection; the International Television Studies Conferences (ITSC) in London sponsored by the British Film Institute and Institute of Education in the summers of 1984, 1986, and 1988, which led to Phillip Drummond and Richard Paterson's *Television and Its Audience* collection[33]; meetings in Michigan in 1983 and 1986 funded by the John and Mary Markle Foundation; the Iowa Symposium and Conference on Television Criticism in 1985; at the University of Wisconsin-Milwaukee's Center for Twentieth Century Studies in 1988; and then the founding of Console-ing Passions: Television, Video, and Feminism, in 1989, although the group would not hold its first conference until 1992.

By the mid 1990s, many involved in the early years of television criticism remarked about the emergence of television studies to such a degree that we can understand television studies to have been called into existence. In his introduction to the fifth edition of *Television: The Critical View* in 1994, Newcomb reflected that "television studies is now an established area of study in many universities."[34] Likewise, from the other side of the Atlantic, Charlotte Brunsdon acknowledged, "If it is now possible, in 1996, to speak of a field of study, 'television studies' in the Anglophone academy, in a way in which it was not in 1970, the distinctive characteristics of this field of study include its disciplinary hybridity and continuing debate about how to conceptualize the object of study 'television.'"[35] Notably, in these quotations, Newcomb and Brunsdon shift from speaking of television *criticism*, which had been the parlance of the textual work that dominated, particularly in the US, before the early 1990s, to television *studies*. This word choice may be coincidental, but we find it emblematic of a general shift that transpires during the early 1990s – at least in terms of US scholarship; some British scholarship had been more open to considering audiences and institutions from the start.

Just as Newcomb noted a new body of criticism in the mid 1980s concurrent with the first sizeable wave of book-length academic studies of television, what is perhaps the first generation of American television studies scholarship appears in the early 1990s. This work, in many cases the publication of dissertation research pursued in the late 1980s, differs from the primarily textual analysis of the television criticism that precedes it. Instead, books by Michele Hilmes, Lynn Spigel, William Boddy, Chris Anderson, Julie D'Acci, and Michael Curtin take on television in a way that expands beyond programming output.[36] Each linked textual analysis with examination of the industrial and cultural contexts that led to particular textual forms. In Britain, as noted above, such work had already begun in the 1980s, but it picked up pace in the 1990s with further work by Morley, Brunsdon, Buckingham, Silverstone, Ann Gray, Justin Lewis, and many more, and it took root in multiple institutional homes.[37]

To a degree, this evolution of television study can be found in the pages of one of its early methodological and theoretical guides, *Channels of Discourse, Reassembled*, 2nd edn.[38] The chapters here primarily chart textual approaches to studying television, very much the methods derived from film and literary studies. Yet a tension exists between the content of the book and what several of the authors, particularly Fiske and James Hay, call for in terms of including examination of industrial context and audience response. In addressing the intersection of cultural studies and television studies, both Fiske and Hay call for television studies to be more than an application of film and literature's textual methods to the texts of television. Yet, there is limited address of methods or theories that would allow this, likely because of the limited research pursuing such approaches at the time the collection was written, as at this time the robust scholarship of the early 1990s was just moving through publication.

By the mid 1990s, then, television studies had become institutionalized into universities to the degree that a first generation of students began training explicitly as "television" scholars at universities such as University of Wisconsin-Madison, University of Texas at Austin, Indiana University, and Northwestern University in the US, Birmingham, Goldsmiths College, University of Westminster, and University of Sussex in the UK, instead of training as film, literature, sociology, or communication scholars and applying those perspectives to the study of television. In many cases, they were trained by mentors not explicitly trained as television scholars but who considered themselves as such. Marking the final stage of academic institutionalization, universities then established more than just the occasional hiring line explicitly seeking "television scholars" at the end of the decade. Thus as Lynn Spigel noted in a 2000 review of recent publications: "television studies is no longer a 'young' academic pursuit. For the past 30 years, a growing body of literature has emerged that – while often drawing on interdisciplinary paradigms – now recognizes itself as a (loosely) organized protocol for understanding television as a cultural, social, political, aesthetic and industrial form."[39] It remains the case that no Departments of Television Studies exist, and television studies scholars tend to meet at small, irregular conferences or have fashioned a small niche in broader academic organizations such as the Society for Cinema and Media Studies and the International Communication Association, rather than developing independent professional organizations. We'll look more at the immediate past of television studies in the Conclusion, but we now turn from the process of how television studies came into being to explaining what television studies is.[40] The following chapters trace the interdisciplinary paradigms we've introduced here in greater detail and enumerate what distinguishes that "(loosely) organized protocol" from others' studies of television.

Distinguishing television studies

Brunsdon notes:

> there is nothing obvious about the television of television studies. This television, the television studied in television studies, is a production of the complex interplay of different histories – disciplinary, national,

economic, technological and legislative – which not only did not exist until recently, but is currently, contestedly, being produced even as, simultaneously, the nationally regulated terrestrial broadcasting systems which are its primary referent move into convulsion.[41]

In a similar vein, Spigel describes TV as a confluence of "technologies, industrial formations, government policies, and practices of looking."[42] These two leading scholars acknowledge a complex matrix of considerations through which an entity known as television emerges. Given this deliberate attention to interconnecting aspects that constitute television, it is thus understandable how the study of such an entity would be diffuse and varied.

Television studies brings together and engages in the difficult task of synthesizing these various traditions. As our subsequent chapters will suggest, it conceives of television as a repository for meanings and a site where cultural values are articulated. It assumes television is a key part of lived, everyday culture in contemporary society and one which may allow us to understand large parts of that culture. It is also an industrial entity produced under specific conditions that require analysis precisely because it is one of our society's prime storytellers, a resource and tool for learning, deliberation, debate, and persuasion, and a site wherein power and ideology operate.

Television is a ubiquitous enough entity that other disciplines would be remiss in their duties if they did not study television at times, and thus other disciplines and approaches frequently inform television studies. Whereas other disciplines may study television with a solitary interest in its programs, its audiences, its producers, or its history and context, television studies sees each of these as integral aspects. As an approach, it is not solipsistic; it is and must be disciplinarily ambidextrous. Granted, individual studies within television studies may analyze only one or two of program, audience, industry, and context out of necessity, but a television studies approach should at the least be mindful of all aspects and see each intricately interwoven with the others. Television studies will not always seek to understand television for the sake of understanding television alone; on the contrary, works of television studies examine the operation of identity, power, authority, meaning, community, politics, education, play, and countless other issues. Television studies, though, starts with the presumption that television is an important prism through which these issues are shared, and hence that a multifaceted and deliberately contextualized approach to the medium and its programs, audiences, and institutions will always help one understand those issues better.

We don't believe that we are pathbreaking in marking off this distinction for television studies. Indeed, what we describe here is fully consistent with the "circuit of media study" offered by D'Acci in her chapter "Cultural Studies, Television Studies, and the Crisis in the Humanities," as well as the approach taught to generations of students, several of whom have been central in defining television studies in the last decade.[43] Rather, these paragraphs attempt a formal articulation of what has operated as a loosely shared understanding among television studies practitioners for some time. Indeed, we are even wary of the consequences of identifying the approach in this way but ultimately view it as potentially useful, particularly for those first attempting to negotiate the many approaches to studying media and television and who share a sense that a common approach to study exists that is not defined by object of study alone. The following chapters anchor this description in particular examples, drawing from television studies' richest works and explaining how and why this work emerges and becomes constitutive of television studies.

Conclusion

From the outset and throughout the months of drafting this manuscript, we've remained curiously ambivalent toward our task. On one hand, we believe that something called television studies exists, and we set out to write this book because it seemed more valuable to help students and colleagues to try to pin down roughly what television studies is than it did to allow it to remain a subjective, "I know it when I see it" classification. We've witnessed far too many of our students develop elaborate contortions drawing from the array of thinkers and works addressed here to explain their approach to study in drafting papers and dissertations, when to most of their audience, writing that they were using a "television studies" approach would have well sufficed.

Yet we're also certain that television studies remains a shifting entity, may be a particularly American construct, or one with some generational specificity. To the first point, we've focused on defining television studies by its approach rather than its object of study because of the proven inadequacy of "medium" based theories and the rapidly changing technological space that makes the future of television-as-it-has-been uncertain but also because, in practice, many studying television have maintained a "big tent" approach to their studies. Perhaps because it has emerged as constitutive of and influenced by so many disciplines and intellectual traditions, many engaging in television studies have not drawn hard boundaries around their work or the subfield. Consider that the journal most centrally about television launched with the title *Television and New Media*. Or that within the academic professional organization Society for Cinema and Media Studies, the Television Studies Interest

Group has been an advocate for the inclusion of scholarship as wide-ranging as sound, video games, and comics. Although such matters occupy a deeply insider space likely irrelevant to most readers, they also speak to the manner with which those studying television are aware of and willingly engage the broader media environment in which they exist. Such a "big tent" approach is decidedly different than that found in the approaches of other subdisciplines that have more rigidly policed their boundaries and tended to exclude new technologies or nontraditional objects or approaches as outside the discipline.[44]

To be clear, though, it is not that we believe television is on the verge of being supplanted by various new technologies or ways of using them so much as we acknowledge that it is suboptimal to identify as specifically with a technology as a term such as television studies suggests. The moniker "television studies" does seem contradictory to efforts to maintain a "big tent" ethic that values cross- and converging media conversations, and such medium-based divides already appear an antiquated intellectual organization. It is here that our other concerns – that of the US-centrism and generational specificity of television studies – emerge. We've taken exceptional pains to trace out intellectual histories in the upcoming chapters because they provide the necessary and important backstory of contemporary conditions. In many places, the distinctions between television and film or between social science and humanities approaches have taken different forms and led scholars to identify their work in different ways in various national contexts. For example, in Britain, for many, "media studies" has served as a primary descriptor of the approach we address here, although such identifications are also fluid, and television studies seems to have more purchase with the generations of scholars who completed studies after the mid 1990s. It is most certainly not our intention to draw fine lines between television studies and media studies, even if we could. Although the nomenclature of television studies might be unnecessary or irrelevant to some readers, we hope this book at least explains how and why the term developed as it has in this particular place.

In terms of the arguments waged throughout this introduction to television studies, we do not suggest there is a need for "television studies" to displace "media studies," or to convince anyone not otherwise compelled to do so to claim the television studies mantle. We are more resolute in the belief that, for television studies to be at all meaningful as a classifier to which some adhere, it should not be synonymous with any study of television. As we've drafted the book, we've loosely referred to the distinction of television studies in our conversations as the "at least two of these" rule, hoping a more refined way to express this classification would emerge. Yet it has not, so we distinguish television studies as an approach to studying television or other media that typically references at least two of the program, the audience, and the industry. Regardless of focus, moreover, television studies takes great effort to specify the context of the phenomenon of study in terms of sociocultural, techno-industrial, and historical conditions.

So it is that, despite these acknowledged misgivings and uncertainties, we endeavored upon this book titled *Television Studies*. We've organized the book into four subsequent body chapters: Programs, Audiences, Institutions, and Contexts, followed by a Conclusion. While an imperfect classification scheme, especially given our mandate of television studies as encompassing "two of these," and while we deviously wish we could buck history and begin with Contexts as that which often glues together the others, this common organization of topics proved most efficient for arranging a diffuse range of interdisciplinary influences. Each chapter endeavors to explain the intellectual roots of studies of Programs, Audiences, and Institutions, while also identifying some key works. The Contexts chapter provides a place to discuss both false starts to the study of television as well as works such as histories that include such a blending of textual, audience, or industrial analysis as to preclude other classification. This chapter also discusses some of the many intangible forces of television that surround and give meaning to its programs, audiences, and institutions. Finally, we conclude with thoughts about the future of television studies' practice.

We have endeavored throughout the book to offer copious bibliographic notes and signposts to other writings in television studies. In some places, this may amount to little more than including an author's name or book title rather than the more sustained discussion we offer of some of the field's more classic works. Such brief mentions are required by the nature of such an introductory volume, but we nevertheless wanted to point readers in the direction of research on various subjects. Thus when a moment in television studies history, or an idea about television, interests the reader, we exhort him or her not simply to take our word for it. As will be argued in the conclusion, it may be too much to ask of prospective researchers that they analyze programs, audiences, industries, *and* context in their projects. Nevertheless, television studies not only asks, but requires, that researchers be well-read about programs, audiences, industries, and contexts, and hence we have seen our task of introducing television studies as including a requirement to gesture toward its ever-growing and impressive body of literature.

1

Programs

Television can command the attention of our eyes, ears, fears, and dreams as can few other sources. Despite the proliferation of competition from a variety of media, television is still arguably the key storyteller in the contemporary industrialized world. Though ratings statistics suggest that we're by no means watching the same stories and receiving the same messages as one another, a great deal of us are tuning in, downloading, or pressing "play" on a daily basis. Between the news, advertisements, regular series, special event programming, broadcasted films, documentaries, and other programming, many of us are awash with stories and messages from television. And at some level or another, surely we all believe that these stories and messages matter, whether because some are beautiful, inspiring, and/or cause for reflection, or because they have another effect or role in the constitution of culture. Granted, we may not believe in the extremities of a "hypodermic needle" approach to media effects wherein television messages are imagined to be injected into a willing patient in need of direction. But surely everyone sees television as responsible for something, whether that something be the dominant political sentiment in a country, pervasive views on race, gender, class, and/or sexuality, what haircuts, fashions, and body shapes are attractive, what is important in life, and so on. Given the role that television is perceived to play in constructing core beliefs in areas from the most crucial to the exceptionally trivial, and given its role in telling us stories and offering us information that matter to us, a key task for television studies is to examine these messages, stories, and information. This chapter will explore various approaches for doing so.

Critical analysis of texts – the television programs themselves – is a central technique for helping us to unpack what this world of images, messages, and representations mean. A wide range of motivations for studying television programming exists. For some scholars, television is interesting because they perceive it as an art form, and thus pick their objects of study with great selectivity, privileging "quality" and "depth." As will be discussed, these scholars have often studied television shows to identify their formal and narrative components and to celebrate their artistry with others. If it's not "art," they're not interested. Other scholars have little if any interest in a program's "artistry," and they look upon a show as a collection of messages, ideas, and suggestions, with their task being to study those messages. After all, nothing that happens on television "actually" happens – everything is a (re)presentation of reality, or a construction of an alternate reality. Even programmers of nonfiction must edit, choose shots, and so forth, thereby still giving us a representation of reality, never the thing itself. As such, everything on television is an image of, play on, and/or a message about reality.

This chapter explores the various ways in which television programs have been studied, why these approaches developed, which have taken root in television studies, and what understanding they offer us of the medium and of society around it. First, though, this chapter will examine an oddity – namely, that while "close reading" and textual analysis are approaches developed in the western humanistic tradition as far back as Aristotle, television wasn't being read closely with any real rigor until well into the 1970s. We will then explore the sites from which television program analysis emerged, before working through a variety of ways that texts have been analyzed since, offering examples from the wealth of work in the field. We pay particular attention to ideological approaches – those that focus on programs' messages regarding power differentials and identity constructions in society at large – as we will argue that this work forms the backbone of television studies' encounter with programs. Attention to how social power is reinforced within television programs often, but not exclusively, distinguishes television studies from other "studies of television" that focus on programs. Finally, the chapter concludes with suggestions for what work remains to be conducted within television studies' engagement with programs.

Throughout, we will use the word "text" interchangeably with "program" or "show." While some readers may have been conditioned to think of texts as books, "text" is the common term in the field. A text is any item of culture that users deem to have enough coherence to treat as a single object. So, for instance, a film is a text, as is a novel, a song, a poem, a comic book, a video game, a painting, a radio program, or, for our purposes, a television program. Textual analysis is a style of analysis developed in and across multiple disciplines for the purpose of studying various types of texts, and hence it will often be important to draw from this wider discussion of how texts in general work, rather than talking of programs and shows alone. In chapter 4, we will complicate the term and what counts as a text in television, thereby moving beyond this chapter's simplified notion of what a text is . . . but that is for that later chapter to explain.

Understanding the late arrival of close analysis

Despite the contemporary prevalence of close textual analysis of television programs and their images, dialogue, characters, and plots within television studies, very little close analysis of television existed until the 1970s. To explain how studies of television went from disregarding textual features to at times excluding consideration of all else requires a careful parsing of the many different approaches to textual criticism that are common in a variety of disciplinary settings. In fact, some might argue that textual analysis has dominated television studies; we would nuance this argument to suggest that textual analyses are the most common approach to *studies of television* but we delimit much of this work as distinctive from the terrain and approach this book defines as *television studies*. Text alone is rarely enough for television studies, even if it is often the first port of call before embarking to context, audience, and/or industry. However, before exploring the various approaches of textual analysis that have emerged in the last forty years, we should at first address their absence for several decades.

Upon the invention of television, a first force restricting the textual analysis of television from developing was the established dominance of social science methods for studying mass media such as radio and print. Industrially and in terms of use, television grew directly from radio. Thus, just as many radio programs transitioned from one medium to the other, so too did many research agendas regarding the effect of mass media that are used daily in the home. Indeed, while radio's role in facilitating Hitler's and Stalin's rises to power had been cause for alarm, for instance, television's addition of images concerned many observers all the more. An effects-based model for studying television was hence the early norm, as the field of mass communications staked an early claim on the medium.

Meanwhile, the humanities traditions of literary and rhetorical criticism that were well established at this time largely disregarded television at first as an inferior artistic form of the masses, not relevant to be considered as art or likely to hold deeper meaning. Even film studies struggled to declare film an art form worthy of textual criticism in its early days, leaving little chance for the decidedly more domestic, everyday, and – in the US at least – commercialized television. Although this would eventually change, and although many of the critical tools most commonly used in textual analysis of television originate from literary and film studies, the acceptance of television as a legitimate artistic form alongside literature and film required difficult – and likely incomplete – negotiation.

Also, to further explain the curious lack of close analyses of television texts in the medium's early days, we should realize that new media are often regarded as monoglot, single-cell organisms, with little attention paid to the infinite minutiae of differences within the medium. One need only witness the sweeping generalizations that accompany the internet and social media in particular today to catch a glimpse of how "television" was itself situated as a medium – rather than as a collection of individual programs – early in its history. Many critics and observers ascribed powers to television as a whole – for example, as will be discussed in chapter 4, "television" was said to be responsible for Kennedy beating Nixon in the infamous 1960 debates, not the choice of camera angles, questions asked, or structure of the specific program. Similarly, though in far shorter supply, glowing and utopian accounts of how "television" would set us all free reduced a wide collection of different programs to a singular entity and force, just as do utopian accounts of the promises of the internet today. "Television" was also treated as a singular entity by some critics because it was regarded as a medical risk, as an item whose radiation could fry children's brains across the world, or that could stunt childhood development through restricting physical action and "real" social interaction; whether the news or *Captain Kangaroo* were playing to such critics was immaterial.[1] We might understand the *urge* to understand television in such grand, sweeping gestures. But studying television is a messy business, and few easy answers exist, requiring a level of distinction and division that early sweeping criticisms evaded at their peril.

Finally, we might also note the sheer *difficulty* of studying early television programs closely, as neither viewers, scholars, nor critics could control the flow or timing of television. Close textual analysis has accompanied literature and literary studies for many years, but a literature scholar often had the luxury of a library of books at hand. By contrast, until the VCR became a ubiquitous technology in the 1980s, close analysis could only be conducted on the fly, during the first screening. Even critics writing for popularly read journalistic outlets faced the odd task of watching something and then writing a review of it for publication the next day, although no one would subsequently be able to see the program reviewed. The pausing and rewinding that are required for high-quality analysis of dialogue and image were simply not available prior to the VCR. Thus, several early analysts of television can regale their students today with stories of sitting down to watch, pen in hand, hoping to keep up if noteworthy events transpired. Such a situation clearly affected the *writing* of textual analyses, but it also no doubt affected the *reading* of them, when many readers would not have access to the program themselves. Television was a largely ephemeral medium, with its images flashing onto screens briefly, then disappearing again, and close analysis of such an ephemeral source requires the slowing down of the medium to a point that was not technically possible and that may conceptually have been seen to compromise the nature of television.

Thus, close analysis of television programs developed decades after the widespread availability of television for a variety of practical reasons, including academic posturing, and arbitrary circumstance.

Prehistory and influences on the textual analysis of television

Textual, formal analysis of television was reasonably new in the 1970s, but textual, formal analysis was by no means a new methodology within the humanities. Rather, multiple other fields and departments were already well versed in textual analysis by the time television studies began to grow. This section offers a brief tour through some of these fields – literary studies, art, rhetoric, film studies, and linguistics – as a way of examining how television studies learned and grew from or in contrast to the other prevailing methods of analyzing texts.

Art and literary studies

Art and literary studies had long worked via close engagement with textual form, engaged in what is commonly called *formal analysis*. Literary studies, in particular, had been governed by the "New Criticism" of John Crowe Ransom and Cleanth Brooks in the United States,[2] and the "Practical Criticism" of I. A. Richards and F. R. Leavis in the United Kingdom,[3] schools of thought that posited the work of literature as an entity best studied through in-depth formal, textual analysis, and that sprung in part from Victorian critic and poet Matthew Arnold's famous belief in Culture as being "the best that has been thought and said."[4] Novels and poems were regarded as dense, intricately worked systems rich with meaning and reflective brilliance and – much as high-school literature education still is today – education in literature involved being taught to close-read deep into the text to find its meaning, and to study the techniques and skills used to saturate that meaning throughout a text in the first place. Literature departments (and Art departments alongside them) had fashioned a well-worn path for early television critics and analysts to follow, and it is thus no surprise that early textual criticism of television often mined programs for aesthetic interpretation.

Just as a literature professor might study how a poem's explicit meaning is made more resonant by its rhyme scheme, word choice, tempo, and/or imagery, formal analysis of television asks similar questions of how meaning comes to the fore. It might analyze how sequent scenes are arranged to construct meaning, for instance, or how a voice-over is used to invite identification with a specific character or otherwise to create a specific point of view. Formal analysis might flesh out audio or visual metaphors in a scene or episode, examining the ducks in Tony Soprano's swimming pool in the pilot of *The Sopranos*, for example. It might interpret characters' names, asking the significance of Tony's family name, or of Horatio Caine in *CSI: Miami*, John Locke in *Lost*, Veronica Mars in the show of the same name, or so forth. It might attempt to make sense of a show's filming style or palette, inquiring into the meaning of *CSI: Miami*'s fondness for deep oranges, *The Office*'s choice to buck the three- or four-camera tradition of sitcom filming and use a handheld style instead, or a soap opera's tight close-ups. Or it might probe deep into a narrative, asking after the effect of *House*'s practice of "false starts" – whereby, for example, a character falling over clutching her chest might prove a red herring, with her brother's ensuing illness forming the focus of the episode – of *The Wire*'s onion-like storytelling structure, with each season adding a new institutional layer of Baltimore society, or of the choice to tell seemingly important background details about characters in piecemeal fashion in a range of shows from *Mad Men* to *Lost*. Formal analysis eschews the idea that anything makes its way into a program "by accident" and thus regards every sound, image, character, plot point, or choice as one worthy of analysis and potentially requiring of explanation. For an outstanding sustained example and discussion of how formal analysis of television works, we recommend Jeremy Butler's recent *Television Style*.[5]

Rhetorical analysis

If the formal analysis practiced in literary and art studies departments stretched back to Aristotle's *Poetics*, so did the field of rhetoric, with its interest in the written and spoken word. Traditionally, though, rhetoric departments studied public address and political speech, and, in many public universities in the United States, were entrusted with teaching public speaking classes to hordes of freshmen. These limited foci would change in the 1960s and 1970s as an increasing number of rhetoricians called for the field to expand. The early 1970s' Wingspread Conference of the Speech Communication Association became the epicenter for a movement of new rhetoricians keen to examine a much wider variety of the manifestations of language and discourse.[6] This new mandate saw several within the field turn to television and other forms of popular culture using a rhetorical analysis that drew from the long history of rhetorical studies, while also more prominently integrating the cultural theory that was elsewhere giving birth to cultural studies and television studies. Rhetoric remains home to a fair degree of television analysis to this day, and numerous rhetorical scholars have contributed to discussions and debates within television studies, especially through the journal *Critical Studies in Media Communication* that serves both areas. However, the field as a whole contributed little to the development of a television studies mode of textual analysis, if only because the brand of formal analysis that those rhetoricians interested in television would practice drew from the same wells of cultural theory and cultural studies as did television studies, and thus could and can look remarkably similar.

Film studies and screen theory

Art and literary studies had willed formal analysis to film studies too. Thus, by the time television analysis began in earnest, film scholars had already developed a host of techniques for interpreting moving images, thereby allowing early formal analysis of television to do and to analyze a lot with techniques developed elsewhere. It is perhaps no coincidence that television studies often grew not simply from fresh ground, as at the Polytechnic of Wales, but especially in universities with strong film programs – such as University of Wisconsin-Madison, University of Iowa, University of Texas at Austin, New York University, University of California, Los Angeles, and Northwestern University in the USA, and Goldsmiths College, University of East Anglia, University of Warwick, and University of Sussex in the UK – where students and faculty could avail themselves of the well-honed techniques of visual and formal analysis of their film studies colleagues (even if they were battling them on other fronts).

However, an especially strong vein in British film studies, dubbed screen theory, proved an early antagonist for early television studies scholars, adopting a line of questioning of the text for which the latter did not care. Screen theory drew heavily from Marxism and psycho-analysis to make sense of how moving images and stories hailed and acted upon their audience, or spectators. For a television studies that, as our next chapter will detail, cared deeply about studying real audiences and that regarded the audience as always potentially transformative, screen theory's insistence that the spectacle of the screen created the spectator, not the other way around, was a bitter point of contention, as was the associated suggestion that a text only had one (ideal) spectator. Famously, for instance, Laura Mulvey wrote of film's "male gaze," wherein the camera seemingly requires us to watch the action as a het-erosexual male, voyeuristically studying the female character from the safety of the darkness of the theater. Women on screen, she noted, were habitually obstacles to action, there to be looked at but dangerous inas-much as they represented emasculation, while male characters acted and moved the plot forward.[7] Here, Mulvey's observations are certainly astute at one level, given that film – and television – often invites us to ogle at women on screen, as is most evident in scenes in which we're introduced to female characters by a camera moving up and down their bodies languorously. Film and television also often reduce women to being obstacles to plot. But to link this to a fear of castration on one hand, and on the other hand to see the gaze as required not offered, is to project a solitary interpretation onto an entire audience. Screen theory took a sociological question – namely, what do audiences do with texts – and attempted to answer it with psychology, yet inexcusably with a psychological analysis without psyches, without humans, and only with texts. As much as early television studies scholars shared a commitment to a neo-Marxist analysis of texts, and to an analysis of them as ideologi-cal beings, television studies' grounding in cultural studies and its commitment to audience analysis made this type of formal analysis impracticable and deeply problematic. Television studies' own interest in ideology would therefore need to find another method.

Linguistics and semiotic/semiological analysis

A fourth approach to textual analysis offered many early television scholars a more amenable way to analyze ideology and form. Semiotic/semiological analysis primarily hailed from linguistics, but also and especially from what various scholars in literary studies, art, philosophy, film studies, and the burgeoning cultural studies were doing with linguis-tic theory.

"Semiology" derived from the teachings of Ferdinand de Saussure, a Swiss linguist whose lectures were recorded and circulated to considerable fanfare, while "semiotics" developed in parallel in the United States largely in the wake of linguists and philosophers including Charles Peirce and Charles Morris.[8] De Saussure noted that all language is arbitrary in that, with few small exceptions, there is no necessary reason why any given language should use the sounds or icons that it does ("signifiers") to describe the concepts within that language ("signifieds"). This point can be illustrated by recourse to other languages that use different sounds or icons for the same concept. However, other languages also illustrate to us a key point of de Saussure's – that concepts are created *through* and *inside* language, not outside them. After all, languages do not all agree on the same distinction and divisions between concepts. Cantonese has two distinct ways to say "thank you," Spanish has no easy translation for "silly," certain states of being can only be described in given languages, and so forth. In other words, Saussure noted that language is a social construct, and, with it, all ideas and concepts are socially constructed. At any given point in time, we may think of a word as a set concept, but in fact it moves and shifts over time – as etymology sections in good dictionaries render evident. All language is open to change, and no concept exists free of language or, hence, of the society around it. Note that to say this is not to say that objects do not have an empirical reality. The chair on which you might be sitting as you read this is definitely there in physical space, but it is only a *chair* because language has been socially constructed in a way that makes you see it as a chair. It could just as easily be called a "table," or for that matter an "aftghast," or subdivided into other terms. Such a concept may seem less important and purely semantic when we're talking about chairs, but if we change the word or phrase in question to a more loaded term, such as "a real man," "love," "justice," or "loyalty," we're once more forced to realize that these signifiers only apply to the signifieds because they have come to take on those meanings socially – there is no "real man," "love," "justice," or "loyalty" outside of language, and no reason why each of these concepts could not be redefined, merged with other concepts, and/or subdivided.

Semiology/semiotics therefore studied texts with a method that was formalist in style, looking at systems of meanings within these texts; however, the ultimate object of understanding in semiotic analysis was language itself, and an entire linguistic system, not the individual text per se. Semiotic analysis examined what any given element within a text signified, but was also especially attentive to how this meaning was created through association, in "syntagmatic" and "paradigmatic" relationships.

A semiotic analysis of the nightly news, for instance, may choose to examine the signs that are syntagmatically grouped together to form a notion of authority and trustworthiness. Namely, the combination of well-groomed anchors wearing suits (thereby signifying orderliness and professionalism), holding a stack of papers in front of them (thereby signifying a ready supply of information and an orderly arrangement of it), speaking in a relatively standardized, distanced diction (thereby signifying an objective unphaseability), addressing the camera directly (thereby signifying nothing to hide, confidence, and assuming a familiarity with the audience) forms a syntagm of authority and trustworthiness. Swapping any one element in this syntagm with a paradigmatically related alternative could produce vastly different, or even laughable results, as with *The Daily Show with Jon Stewart*, when Jon scribbles on his notes (instead of arranging them neatly), makes faces at the camera (instead of staring at it robotically), and/or swears (instead of keeping "professional," newscaster diction). Or we might imagine how little authority a newscaster wearing a T-shirt and jeans might conjure. On one hand, semiotic analysis allows us to see the rules by which the language of culture works: noting, for example, that suits are associated with decorum and professionalism more than are T-shirts. On the other hand it allows us to see sites wherein those rules are written and maintained in the first place. After all, one might imagine another culture – or pockets within our own – in which those in suits are distrusted as putting on airs, and hence in which they signify something else and in which "authority" is created by different syntagmatic groupings. Semiotic analysis might also allow us to see how the nightly news sets its own rules for authority that might operationalize elsewhere in the program, as when guests or interview subjects wearing suits may be accorded more trust than those not doing so.

Differing motivations for analysis: Aesthetics and ideology

Each of the above fields worked with different tools for textual analysis, but, since each tool was developed with different uses in mind, they have proven to be of varying utility to television studies. One key distinction lies in whether given methods ruled out or disallowed other methods, as did screen theory with audience analysis, for instance. But another key distinction lies in what the methods could be used *for*, whether to ascertain and evaluate artistry and aesthetics on one hand, or to analyze the workings of ideology and power on the other.

Traditionally, art and literary studies were disciplines motivated by the search for, evaluation, and study of "beauty." As noted above, Matthew Arnold had argued that art (or, to him, "Culture") had an ennobling and civilizing effect. Studying art was thus intended to refine one's mind, open up room for the contemplation and experience of the sublime, and take one away from the quotidian pursuits of the work world, toward a higher, more reflective plane of existence. Similarly, *teaching* art was a process of encouraging others to pursue reflection of such things. Toward this end, formal analysis had been developed by New and Practical Criticism as ways of "close reading" a text, that is, of getting close to it, excluding external filters, and to study its minutiae of form, structure, and arrangement while "up close." As such, in its pure form, formal analysis had often been used in the pursuit of aesthetics, with the text in hand as the object of study.

Television long displeased critics, who found it unworthy as an art form, but gradually some programs began to attract significant interest from some in English and film departments working within the aesthetic/formal tradition. Since it presupposes the positive evaluation of a program, aesthetic analysis has tended to conglomerate around a few television shows, and thus works in spurts. In recent years, for instance, *Buffy the Vampire Slayer* captured many an English professor's heart, leading to the long-running online academic journal dedicated to work on *Buffy – Slayage: The Journal of the Whedon Studies Association*.[9] *The Sopranos* similarly captured significant attention, and most recently *The Wire* and *Mad Men* have garnered such notice. Several hybrid academic-lay presses have specialized in edited collections on such "landmark" shows. While contributors to these collections at times engage in the types of audience, industrial, or contextual analyses discussed in chapters 2, 3, and 4, or treat texts ideologically, as will soon be discussed in this chapter, many engage enthusiastically with the artistry of the series in question.

Though this work often informs television studies, and may even at times be conducted by scholars who at other times pursue lines of inquiry more consistent with television studies, it is more commonly found in literary studies departments as a correlate to the traditional mission of such departments to analyze aesthetics. By contrast, television studies took its lead from the transformation experienced by many literary studies departments and units across the humanities beginning in the 1960s and 1970s, with the arrival of cultural theory, or what is at times simply called theory. In many ways, television studies' method of critical textual analysis grew out of and alongside semiotics with its broader interests in how a text might tell us something about the cultural system that surrounds it more generally.

Once theorists asserted that language is arbitrary and meaning a social construction, many scholars turned to analyzing language as anything but an innocent system. Instead, language was seen as an outgrowth of an ideological system and as a system of power, and all texts became players in the maintenance or contestation of that system. In other words, for example, if the phrase "a real man" has only taken on meaning culturally and linguistically, and is by no means an objective reality, how then did it become as it is now, how does it stay defined as such, and/or how might its meaning be destabilized and changed? Cultural theory drew from the writings on ideology by Karl Marx, Louis Althusser, and Antonio Gramsci in particular that suggested any society has a dominant ideology, organization of power, and systems of beliefs regarding what constitutes "common sense," and that texts and the social apparatus in general are organized in such a way to protect that system and ensure its vitality.[10] Semiotic/semiological and formal analysis, therefore, could be used to explore not only aesthetics, but also a text's relationship to dominant ideology – its impact on and place in the culture and power networks that surround it.

A landmark, early example of this use of semiotics is seen in the French literary theorist and philosopher Roland Barthes' *Mythologies*.[11] *Mythologies* is representative of several other projects of this time in semiology/semiotics and literary theory in three key respects. First, since Barthes wanted to know how meaning was constructed, he found it insufficient to look solely at literature and at the world of high culture. Individual essays in *Mythologies*, for example, examine toys, margarine, wine and milk, photo exhibits, and discussions of Einstein's brain. Thus whereas the former task of literary studies was to find value within the privileged realm of high, bourgeois culture, Barthes and others' theory required them to look at a wide variety of cultural objects. Second, since semiotics posed that all concepts were socially constructed, literary and social theory surmised that "value" must similarly be subjective – or at least intersubjective – and open to redefinition, not immutable or divine. This move destroyed the magic circle that surrounded Art and Literature, and rendered their categorization as problematic. Third and arguably most importantly, semiotics' ultimate goal, through Barthes and others, was to explore how *ideology* worked in society, and to see what texts could tell us about the work of power – about how certain notions calcified, and about how hierarchies were created between concepts.

Meanwhile, a second strand of cultural theory had developed within and around anthropology, as structural, formal analysis was similarly being used by the likes of Claude Lévi-Strauss, Clifford Geertz, and Victor Turner to analyze the symbolic functions of rituals and totems.[12] Through applying the term "mythology" to popular culture in the West, Barthes created an easy bridge between this work – with its primary interest in understanding Other, "tribal" cultures – and the nascent analysis of television's own rituals, symbolism, and reinscriptions of power. James Carey and Roger Silverstone in particular would mine this work with skill, as their early work framed television as myth and as storyteller.[13]

Close reading was still a key method in this work, but it was now conducted with a radically different purpose: to reveal not its artistic machinery but its ideological machinery, and to understand the deep structures of culture. While this theory may have begun predominantly in literary studies, linguistics, and anthropology departments, it mandated the study of popular culture, not just high culture and not just Other cultures, thereby opening the door decisively to the study of television as one of the most popular media around. Literature departments did not merely bow to this, and many professors within such departments still saw their role as the engagement with aesthetics and form, but all of a sudden the academic rationale for the close reading and analysis of television presented itself even – and perhaps especially – to those who refused to see it as a beautiful object. Semiotic analysis worked with a specific vocabulary that sought to explain metaphors and deeper meanings not only in the "first" and "second" order – whereby, for instance, in *House*, Dr House's cane signifies a physical ailment or handicap, which jars with his bravado to further signify an inner weakness – but also in the "third order" of what Barthes called mythology or deep structure and ideology, wherein such meanings speak to society more generally – so that, on one hand, House's bravado may signify a broader notion of how men are supposed to act and his disability represents a challenge to traditional scripts of masculinity, or, on the other hand, his depiction speaks to wider societal representations and beliefs of the frustrations, impotencies, and scarring that "disability" is supposed to entail. Semiotic analysis, in other words, digs into a text to make sense of what's around that text and to see how it is "written" by ideological structures and messages.

Semiotics also proved a jumping-off point for a rich assortment of theories of how texts work ideologically. In semiotics' wake, and drawing from the political theory of Marx, Althusser, Gramsci, and others, came numerous other theories for how language enacted power on an everyday, textual level. For instance, working with the idea that all meaning can only be constructed in relation to other concepts – so that, for instance, "love" only has meaning in relation to words such as "friendship," "hate," "lust," and so forth – that in turn are relational, Jacques Derrida posed that a system of *différance* rendered all language fatally slippery, and he saw close reading as a way to "deconstruct" the assumptions upon which any text was built.[14] Michel Foucault wrote of concepts and institutions taking on meaning and being granted disciplinary power at certain moments in time, and he proposed a method that was equal parts historiographic analysis and close textual analysis and considered close reading as a way to understand how such "discourses" calcified, and of examining how counter-discursive raids could be made.[15] Multiple feminist and postcolonial scholars focused in particular upon how texts constructed our ideas of, respectively, masculinity and femininity, and racial, ethnic, and national identities. The force of this and other work profoundly destabilized prevailing notions within the academy of how identity works, challenging previous Enlightenment era ideas of a uniform and pre-constituted self, and instead suggesting that identities were fashioned as a project, by ourselves but also by the multiple texts, discourses, and institutions around us.[16]

This revolution of semiotics and theory transformed how many within the humanities made sense of their role as professors and analysts. If the Arnoldian project of teaching and understanding beauty had once been dominant, it was now rivaled by a concern for how texts created our identities and the world around us, and hence for how texts could serve as the site where identities and the world could be changed. Television studies would be born in and from this moment in which it became vital to inquire into a text's ideological role. Formal analysis would still prove important, but television studies tended to engage in formal analysis primarily as a means to the end of determining any given show's place within a network of power.

Television studies and critical analysis

To further understand why television studies has emphasized critical analysis of its texts, it is helpful to consider some of its earliest voices. Horace Newcomb's *Television: The Most Popular Art* was one of the first serious books about television, and, reflecting on the book thirty years after its publication, Newcomb explains that it considers two questions: "how does television tell its stories?" and "what is the relation of television's stories and storytelling strategies to American – and, by implication, any other – society and culture?"[17] As this language of "stories" and "storytelling" suggests, Newcomb trained in literary studies in the 1960s, but he had long been an avid watcher of television and was intrigued with the just emerging academic attention to popular culture as he completed his degree. Newcomb's belief in the complexity and significance of television had very personal origins. As a boy and teen growing up in segregated Mississippi, he had strong firsthand experience that suggested to him that television had important social consequences beyond those of instigating violence or anti-social behavior, as most of the psychological research had focused on. Newcomb felt that the images of a broader world that television brought into his world and the horrific images of injustice in the South that television newscasts shared with homes around the US played a key role in challenging the racism that dominated Southern culture. He writes:

> Growing up in Mississippi in the forties and fifties meant growing up in a closed society. Television opened a vast array of options to that closure, most crucially in the way it dealt with "race." Sometimes it presented issues in veiled forms, as when Matt Dillon defended a minority character on *Gunsmoke*. Sometimes it took issues by the throat, as in *The Defenders* or in a particularly vivid episode of *Dr. Kildare*. At other times, and increasingly in the years in which I was watching less but thinking more, it pushed terrible images into our living rooms. The Freedom Riders pulled from buses and the students beaten at lunch counters were being filmed very close to my home, and this had an enormous impact, radically altering the ways in which I conceived of "race relations," leading to some considerable degrees of personal and social discomfort, and to minor activism.[18]

Newcomb's guiding questions of "how does television tell its stories?" and "what is the relation of television's stories and storytelling strategies to American society and culture?" also illustrate the multifaceted ways that examinations of television programs might explore the politics and the culture of the worlds they represent without explicitly focusing on matters of power or ideology.

Similarly, Christine Geraghty recently recounted her introduction to the study of British television as a member of a feminist study group composed by the British Film Institute seeking to investigate film theory in relation to feminism.[19] The group was mostly women who were not full-time academics and wasn't connected to a university. The group settled on the television series *Coronation Street* in 1976 largely out of convenience – some of the women had babies and it was too difficult to take them around to the theater – and began watching and analyzing out of a sense that what was happening on screen in the stories mattered to women and society in important ways and that it was vital to develop a more accessible language for talking about theories of media and gender. As she recalls, it was chosen not out of a sense that it was "good" television: they liked talking about it more than watching it. Geraghty described her introduction to the study of television as a crucial but unsuccessful moment that was symptomatic of the beginning of television studies.

John Hartley too has written of how his own initial interest in television was driven by a sense of how much it mattered. Critics of television often make the dangerous mistake of discussing television as something "out there," removed from everyday life, and somehow impinging upon it, but Hartley notes how tightly woven television is into daily life, and especially into the homes of so many. In a postscript to *Uses of Television* – a book whose title is an homage to Richard Hoggart's famous *Uses of Literacy* that studied the vitality and meanings of working-class life – Hartley describes his upbringing in a poor household, and insists that "With a home and family like ours, I couldn't look at contemporary popular culture with lofty metropolitan disdain or artful critical contempt. With my history, suburbanality is not to be sneezed at; not envied or scorned, not over- or under-valued, but not to be taken lightly either."[20] While Newcomb's reflections on his turn to television highlight television's role in the grand politics of civil rights and protest, Hartley's complementary reflections highlight how television is no less operational in the politics of the everyday, addressing, as he notes, "people who cannot be certain of their origin, class, faith, sexuality, family, housing, history. It revels in us."[21] Hartley would begin his academic career intending to study history, and start a PhD on literacy and individualism in Shakespearean plays and England, but eventually turn his interests to media, writing another of television studies' founding books, *Reading Television*, with John Fiske while both worked at the Polytechnic of Wales. Another scholar trained in formal analysis, in other words, found himself drawn to the hugely important yet hardly studied medium of television, here as a means of understanding how home, family, and identity were fashioned.

Clearly, Newcomb, Geraghty, and Hartley, along with the members of the CCCS and other early innovators in television studies, were among a generation for whom television had played an important role in everyday life since childhood, unlike the previous generation of media researchers, who had come of age with newspapers, radio, and film. As charted in other chapters, as television studies moved forward, the new field showed interest less in the aesthetics and evaluation of television, and more in television's role in everyday life. Admittedly, some scholars have looked at aesthetics *and* social role, and others have allowed their research projects to be dictated in part by personal aesthetic preferences – as will be discussed at the chapter's conclusion. But television studies' engagements with programs have more usually been from the perspective of ideological, critical analysis for reasons that have a lot to do with the personal biographies of its earliest voices, their key experiences with the medium, and the sociohistorical context of the times in which they began to seriously consider television. As it is now, television was seemingly everywhere, its narratives and characters pervasive, and a clear – even preeminent – part of popular culture. If identity and agency, ideology and power, worked through this realm of the popular, the close analysis of television would tell us how such entities worked. Similarly, if we wanted to *change* society and culture, an understanding of the entire television system – not just its "better," landmark programs, but anything with a viewership – could help us better understand the dominant ideology and how to change it. As such, critical analysis and close reading of television was, and has remained, part of a deeply political project, contributing to a general audit of how power works.

By means of conducting this audit, television studies has featured textual analysis since its first days, as early scholars attempted to bridge the emphases of the textual tradition of literature, various cultural theories, and the particularity of television. Fiske and Hartley's *Reading Television*, for instance, offered two early chapters on semiotics, "The Signs of Television" and "The Codes of Television," together detailing Barthes' approach to semiotics and engaging in preliminary, illustrative analysis that took a small shot sequence from the British documentary drama, *Cathy Come Home*, and analyzed how the composure and juxtaposition of these shots created meaning that reinforced the ideological argument of the program.[22]

At stake in such early work was not simply a reason to look at television closely but also a vocabulary for what was then a new exploit; as Fiske and Hartley argued, "we have no fully formed language of appreciation to 'read' [television] by. The tools of literary and dramatic appreciation are by now very sophisticated. But these tools will not necessarily do for television."[23] And thus the semiotic analysis of television began to engage with the medium's unique form and visuality as a separate language and sign system from literary studies, wherein semiotics first made such a splash. As with other semiotic analysis in the vein of Barthes and Claude Lévi-Strauss, though, a keen eye for structure and dominant ideology was key. Fiske and Hartley noted:

> It is by no means natural for television to represent reality in the way that it does, just as it is by no means natural for language to do so. Both language and television *mediate* reality: there is no pristine experience which social man can apprehend without the culturally determined structures, rituals and concepts supplied to him via his language. Language is the means by which men enter into society to *produce* reality (one part of which is the fact of their living together in linguistic society). Television extends this ability, and an understanding of the way in which television structures and presents its picture of reality can go a long way towards helping us to understand the way in which our society works.[24]

Here, Fiske and Hartley are clear: the close analysis of television will help us explain how reality is fashioned, who makes it and how, where society comes from and how it works.

Television as a cultural forum

Another television-specific approach to understanding its texts was developed by Newcomb and Paul Hirsch, who sought a way to theorize the many ideological contradictions within texts. Their framework of viewing television as a "cultural forum" defied attempts to simply read surface ideologies from television programs and, while positing that "television is central to the process of public thinking," stressed the need to consider television's ideological work as a process rather than the static thing of a single series or episode.[25] Although vague regarding the nature of power, Newcomb and Hirsch argued that, "A cultural basis for the analysis and criticism of television is, for us, the bridge between a concern for *television as communications medium*, central to contemporary society, and *television as aesthetic object*, the expressive medium that, through its storytelling functions, unites and examines a culture."[26] Thus Newcomb and Hirsch sought to emphasize the distinction of television as a medium that encompassed both the everydayness and commonality of television to which tools of critical analysis could be applied. Of television, Newcomb and Hirsch argued, "In its role as central cultural medium it presents a multiplicity of meanings rather than a monolithic dominant point of view"; and therefore, that efforts to explain its cultural work must place an emphasis "on process rather than product, on discussion rather than indoctrination, on contradiction and confusion rather than coherence."[27] Such interventions began to specify the tools for textual analysis of television that distinguish textual analysis of television programs consistent with television studies from those textual studies of television that do not account for or address the specificity of the medium.

Polysemy – one show, many meanings

Fiske in particular would also prove instrumental in introducing another key term to television analysis, that of *polysemy*. Much textual analysis is motivated by the attempt to uncover a program's meanings. However, early on in television studies' history, Fiske and others identified polysemy as an important consideration in the analysis of such meanings. Polysemy was proposed by Barthes, especially in his later writings, as the theory that no text could effectively police just one meaning (mono-semy), but rather that all were open to interpretation in a variety of ways (hence, polysemy). Barthes further posed that some texts would be espe-cially "writerly," by which he meant that they invited the reader to create meanings too, to be a writer.[28] Through processes of intertextuality (dis-cussed further in chapter 4), Barthes regarded all texts as potentially open to different resonances and readings. Certainly, it is in part through Barthes that the word "text" was willed to television studies, and Barthes was clear to distinguish between the "work," as that which a producer creates, and the "text," which only occurs in the reading, which only truly comes to life once a reader gets involved. Getting involved will always entail some form of personalization and transformation, meaning that in Barthesian terms, a text is always already a product of the work and an audience interacting. A text "asks of the reader a practical collaboration" and can be "experienced only in an activity of production."[29]

Fiske became an especially vocal proponent of this notion of poly-semy, extending it to suggest that we all live in what he called a "semiotic democracy," in which texts may well come with intentions, meanings, designs, and signs, but in which we can change those signs and do with them what we want.[30] Popular culture, he argued, can only be popular in the first place because an audience has found personal meaning for a text, and thus has domesticated the text in some way. Though Fiske has subsequently been criticized for opening the door of textuality *too far*, he certainly did wish to open it: "Television," he wrote, "is not quite a do-it-yourself meaning kit but neither is it a box of ready-made meanings for sale."[31] Needless to say, polysemy poses a significant challenge to our examination of programs, since it requires that analysts be aware of the multiple readings that texts might take on. On one level, of course, anyone who has ever had their words misunderstood can appreciate how easy it is for polysemy not only to creep into any communicative act but to vastly transform meaning in the process. On another level, however, polysemy means not only that "misunderstandings" will happen, but also that active and purposeful play with meaning will occur. And thus the textual analyst must always be aware of how television can be read in different ways, how its messages may play to different audiences, how varying life experiences or past viewing experiences will recode what is being watched, and so on. Precisely because, as will be argued, audiences are so unpredictable, texts are similarly unpredictable. This should not stop analysts in their tracks, and indeed Fiske quite gleefully practiced textual analysis in a terrain of polysemy, examining how various texts of popular culture might be interpreted differently. But it should give all textual analysts cause to be open to other readings and to pay close attention to textual attributes that might make "writerly" moves easier or more difficult. And ultimately, since this openness leads directly to the power of the audience, polysemy demands that no definitive, closing statement about the text be made until the audience has been analyzed. With this in mind, our next chapter turns to television studies' history of audience analysis, research, and theory.

Examples of critical analysis of television

First, however, it is high time that we offer examples of how critical analysis works. Critical analysis of television programs has followed a wide variety of topics and themes, and much of the rest of this chapter will provide several examples of this work, and especially of its attention to representations of various identity markers. Importantly, though, much of this work has simultaneously engaged in industrial, audience, and/or context-based analysis. Indeed, it is worth returning briefly to screen theory to note its fate: it failed to take root in television studies largely because it refused to take the audience seriously. By contrast, the below-discussed projects show a critical awareness of audiences, industry, and/or context, often including sections on them within the project. But for the purposes of illustrating how textual analysis has worked in television studies, in this chapter we restrict our attention to textual, *program* analysis within these projects.

To make sure our terms are clear, ideology – or the ideas about the world – is part of television texts even though we rarely notice it. Dominant ideology is often thought of as "common sense" or just the way things are. It describes systems of belief that are widely shared in a society at a moment in time, which come to take on extraordinary power because they are normalized by everything from schools, to religious organizations, to the content of popular media such as television. The dominant ideology is not fixed; neo-Marxists such as Althusser and Gramsci contend that those in power must constantly work to reassert it in order to maintain a hold on common sense. Consider that in television's fairly brief lifetime, the dominant ideological perspectives regarding equality among men and women and different ethnic groups have experienced marked revision. More recently, television has been one of many spaces of contestation of the dominant ideology regarding rights of gays and lesbians, who had previously been absent or unmentioned on television, while others such as transsexuals still remain largely invisible. Importantly, examinations of dominant ideology need not be identity based. Examinations of contemporary children's shows, for example, now indicate a profound attention to environmental messages and attitudes about conservation that are also examples of ideologies, or we might examine how belief systems such as Catholicism or capitalism are represented. Some providing introductions to textual analysis, such as we do here, attempt to subdivide textual and ideological analysis much more precisely than we do. Rather, we consider any work that examines the construction and depiction of power relations in a text – be they related to class, nation, race, gender, sexuality, or exploring belief systems – as characteristic of critical, ideological analysis.

"Critical" analysis, let us be clear, need not take the form of a damning rejection, and in this respect "critical" does not have the same meaning as in the everyday usage whereby "being critical" means "being negative." Instead, critical analysis pries under the surface for deeper meanings and connects these meanings to broader social analysis and commentary. Such a process may very well contribute to a scathing critique of a text and its politics, as television presents us with a great deal to be attacked and resisted. But it need not always do so. Ultimately, we take the position that analysis is truly critical when it is open to exploring a wide variety of issues, when the analyst has been open to being surprised by his or her textual analysis, and hence when it leads its readers to a better understanding of the text and of how and why that text matters.

Most critical analysis of television has focused on some aspect of identity. Much of this research draws from a similar neo-Marxist theoretical framework that presumes television to play an important role in establishing systems of belief. One challenge for this work has been to further ground its theoretical framework in terms of theories about how media work in society. Early critical analysis often drew from the social science research and language of "positive" and "negative" representations. This was largely replaced with perspectives regarding making dominant ideology uninhabitable in the work of Stuart Hall and others at the CCCS.

As television content has changed in accord with various social movements and expanded exponentially into a multiplicity of niche channels, some of these analyses have struggled to theorize the operation of ideology in the increasingly diverse representational fields now common. In the 1970s and 1980s, sexist and racist representations were readily available and it was easy to argue what was wrong with consistently featuring women as sexy love interests or blacks as criminals. By 2010, the representational field had become diverse and complicated. A multitude of women could be found across shows, and even a single show might offer a number of characters that aspired to a far greater array of goals; in this context, how do we make sense of one character who wants to find a husband if she is "balanced" with a best friend driven by career goals?

Or how could we understand the continued centrality of white characters even when police procedurals stopped uniformly casting black actors as criminals and increasingly cast them in culturally powerful, but narratively insignificant roles such as judges? At the same time, much reality television continues to traffic in stereotypes otherwise excised from most fictional television.

Gender   A desire to expose the ideology present in television texts has long been a central driving impulse of television studies. Notably, the slow turn to studying television as an important popular media form that began in the 1970s occurred alongside considerable feminist activism and contesting of the ideology surrounding women's gender roles. As a result, much television studies research has a particularly feminist perspective that can be traced to the beginning of television studies; Charlotte Brunsdon notes that sustained attention to feminist research was present even in early television criticism, and Newcomb acknowledges "feminist theorists have been among the most active and perceptive in the study of television."[32]

Much of the first scholarship looked back at women in television's early years to analyze evidence of their agency or tensions in the way gender roles were recalled. Patricia Mellencamp analyzed the gender politics of *I Love Lucy* and *Burns and Allen* to illustrate how the series showed Lucy and Gracie to perpetually try to break out of the domestic bounds that confined them, using comedy to contest their confinement.[33] Similarly, Kathleen Rowe argues for the feminist subversion exhibited by the then-contemporary "unruly woman" character exemplified by Roseanne Arnold in *Roseanne*. Unruly women characters, she argues, provide women with a way to disrupt dominant gender hierarchies, as their denial of socially produced beauty standards and agency as joke-makers inverts structures that often oppress women.[34] More contemporary unruly women might include Holly Hunter's Grace Hanadarko character on *Saving Grace* or *Damages'* Patty Hewes.

A considerable amount of feminist television scholarship focused its analysis on women portraying characters who were wives and mothers. Mary Beth Haralovich analyzes the mise-en-scène of *Father Knows Best* and *Leave it to Beaver* to illustrate how the shows constructed a particular image of the housewife consistent with those offered by suburban housing development and the consumer product industry at the time.[35] Then, as television increasingly acknowledged changes in gender roles, much scholarship turned to assessing constructions of women's liberation. Such analyses often focus on female characters, character types, or a depiction of a character's subjectivity – as in the "new woman" example of *The Mary Tyler Moore Show*. Using this approach, Judith Mayne explores how feminist content disrupts the narrative organization and the representation of law in *L.A. Law*, arguing that feminism structures the narrative as a "door that swings both ways," often providing the text with its open-endedness as a result of presenting discourses that suggest the radical difference between women and men according to the law, while also exploring the applicability of the law to men and women alike.[36] Likewise, Danae Clark considers the strategic use of narrative form, representational codes, and structures of looking to suggest *Cagney & Lacey* as a feminist text.[37] She argues that "*Cagney & Lacey* empowers women and encourages women-identified constructions of meaning" through a narrative form that hybridizes the police genre and conventions of soap opera, through "the text's refusal" to define the characters solely as private or public figures, and by providing an "alternative viewer-text relation that breaks up traditional structures of looking."[38] Other examples include Jeremy Butler's analysis of *Designing Women*, in which he examines the series for evidence of feminist discourses in its dialogue and within the narrative structure; or Lauren Rabinovitz's examination of "single mom" sitcoms, which analyzes "single mom" feminism as a representational trend, examining discourses in *Kate and Allie* and *One Day at a Time* as prototypes of the single mom sitcoms that were prevalent between 1975 and 1985.[39]

Critical textual analysis is a fairly big tent, under which research taking a wide array of subfoci can be categorized. Bonnie Dow's book tracing feminist discourse longitudinally across the series *The Mary Tyler Moore Show*, *One Day at a Time*, *Designing Women*, *Murphy Brown*, and *Dr. Quinn, Medicine Woman* argues that the shift in feminist discourse from *The Mary Tyler Moore Show* to *Murphy Brown* illustrates an obsession with feminist identity and a gradual reduction in the engagement of feminist politics.[40] Dow, a rhetorician, emphasizes the way feminist discourse is constructed, evident in analysis of "the intersections of . . . textual strategies – genre, plot, character development, narrative structure – with the confluence of discourses, produced by and about feminism, in the time period during which they were produced and originally received."[41] In her analysis of late 1990s dramas, Amanda Lotz presents a critical analysis focused more on narrative to explore how certain categories of stories and themes became preponderant in the subgenre of female-centered dramas, exploring the politics of these themes and how some of the new variation in women's characterizations dismantled long-powerful stereotypes.[42] Or Tania Modleski explored the narrative form of soap operas and why their formal strategies might be appealing to women viewers, considering features such as stock character types and its ever-unresolved form.[43]

More recent feminist critical analysis has been significantly engaged with questions of "postfeminism," a term with contested meaning and uncertain implications for feminist analysis. Although a considerable number of feminist textual analyses appear each year, the area has become considerably stymied in identifying new directions and moving beyond what Charlotte Brunsdon categorizes as "Ur" feminist article in which scholars acknowledge the regressive aspects of a favored text but then identify a variety of simultaneous "progressive" aspects.[44] Some have also worked to explore other categories of women – such as depictions of girls and teens – or considered once-underexplored genres such as factual television.

Class and nation   Another early focus of critical analysis considered representations of nation and class. One of the first books of television studies analysis, Charlotte Brunsdon and David Morley's *Everyday Television*, took the popular British news journal program *Nationwide* and analyzed it with particular attention to its messages regarding class and nation. The rationale behind the program choice was that the show posed " 'ordinary people' as its source, and thus represents historically-determined and necessarily political positions simply as a set of natural, taken-for-granted 'home truths.' "[45] *Nationwide* was fond of domesticating issues, they noted, by presenting "an average person's" attitudes or responses to policy and society and thereby placing all the more importance on how the show decided to construct this "average person." Who was the "average" Briton and what was his or her "average" experience of life in the nation? Brunsdon and Morley noted that in answering such questions, *Nationwide* often erased class from the picture in favor of highlighting interview subjects' regional identities: "spatial difference replaces social structure and the nation is seen to be composed not of social units in any relation of exploitation or antagonism but of geographical units often reduced to regional stereotypes or 'characters.' "[46] Their critique of the show's textual strategies to erase not only class but race and gender too sought to make sense of how patriarchy, elitism, and racism were rationalized, or at least watered down, through being translated to the language of regional difference, "the way things are," and to British "common sense."

Such work proved especially important in the UK, where the BBC was explicitly entrusted with broadcasting the nation to the nation. In the US, the grandiose titles and rhetoric of the *American* Broadcasting Company (ABC), *National* Broadcasting Corporation (NBC), and *Columbia* Broadcasting System (CBS) certainly claimed to speak the nation to the nation, but in the UK this mandate was much more clearly stipulated by the BBC's charter. British television scholars thus became all the more interested in, and dispirited by, the degree to which the nation was constructed in only some citizens' images, often far more so than their American peers. Stuart Hall wrote an article entitled "Which Public? Whose Service?" in which, as the title suggests, he criticized the BBC's "public service" programming as excluding vast swathes of the population.[47] Given that Britons with televisions are required to fund the BBC through a television license fee, due annually, questions regarding the value of this service and its ability to address the whole nation have been especially pressing. However, even in the United States, ABC, NBC, CBS, FOX, and The CW enjoy signal monopoly – meaning that no other individual or corporation can legally broadcast on "their" part of the spectrum – because they are seen to be providing broadcasting in the "public interest" in return. Thus, while questions of nationality have been less common in American television studies, we might also ask how "America" as a concept is created. Who is American and who isn't? Where is America "more" American, or "less" American? And how does America intersect with other depictions of class, race, gender, and sexuality? For instance, when "American values" is often code word for white, Christian, heterosexual, middle-class values, the utility of nation as an identity marker shows itself no less devious than in the UK.

With this in mind, Victoria Johnson's recent book, *Heartland TV*, turns its attention to a specific regional construction, that of "the heartland," usually taken to mean Midwest America. Johnson acutely notes that the term serves a paradoxical double duty, on one hand referring to a place where hicks live, white working-class folk who don't understand or appreciate progress, while on the other hand – and occasionally at the same time! – reverentially referring to a salt-of-the-earth, honest working folk who constitute the moral and ethical heart of the nation. Representations of the Midwest are thus densely loaded, she observes, sliding between admiration and dismissal. All the while, though, a racial, classed, sexualized, urban Other is elided from this discourse, so that, for instance, Chicago sits uncomfortably in the Midwest representationally even when it centers it geographically, and so that the queering of Midwestern characters carries great potential significance.[48]

Race and ethnicity   If class has proved a vital identity marker in both British society and British television studies, Johnson's is a relatively rare examination of class and nation in the American context. More common have been studies of gender, sexuality, and race. Indeed, in both the UK and the US, as neo-Marxist approaches turned the tools of critical analysis on identity constructs beyond class, race too became a central area of investigation. For television studies, Herman Gray's *Watching Race* remains an exemplary study in terms of its carefully contextualized critical analysis that places its textual objects in the social and political milieu of the 1980s and addresses television's industrial context as well. Gray examines television as one of the places in the cultural terrain upon which the culture at large struggles over ethnic identity, specifically over the meaning of blackness. The work begins by contextualizing its texts within the historical moment of Reaganism and the political economy of the end of the network era in relation to changes in representations of African Americans and blackness. The institutional change is a necessary element in his judgment for understanding the textual shifts evident in the late 1980s and early 1990s. His textual analysis then proposes a taxonomy of three representational strategies before launching into four chapters of case studies that explore how various series offer assimilation, contestation, and parody.

Gray's book remains a standard-bearer in terms of contextualized textual analysis. Many others focusing on race have tended toward more description than analysis. Darrell Hamamoto's *Monitored Peril* focuses more on textual analysis alone in its efforts to trace the history of Asian American representations on US television.[49] Many others have offered broad and sweeping descriptive accounts or generalized histories.[50] Following on these efforts to chart the broad history of representation, subsequent scholarship has increasingly turned to more specific phenomena. Kristal Brent Zook follows Gray's form in *Color by Fox* to blend institutional analysis with textual analysis of the Fox Network's strategy for achieving parity with the Big Three networks by serving underrepresented African Americans.[51] Or in *Laughing Mad*, Bambi Haggins examines African Americans' use of comedy – much of which was broadcast on television – to transcend racial boundaries and how this comedy that came into the home was used to mediate racial tensions and ignorance.[52] Beretta Smith-Shomade focuses on representations of black women on television, considering the particularities of this identity group often unaddressed in feminist scholarship or generalized studies of African-American representation.

Important critical analysis of race has also attended to news representations, an area generally lacking in television studies. Jimmie L. Reeves and Richard Campbell's *Cracked Coverage* offers detailed analysis of the discrepancy in television news frames for relaying stories about the cocaine epidemic in America depending on the ethnicity of the drug users.[53] And in chapters of *Media Matters*, John Fiske attends to various factual media and their constructions of Anita Hill's allegations during Clarence Thomas's Supreme Court hearings and the coverage of the Rodney King beating and trial.[54]

Sexuality   Sexuality has provided another focus of critical analysis of identity. As television has incorporated a greater range of gay characters, so too has the scholarship about gay representations expanded.[55] Ron Becker's *Gay TV and Straight America* provides analysis of what he terms "gay-themed TV" amidst the complicated and contested political field of the 1990s in which college student Matthew Shepard was beaten to death for being gay while the country laughed at a growing array of gay characters, as well as changes in the television industry that afforded gay representations salience not only to those whose lives they mirrored, but also to the demographic of straight audiences accepting of broader depictions of sexuality.[56] Although Becker's remains the only book-length study focused on television, some published articles consider television and sexuality, while other books include television among a matrix of other media important for assessing gay representation. A recent collection, *Queer TV*, also expands this work.[57]

Politics   Critical analysis, though, has not served solely to explain identity markers. Rather, one could analyze representations, and the ideology, of almost anything. We might ask, for instance, how are professors represented on television, or how is love represented? What does happiness look like when televised? How does television deal with birth, or death? Endless possibilities present themselves. Of course, many such projects could be subsumed under the broad mandate of an interest in gender, race and ethnicity, sexuality, class, or nation, since those representations likely impact these various identity markers. Another key area for analysis, though, lies at the level of television's representation of politics. Here, and despite all the pop analyses of the wonders or ills of certain news programs, too little formal analysis exists, with Brunsdon and Morley's *Everyday Television* a relatively rare exception that is joined by several others, John Corner's discussion of news amongst them.[58] What one finds more of, however, is analysis of political entertainment. Certainly, *Everyday Television* fits, and perhaps created, this mold. But especially in recent years with the rise of some intelligent, thoughtful, and politically savvy entertainment programs, some within television studies have offered helpful analyses of such texts. Jeffrey Jones's *Entertaining Politics* stands out here, which in its first edition looked at Dennis Miller, Bill Maher, and Jon Stewart, but in its second edition added the television shows of Michael Moore and *The Colbert Report* in particular.[59] Here we see how critical analysis need not simply be a matter of finding problematic representations and critiquing texts' inclusion of them. Jones, by contrast, uses formal analysis to make better sense of exactly how this brand of political entertainment is able to succeed, and to tease out its strategies. Stewart and Colbert in particular are cunning, wily analysts of the media in their own right, attuned to how best to undercut and counter the policies and politicians they attack. In many ways, Stewart, Colbert, and their writing teams engage in their own careful formal analysis, as several of their richly satiric clips suggest, as they focus on specific words or uses of images employed by politicians and newspeople. In one such instance, Stewart eviscerated Fox News' crude caricature of "liberals" by cleverly applying this caricature to Fox News itself, and by matching, one for one, instances of its statements regarding "the liberal media" with its own present behavior. Representational and formal analyses, thus, can at times be complementary, working with one or more shows to shed light on the textual strategies of yet other shows.

What next? New directions for textual analysis

Having examined textual analysis to the present, however, what might be its next steps? Part of our answer to this question takes the form of the remaining chapters, as we argue that textual analysis, while not requiring of audience, industry, and contextual analysis to be of value, can nevertheless benefit from a multipronged approach.

Another answer comes in the form of a gentle call for a better integration of aesthetics. As much as we see little room for fetishized analysis for its own sake within television studies, we would welcome a more successful reintegration of aesthetics and critical analysis, and we regard this as a key frontier for the field. This frontier has only loomed larger as a recent spate of programming has caused many to marvel at the quality of today's television. Discussions of *The Wire*, *Lost*, *Friday Night Lights*, *Breaking Bad*, *The Sopranos*, *Six Feet Under*, *Mad Men*, and many other shows are often replete with assertions of the shows' artistic excellence. Thus the vocabulary of artistry and aesthetics is significantly more prevalent in everyday talk about television than arguably it has been at other points, save of course for many moments in history when the medium's alleged *lack* of artistry was touted. Not only does this surge in "aesthetic talk" require our engagement with aesthetics if we are to truly triangulate the discourses that surround television programs, but it also colors our own choices in television studies of what to study. A banal yet important point not heretofore mentioned in this chapter is that formal analysis of television takes a lot of time, especially for long-running shows. One should only expect, then, that some scholars will work most closely with programs that they like, or alternately with programs that they feel the need to attack. In either situation, we see some television studies motivated by an urge to proselytize, with the show in question's perceived surfeit or lack of aesthetics playing a key role in inspiring the research project. If such choices are made without explicit acknowledgment, as indeed they often are, we are once more left with a situation in which a clearer, more explicit, and rigorous discussion of aesthetics may help television studies as a field to move forward.

Aesthetics have often been avoided with due reason. First, as noted, a program's ideological role has often been deemed more important. Second, especially when public (mis)understanding of television studies is often that scholars sit around and talk about what shows they like, television studies has often found it rhetorically important to focus more definitively on sociocultural importance and to leave the realm of aesthetics alone. Some who write popularly on television positively gush about how wonderful this or that program is, and few in television studies wish to have their scholarship confused with such gushers, even if this position risks overcompensation. Third, cultural theory posed hard questions about art and aesthetics, seeing them as the provisions of the upper classes (as will be studied further in chapter 2) and as evaluative schemes used to reduce to nothingness the tastes of the working classes, women, children, and other marginal groups. Art therefore became a dirty word. It is not our suggestion that cultural theory's careful engagement with the politics of taste and distinction be dismissed. On the contrary, we would like to see television studies wrestle with such analysis anew, in order to better analyze the discourse of art and aesthetics that surrounds discussion and studies of television. After all, surely we cannot reduce all declarations of a show's artistry to the politics and performance of superiority, and surely therefore more work exists for television studies at the level of interrogating how art and the sublime work, why and how we experience them, and why and how we claim them on behalf of certain programs or types of programming. We can, in other words, engage with what many have called "quality television," maintaining a healthy critical distance and skepticism of the notion of "quality" that undergirds such a phrase, and that distinguishes television studies from gushing, gleeful praise, while also examining the processes by which shows are both branded and deemed as "quality."[60]

Television studies will also need to respond to the dissemination of television via social media by examining units *smaller* than the individual show that travel as such. Even prior to the internet, multiple shows were designed to allow viewers to dip in and out of them, each a collection of segments more than necessarily a coherent whole. From variety and sketch shows to late night talk shows, morning shows, and the news, some of television's programs throughout the medium's history may more profitably be analyzed at the level of the segment.[61] In an era of social media, moreover, many such shows are experienced all the more often in segmented forms, as Hulu, YouTube, Facebook, embedded clips in blogs, and other platforms allow viewers to circulate segments ripped from the remains of the text. Thus, shows such as *The Daily Show with Jon Stewart* and *Saturday Night Live* may best be understood and appreciated at their Facebook-embedded level rather than as distinct programs. Tina Fey's Sarah Palin impression achieved a ubiquity through endless links and embeddings that *Saturday Night Live* could not manage on its own, to the point that it may now be bizarre to study those sketches within the context of the episodes in which they appeared. If textual analysis has expanded to encompass collections of texts in the form of genres, it should also contract to make sense of segments.

Another huge frontier for television studies is simply to study much more television. Whether due to unacknowledged biases regarding quality and/or to a sense that prime time matters above all else, television studies has at times doggedly clung to prime-time television from the broadcast networks and a limited number of other boutique channels. Thus, as Frances Bonner importantly observes, studies of "ordinary television" are somewhat lacking.[62] As time goes on, and as "television" is constituted of more and more channels that attract yet larger proportions of the audience, this blind spot becomes all the more egregious. Increasingly more shows and genres elude the field's gaze. This is not to say that television studies should abandon its interests in the latest HBO, ABC, or BBC critical darlings, but such shows do not suffice if the field is after a full picture of television's relationship to society at large.

The potential findings of studying more "ordinary" television are abundantly clear in several exceptions to this trend. Fiske, for example, proved instrumental in the early days of American television studies largely by analyzing the more banal texts of quiz shows, *Hart to Hart*, and wrestling, rather than simply the marquee productions of the day such as *Hill Street Blues*.[63] Working in this vein, Kevin Glynn's *Tabloid Culture* offers a strong and compelling analysis of the workings of class in television viewership by studying numerous instances of "trash television" – alien abduction videos, tawdry talk shows, and the like.[64] And Derek Kompare's *Rerun Nation* embarrasses television studies by noting the ubiquity of reruns and yet their relative absence from discussion; Kompare's book is largely historical, with little close analysis of texts, but it poses the important question of what meanings shows take on in their syndicated afterlives.[65] What do *I Love Lucy*, *Seinfeld*, *Friends*, *M*A*S*H*, *Roseanne*, *Little House on the Prairie*, *The Cosby Show*, or season-one episodes of *Law and Order* or *CSI* mean in 2011? To rework the old riddle, what noise does a tree make if it falls several times a year in stripped scheduling?

Television studies should also conduct more work examining the medium's diverse genres. Sports programming, late night television, morning shows, movies of the week,[66] and religious broadcasting,[67] are all examples of television programming that has largely gone unconsidered. Advertising has also, and shockingly, largely disappeared from television studies' field of analysis, as many scholars can comfortably write about and teach ads' effects on other programming, but few examine the ads themselves.[68] And if television studies' early days were marked by a fervid interest in soaps (as discussed in chapter 2) and the news,[69] more recent work has often underplayed the importance of these genres, and we would welcome a return to them. Finally, yet not insignificantly, "television" is not just American television, nor American and British television, and while global media studies have often been structural and industrial in character, more textual analyses of the world's television would help destabilize the Anglo-American hegemony in the field as a whole.

Inevitably, there will perhaps always be more television than there are scholars to study it, meaning on one hand that the field will always require finger-wagging reminders to cover a wider variety of shows, but, on the other hand, that there will always be un(der)explored territory on which new scholars can make their mark.

2

Audiences

As much as television's programs matter, much of their importance is only felt inasmuch as an audience is there in the first place. To say that a program "does" or "means" something is to assume it does so *to* an audience. We might often convince ourselves that commercial television is the business of creating and selling *shows*, but in truth it is the business of creating and selling *audiences*. Audiences are the central commodity in a commercial television model, as channels sell potential viewers to advertisers, whereas in a public broadcasting model, the system exists solely for the edification, enlightenment, and entertainment of audiences. However, knowing that audiences matter doesn't solve the more tackling issue of working out exactly *how* they matter, and how they behave. After all, so many different types of audiences exist, not only audiences of millennials, longshoremen, African Americans, Canadians, fans, or so forth, but also hypothetical audiences, ideal audiences, assumed audiences, numeric audiences, potential audiences, individual audience members, and audience communities. Thus studying audiences has long proven to be a difficult and highly contentious task. Moreover, since so many roads in television studies lead back to the audience, many statements about programs, industries, and context assume and imply a great deal about audiences, meaning that audiences are often being invoked and constructed even when the individual study ostensibly has little to do with audiences. In this chapter, we will trace the history of television studies' varying engagements with audiences and in the process will discuss numerous methodologies for studying audiences.

We begin by looking at the analysis of audiences that preceded television studies by way of setting up the impasses and problems that audience studies in a television and cultural studies vein subsequently attempted to overcome through a different methodology. This methodology is then discussed in detail, as we look first at the Birmingham Center for Contemporary Cultural Studies (CCCS) and its sizeable imprint on audience studies, and then at the "active audience" paradigm that grew in part from CCCS and in part from a new generation of audience researchers elsewhere too. Arguably the most thriving sub-area of audience studies throughout television studies' history has been work that examines fans and fandom. Given the degree to which crude accounts of the media allotted a special place of ignominy and infamy for fans as the supposedly passive dupes lost in the media system, the rhetorical importance of studying actual fans saw this sub-area take on a life of its own. We will chart some of the further reasons for this growth before attending to a backlash of criticism that faced fan and audience studies in the early nineties and beyond. Following this backlash, audience studies branched into numerous other areas, as did fan studies more specifically, and the remainder of the chapter will cover these various areas, focusing particularly on television studies' examinations of the audience in everyday life, user-generated culture, global and diasporic audiences, and rituals of television use. Finally, we close with a call for audience work to expand into several underexplored areas.

A prehistory of television studies' engagement with audiences

As noted in our Introduction, what we are calling television studies did not inaugurate the study of audiences, as instead audience research had been conducted for several decades prior, with a heavy social scientific inflection. Especially in the wake of the unprecedented mastery of propaganda that characterized the years surrounding World War II, many scholars realized the utter importance of examining exactly how such mediated propaganda worked when it reached its targets. This research was often survey based and quantitative by nature, and/or involved experimental settings, conducted within the paradigm of what is called "mass communications." The style of such work should be familiar to all readers, since it is still going strong to this day, and the press has long been fond of reporting on it, especially since it can frequently offer its findings in the form of sound-biteable dictums with the heft of numbers, percentages, and determinate statements about media effect behind them. When one reads that such-and-such a university has "proven" that television leads to more permissive ideas of sex or violence, for instance, with X percent of those studied showing a prominent change in sexual or aggressive behavior, one is reading effects work.

However, while much of this research was at least initially motivated by an interest in how successful various forms of propaganda and governmental messaging were, and by a concern for the dangers of mass media, numerous researchers soon began to report instances in which a message backfired, or they found other challenges to the idea that audiences were simply consuming everything in the way that the message's creators intended. Studying audiences of *The Man with the Golden Arm*, for example, Charles Winick found that, despite the film's apparent anti-drug message, many young drug-using viewers identified with Frank Sinatra's drug-using character, and hence missed the film's supposed message, instead seeing the movie's treatment of Sinatra's character as making drug use somewhat cool.[1] Similarly, Eunice Cooper and Helen Dinerman examined how audiences reacted to a US government-released anti-fascist, anti-discrimination film, *Don't Be a Sucker*, with some finding the Nazi German hero substantially more charismatic than his American opposite, and hence identifying more with his struggle.[2] These and many other studies formed a paradigm of research referred to as "uses and gratifications," whereby researchers gradually began to examine what uses audiences had for media, and how they used the media to gratify personal interests and desires. The paradigm looked at the text's encounter with an audience through the eyes of the audience, situating them as individuals with pasts and with intended uses for the text, rather than as patients waiting to be injected with messages by the media, as prior research had been guilty of doing, leading to the pejorative categorization of that earlier research as conducted within a "hypodermic needle" paradigm.

Looking back on both hypodermic needle and uses-and-gratifications research through a television studies lens, though, many of these studies offer more questions than answers. What precisely *is* more aggressive behavior, in the case of violence research for instance – does pleasure in the death of a fictional character equate to pleasure in seeing someone hurt in real life? In other words, what different roles do violence, sex, or any other topic play in our everyday lives? Why might people seek out certain content in the first place? Or, in the case of the above-mentioned uses-and-gratifications studies, what role does identification with a star or character play in media consumption? How did context of viewing matter? Winick, for instance, noted that price of the movie affected responses. Where are viewers doing their watching, with whom, and how does this change their responses? What meanings do these films have for the viewers weeks later, not just immediately following viewing?

How do they talk about them, and how might the movies' messages be further negotiated by what others have to say? A methodology that could answer more of these questions might be better enabled to understand not only the nature of the interaction between text and audience, but also further issues such as the role of celebrity in contemporary society, social meanings surrounding drug use or discrimination, and so forth.

The CCCS intervention

The beginnings of this more nuanced methodology took root in Birmingham in the 1970s at the Center for Contemporary Cultural Studies. As noted in the previous chapter, the Center was greatly influenced by semiology and its attempts to examine popular culture as a language, but, whereas many semiologists had discussed audiences only as hypothetical, Stuart Hall's Encoding/Decoding model shifted focus to balancing out the "encoding" and construction of messages with the "decoding" of them, or with how audiences interacted with them and shaped meaning themselves. Hall noted that "there is no necessary correspondence between encoding and decoding," meaning that what is put "into" a text would never necessarily determine what was taken "out" of it: encoding "can attempt to 'pre-fer' but cannot prescribe or guarantee [decoding], which has its own conditions of existence."[3] Encoding and decoding are each separate determinate moments, argued Hall, and while the former would always in some way prefigure the possibilities of the latter, it could never wholly control it. If it did, we would all believe everything that every program told us. As such, Hall proposed three key possibilities: either a decoder would adopt the "dominant-hegemonic" position, falling in step with what the encoder wanted, s/he would adopt an "oppositional" position and read against the encoded text's grain, or adopt a "negotiated" position somewhere in between. Hall's model enjoys significant intuitive purchase, to the point that it may seem somewhat banal and obvious to a reader today, but its importance in inspiring a wave of qualitative audience research cannot be understated. The model was also tied to Hall's and the Center's use of Antonio Gramsci's notions of ideology and hegemony. Gramsci saw ideology as working not only by force, but also by seeping into the "common sense" of a society, by seeming natural – much as one rarely considers one's own accent as anything but "normal" – and hence by working at a micro level in countless cultural interactions and messages of popular culture.[4] Hall's model posited the study of decoding as the study of how power works in society, not simply of how any given message works. If one was to understand how dominant meanings of class, race, gender, politics, and social values were created and maintained, and of how they might be challenged, one needed to understand the moment of decoding.

The Center's project was by no means relegated solely to television. Prominent early research from CCCS members, for instance, also examined punk and other musical subcultures,[5] and young girls' use of magazines and fashion.[6] However, given the nationalizing force and mandate of the British Broadcasting Corporation (BBC), and of television in general in 1970s England, particular attention was paid to television by numerous members of CCCS. The project most clearly tied to the Encoding/Decoding model was the Center's analysis of a popular news magazine program, *Nationwide*.[7] As noted in our previous chapter, David Morley and Charlotte Brunsdon first analyzed the show's textual strategies, especially its construction of nation, but they then conducted focus group analysis of the decoding of the program. They showed episodes of the program to groups that were united by class positioning, with, for example, a group of shop stewards, another of teacher training college students, and another of managers. The group format, they hoped, would show "how interpretations were collectively constructed through talk and the interchange between respondents in the group situation – rather than to treat individuals as the autonomous repositories of a fixed set of individual 'opinions' isolated from their social context."[8] They then looked for evidence of watching within the dominant-hegemonic, negotiated, or oppositional positions, and found significant evidence to back up Hall's model. The managers were often only too willing to accept the dominant-hegemonic position, for instance, ensconced as they were in that position of privilege in society, whereas working-class groups often felt the need to oppose the hegemonic values on offer in *Nationwide*, or at least to negotiate with them. In other words, rather than finding that working-class individuals accepted bourgeois values at face value, they found *Nationwide* to be a site of friction and the process of watching it to be one in which some of those values were contested, some accepted, some negotiated.

The *Nationwide* studies proved highly influential. As Morley and Brunsdon have reflected, at the time, the textual analysis that preceded the audience analysis drew much of the attention.[9] Indeed, the very choice of what program to study was important, given that it fell much lower on scales of supposed cultural value than did, for example, *Panorama*, the BBC's more "austere" news magazine. But, as Morley has argued, "there is, in television, no such thing as 'an innocent text' – no programme which is not worthy of serious attention, no program which can claim to provide 'only entertainment' rather than messages about society."[10] Thus, not only was their analysis of its construction of "common sense" relevant, but their choice of program signaled very clearly that all programs were worthy of, perhaps even *requiring of*, analysis. So, too, with audiences, and while uses-and-gratifications research had often been drawn to "message films" and other media with seemingly clear intentions, the CCCS demanded that audiences for the multiple minutiae of the world of popular culture would reveal how power, social values, and "common sense" were constructed and contested.

In many ways, Morley and Brunsdon serve as spectacular examples of the quick maturation of audience research and theory within television studies. For his part, Morley's next book, *Family Television*, began with an honest admission that the *Nationwide* project had involved screening television in an unnatural setting, and thus he set out now to examine how consumption occurred in the family home.[11] This represented a quick learning curve of realizing a need to discuss television as it was actually watched, not television as it is watched in a laboratory or experimental setting. But it also moved beyond the *Nationwide* study's anchoring to the Encoding/Decoding model, as Morley examined a broad range of responses to and uses of television. His work here was co-influential with numerous German researchers, Hermann Bausinger in particular, who similarly examined the place that television occupied in the home. Bausinger, for instance, writes of a family where the father regularly came home from work angry, turned on the television, and watched in stoic silence until in a more pleasant mood, and where the mother often watched sports with her son, not out of interest, but simply to connect with him; analysis of this family's viewing experiences would risk missing the point of the viewing if it focused solely on the programs they watched and not on the important frames of viewing.[12] Similar work was also being conducted in the United States by James Lull from a slightly more quantitative, survey-based tradition, yet also concerned with how television as technology fitted into the patterns of everyday family life.[13] Soon this led to a burgeoning new form of television studies that examined relationships with the technologies of television. As did Morley in *Family Television* and in subsequent work with Roger Silverstone and Eric Hirsch, much of this work focused on gender. Morley, Silverstone, and Hirsch examined how, for example, remote controls became totems of masculine power in many families, and how program selection enacted power hierarchies within the home.[14] Ann Gray, meanwhile, studied ways in which the VCR was allowing women to navigate gendered expectations of their television consumption and of their behavior in general.[15]

For her part, Charlotte Brunsdon's work following the *Nationwide* project was intrinsically linked to feminist media studies. Indeed, as we will see, feminism and audience research within television studies have been closely connected. Morley has since noted that the CCCS's original decision to study *Nationwide* was not arrived at easily, as numerous team members had wanted instead to study soap operas, as a yet more culturally "lowbrow" product than *Nationwide*, and as a genre that more explicitly invited discussions of *gendered* power than did *Nationwide*.[16] Brunsdon, though, was one of several British and American scholars to study soaps in the wake of the *Nationwide* project. Related to this, Brunsdon has continually examined issues of taste, and of how television technologies – such as satellite dishes – genre, and individual programs become lightning rods for cultural distinctions, and she has examined the cultural politics of taste in relation to television and film.[17]

The active audience

In the 1980s, audience research and theory in television studies flourished, opening doors to more fruitful analysis of audiences, while also complicating notions of the text by pointing out its contingency on audiences and hence its multiple variations. Audience research and theory of the 1980s rejuvenated studies of television, and in many ways created television studies as a field. As with the work by the CCCS, much of this work was politically motivated, and it had something to prove.

Most notably, audience research was taken up with particular relish by feminist media scholars, who saw in it a way to test both their own suspicions of seemingly anti-feminist genres, and widespread vilification and ridicule of women's genres in general. Though not a discussion of television, Janice Radway's *Reading the Romance* was an important book, as Radway first walked through a standard feminist critique of romance fiction as patriarchal, but then turned to audience research that revealed intelligent women using this fiction in interesting ways and forming communities whose tenor and character were nothing like the picture of squealing housewives that popular accounts imagined romance readers to be.[18] Within the burgeoning field of television studies proper, a great deal of work was being conducted on soap operas. Dorothy Hobson, for instance, examined British soap audiences and the ways in which program choice and viewing styles were inflected by gender.[19] Ien Ang conducted research on *Dallas* in the Netherlands, not only challenging myths of the show's march of cultural imperialism through the world (as would Elihu Katz and Tamar Liebes a few years later), but also treating *Dallas* as a *practice* of watching, not a text, and thus as an "enigma" that could not be solved by textual analysis alone.[20] And several other researchers found particular interest in soap viewers.[21]

But if women were one derided audience often deemed cultural dupes, another was children, and David Buckingham took aim at the simplicity of discourse that reduced child and teen television viewers to blank slates. Laying down the gauntlet, Buckingham began his examination into child and teen viewers of the British soap *EastEnders* by arguing that "The assumption that critics are able to 'see through' television, while ordinary viewers cannot, is both arrogant and patronising."[22] Buckingham interviewed numerous child and teen viewers of the series and found a broad variation in what meanings they pulled from it, but a consistent savviness of interpretation. "[I]n general," he concluded, "the children appeared to be able to apply their own moral and ideological frameworks to the programme without feeling that it was encouraging them to adopt different ones," and he noted significant pleasure drawn from "questioning and in many cases ridiculing the artifice" of *EastEnders*.[23]

What these and other researchers argued for, then, was the utter inadequacy of reading a program's cultural or political uses to an audience off its surface alone. As Justin Lewis was to note, unless an audience is present, the program is like the proverbial tree falling in a forest with nobody there to hear it, and thus "textual analysis has, unfortunately, become alarmingly presumptuous."[24] He insisted, "The question that should be put to textual analysis that purports to tell us how a cultural product 'works' in contemporary culture is almost embarrassingly simple: where's the evidence? Without evidence, everything is pure speculation."[25] As such, audience research was posited as a potential rejoinder to whatever theories or concerns textual or industry analysts might have. As Lewis also noted, it is not enough "to say that people use TV programs for various purposes: we need to understand that this changes the nature of what is being watched."[26] In other words, the process of viewing is always a potentially *transformative* event, one that can change the nature of the program being watched. Audience research, therefore, was not simply about seeing whether one's predictions for a program came true; it was about seeing what happened to the program, what it became, and, importantly, what new or different meanings accrued to the program in the process of viewing. Or, more boldly and to others, as with Ang, audience research was about studying the *practice* of watching as its own text, and as an entity unto itself. In contrast to seeing the audience as a byproduct of the program, this generation of audience researchers insisted on the importance of seeing audiences as cultures. Certainly, the ethnographic method employed by many of them – interviewing, observing, sitting in with, and discussing television in their subjects' natural environments – borrowed from anthropology with its similar interest in cultures as systems of meaning. In doing so, they looked beyond the questions of whether a program was successful in doing this or that, and saw television, and television audiences, as points of access to understanding how society worked in general – how taste worked, how class, gender, or race worked, how familial power was exercised, and so forth. Morley was fond of noting in his teaching that if anthropologists had long considered food and meals wonderful nodes of access to a culture, television and television-watching practices had become a similarly helpful node.

It is this notion of studying cultures that was central to one of the more famous, or perhaps infamous, television studies researchers, John Fiske. "Popular culture," he wrote, "is not consumption, it is culture – the active process of generating and circulating meanings and pleasures within a social system."[27] Most dramatically in *Television Culture* and then in the pair of books *Understanding Popular Culture* and *Reading the Popular*, Fiske noted the fundamental openness and hence "polysemic" quality of all texts (see chapter 1).[28] But he also drew a sharp distinction between "mass culture" and "popular culture," noting that the former was the product of the culture industries, whereas the latter reflected what audiences did with it, and what culture they produced on top of it. "Culture is a living, active process: it can be developed only from within, it cannot be imposed from without or above."[29] Audiences, he argued, were "active" in creating their own meanings, and in "excorporating" items from mass culture and finding ways to use them. Fiske drew on Michel de Certeau's idea of audiences as "making do" with a mass culture not of their creation,[30] but one that through acts of bricolage, repurposing, and personalization could become domesticated. Texts, in short, were "resources," and where "Every commodity reproduces the ideology of the system that produced it," to consume was not necessarily to accept that ideology, but rather could be "a refusal of commodification and an assertion of one's right to make one's own culture out of the resources provided by the commodity system."[31]

As did much audience work of the 1980s, Fiske also drew on the politics of taste and distinction laid down in Pierre Bourdieu's *Distinction*. Bourdieu had studied taste cultures in France and saw their roots not in aesthetic superiority or inferiority, but in, an at times unknowing, class politics. He argued:

The denial of lower, coarse, vulgar, venal, servile – in a word, natural – enjoyment, which constitutes the sacred sphere of ["high"] culture, implies an affirmation of the superiority of those who can be satisfied with the sublimated, refined, disinterested, gratuitous, distinguished pleasures forever closed to the profane. That is why art and cultural consumption are predisposed, consciously and deliberately or not, to fulfill a social function of legitimating social differences.[32]

Bourdieu saw taste as a form of "cultural capital," working as a sign and a divider of class. Taste is taught to future generations amongst the wealthy and middle classes so that they might see themselves as entitled to their higher place in society when compared to the lower classes whose tastes are coded as barbaric, low, and degraded as a way of explaining their existence at the bottom of society. In the wake of Bourdieu's theory of distinction, everything that had previously been considered "lowbrow" and thereby labeled as unworthy of examination now required and invited study. Wrestling, soaps, quiz shows, and cop shows weren't inherently "crap," much less television itself; they had been *coded* as crap in order to denigrate their viewers, but closer analysis of these programs and their viewers was now required. One might think, for a parallel, of how some American historians were forced to revisit vast swathes of the nation's history when notions of the Native American as a lesser, uncultured savage were discredited as pure racism. Historians needed to tell those stories again and anew. Similarly, academia was now faced with the embarrassment of having largely ignored the culture and meanings of all but the bourgeois; thus, Bourdieu's work initiated a period of considerable study of audiences' "lowbrow" and "middlebrow" tastes.

Fiske's work in particular certainly romanticized audiences, borrowing Michel de Certeau's metaphor of audiences as engaged in "semiotic guerrilla warfare" with the cultural industries, using "tactics" against the "strategies" of Hollywood and of Madison Avenue. He also offered numerous examples, especially in *Understanding Popular Culture* and *Reading the Popular*, of, for instance, teenage girls seeing a strong female figure in Madonna's 1980s "material girl" image, of wrestling fans enjoying the pleasures of carnival and play, or of mall or beach patrons making their own culture. Fiske was by no means the only person lodging such arguments. But he was a remarkably accessible writer, with a gift for turning and repurposing the high theory of Roland Barthes, Mikhail Bakhtin, Michel Foucault, and Pierre Bourdieu into simple and persuasive arguments. By most accounts, too, Fiske was a remarkable teacher and a charismatic figure, and in his travels through Welsh, Australian, and ultimately American academia, he gained many followers and colleagues in arms. Thus, Fiske came to enjoy a central position in discussions of television programs and audiences in the 1980s and into the early 1990s. As will be discussed shortly, he also became the lightning rod for criticism of active audience theories and of what were perceived to be the excesses of an audience-centered model of analysis.

Early fan studies

In the meantime, though, the late 1980s gave birth to studies of fandom. Such a move was a rhetorical necessity: if audiences had previously been discounted and regarded as dupes and mindless automatons, fans were seen as those most completely lost in the system, and thus any response to such theories could best be lodged by noting intelligence and resistance in fans. Such was the argument suggested by Henry Jenkins in his landmark work of fan studies, *Textual Poachers: Television Fans and Participatory Culture*. Jenkins's title alludes to a chapter in de Certeau's *The Practice of Everyday Life*, in which reading is described metaphorically as "poaching," squatting on land not of one's own making, yet with a disregard for the posted rules of that land. Fans and consumers, Jenkins states, "are selective users of a vast media culture whose treasures, though corrupt, hold wealth that can be mixed and refined for alternative use."[33] His subtitle suggests the degree to which Jenkins was interested in fans as co-producers, not merely consuming, but producing through that consumption. On one level, this production was literal, in the case of fan fiction, fan songs ("filk"), and fan art based on the characters and themes of beloved stories. But on another level, Jenkins wrote of consumption as itself a constitutive act of the text, and of fans as co-authors. Echoing Fiske, Jenkins noted that fan modes of consumption may be coded as particularly garish by bourgeois culture, given its preference for aesthetic distance, and distrust of passionate consumption, which led to an interest in fans as a particular subculture.[34] The fans that Jenkins studied were predominantly women, too, and thus his work connected with and continued feminist media studies' interest in the audience as a site for cultural negotiation and resistance. He observed that women in particular may have been forced to read as poachers: "The school girl required to read a boy's book, the teenager dragged to see her date's favorite slasher film, the housewife forced to watch her husband's cop show rather than her soap, nevertheless, may find ways to remake those narratives, at least imaginatively."[35]

By way of illustrating this process of "remaking," Jenkins paid particular attention to fan productivity. Here his work was matched by Camille Bacon-Smith's *Enterprising Women: Television Fandom and the Creation of Popular Myth* and Constance Penley's article, "Feminism, Psychoanalysis, and the Study of Popular Culture," also published in 1992.[36] All three examined how, for instance, fans could use fan fiction as a way to alter stories to their liking, making room for women's concerns in otherwise overtly male narratives, or valuing and amplifying such concerns when they did exist. Fan writers, wrote Jenkins, "do not so much reproduce the primary text as they rework and rewrite it, repairing or dismissing unsatisfying aspects, developing interests not sufficiently explored,"[37] while Penley later defied notions of fans as passive viewers by writing that:

> there is no better critic than a fan. No one knows the object better than and no one is more critical. The fan stance toward the object could even be described as the original tough-love approach. The idea is to change the object while preserving it, kind of like giving a strenuous, deep massage that hurts at the time but feels so good afterwards.[38]

Important to all three writers, however, and to the growing numbers of fan studies scholars who would follow their lead, was the notion that fan readings were communal, not simply individual. Just as Morley and Brunsdon had examined *groups* of *Nationwide* viewers in order to see how meanings were created not only in response to the show, but also within a discursive setting, fan studies paid close attention to how fan conferences, fanzines, the circulation of fan fiction, and other communal practices worked to establish versions and readings of a program that could be shared and that would have particular meaning to a given community. All programs, they noted, took on a whole new life in the communities that grew around them.

Writing in a collection on fans, John Fiske would argue that distinct from the financial economy of media was a "shadow cultural economy" that worked by its own rules, giving power to different individuals and groups, yet serving no less of a role in the movements and meanings of a text. If Bourdieu saw cultural capital as dividing one group from another, Fiske wrote of "popular cultural capital" as privileging certain fans within their own communities, and hence of creating secondary hierarchies outside of those dictated by the industry and bourgeois society.[39] "At the point of sale," he wrote, "the commodity exhausts its role in the distribution economy, but begins its work in the cultural."[40] The combined weight of early fan studies and of active audience theory therefore significantly complicated notions of how consumption works as an at-times separate system, and of how power works within the practices of consumption. Jenkins, Bacon-Smith, and Penley all showed how some *consumers* can be simultaneously audiences of a television program and yet *producers* of a fan text, or audiences of both a television program and a fan text. In a dramatic reversal, early fan studies work flipped the polarizing lens through which scholars had been invited to see fans, from regarding them as obsessed losers eating whatever scraps the television industry fed them with glee to regarding them as especially resistive, reflective, and savvy critics, intent on repurposing narratives for their purpose.

The attack on active audience theory

Active audience work and early fan studies enjoyed moments in the sun, but they were soon beset upon by critics. In particular, a cultural studies conference in 1990 at the University of Illinois at Urbana-Champaign played host to a barrage of criticism against Fiske in particular, as did several articles published around the time, most notably William Seaman's "Active Audience Theory: Pointless Populism" and Meaghan Morris's "Banality in Cultural Studies."[41] One concern was that in an attempt to study the cultures of the lower classes and of marginalized subcultures, active audience work had at times instead gravitated toward examining the viewing pleasures of the comfortably middle-classed. The more vociferous attack saw active audience studies as woefully reducing media power to a matter of how one read a text while ignoring larger-scale issues of who owned the media and what their politics and ideological leanings were in the first place. Seaman took issue with the notion that *some* resistant readers would ever be sufficient, arguing that their isolated resistance by no means ensured that the program's effects would not still be felt by others, or indeed by a majority, thereby rendering the resistant reading little more than a footnote. For example, he countered the suggestion that some women watching *Charlie's Angels* may be "poaching" on the program to read it in feminist ways by arguing that even if such creative consumption was occurring, many male viewers were still likely consuming it wholly within the dominant reading, thereby ensuring the text's complicity with patriarchy. He also countered that Fiske's insistence that audiences "interacted" with texts "suggests that the viewer has some 'effect' on television, on the television program she or he is interpreting. Clearly this sort of 'interaction' is not taking place."[42]

Firmly drawing the battle lines, Seaman wrote of active audience theory's optimism in consumers' abilities to deflect programs' and their producers' ideology:

> Such pandering is familiar and easy to spot when the spokespersons involved are representatives of the major networks or of the advertising industry. It is puzzling when precisely the same sorts of "arguments" are made by academics. At best they reflect a misguided or twisted form of "deference" to "ordinary people." At worst, they only masquerade as deferential respect for the desires of the "masses";

frequently they constitute a deceitful reliance upon the symptoms of a system of indoctrination as a warrant for dubious claims about "resistance" and "opposition."[43]

He closed his essay with moralistic fervor, stating that, "It is imperative that communication scholars resist the pernicious features of this new trend in cultural studies."[44] For their own part, David Miller and Greg Philo label active audience research as a definitive "wrong turn in media studies" that clearly required the subsequent "rescuing" of a right-headed notion of media power.[45]

It is our belief that, while these critiques may have served a rhetorically important purpose, many were ill-spirited in the degree to which they reduced active audience theory to a caricature of itself, and to a straw man. On one level, they draw important attention to precisely who we mean by "the audience," if said audience is "active." For *some* audience members to be active is perhaps not enough. As Celeste Condit also noted in a study of two students, one pro-choice and one pro-life, watching a pro-choice episode of *Cagney & Lacey*, we must also remember that reading against a program's grain takes work, and that many viewers may find this too much work with too little payoff.[46] Scholars from a more quantitative research tradition – or those accustomed to its norms – therefore challenged the small sample sizes in active audience research, wondering about generalizability. Morris, meanwhile, noted the "banality" of observing that resistance occurs, when in fact the more interesting and important topic for examination may be the resilience of the program and of the producer even in the face of pervasive textual resistance and audience activity.[47] Moreover, though most examples of active audiences framed their activity as progressive, and hence the audience as marginal and subcultural, surely activity could also be regressive and a strategy of the mainstream to read against texts that may themselves be resistant. Philo and Miller in particular are also correct to note that Fiske rarely engaged with any rigor in actual audience research to confirm his theories. Ironically and problematically, then, a theory that posited that meaning could not be read off the program alone often relied on readings gleaned from the program and not an actual audience. Other active audience researchers, though, often did engage in considerable audience research, as did Jenkins, limiting the scope of this criticism.

On another level, however, criticisms of active audience theory ignoring broader social and industrial processes are weak. Both Fiske and Jenkins are unequivocal in framing their arguments within an acknowledgment of the grander powers that the industry alone possesses. As romantic as metaphors of semiotic guerrilla tactics, poaching, and "making do" may seem at first blush, Fiske and Jenkins still acknowledge that audiences are stuck in a system not of their making. Jenkins noted point-blank that, "Nobody regards these fan activities as a magical cure for the social ills of post-industrial capitalism. They are no substitution for meaningful change, but they can be used effectively to build support for such change."[48] Fiske's rhetoric regarding "semiotic democracy" is admittedly fervid in *Television Culture*, but his future books all add important and major provisos and warnings regarding industry power. In short, despite believing in its potential, neither argued that audience power and resistance is ever *enough*. For his part, Morley has also noted that "The power of viewers to reinterpret meanings is hardly equivalent to the discursive power of centralized media institutions to construct the texts which the viewer then interprets, and to imagine otherwise is simply foolish."[49]

The critiques also risk abandoning vital ground in their rush to insist on the powers of the industry. They served as an important reminder that the industry and production hold considerable power in the construction of meaning, a reminder that would help inspire subsequent waves of television studies analysis of production – as detailed in chapter 3. But in positing that the text–audience relationship was a "micro" level issue of little significance when compared to the macro-level issues of production and labor, they offered an unhelpful and inaccurate picture of the relationship between political, cultural systems and how people interact with them. In responding to criticism from James Curran that a "new revisionism" in audience research discounted structural processes and determinants in favor of studying the "micro" level agency of the audience, Morley argues that, "structures are not external to action, but are only reproduced through the concrete activities of daily life, and must be analysed as historical formulations, subject to modification."[50] In other words, the "macro" can only be constructed by and out of the "micro" in the first place, and a model of power that excludes human beings and everyday social interactions is a nonsensical one. Just as a cake does not precede flour and eggs, "society" or "culture" cannot precede the "micro" – they are made up of it, and thus larger, "macro" forces always rely deeply upon "micro" forces. By consequence, change will either require revolution and a wholesale reinvention of an entire society's power structure, or will require constant toggling and small incursions at the micro level. While the former option may make for better dreams and is doubtlessly a purer, less compromised endeavor, Fiske and others were perhaps more practical and realistic in their understanding of the necessity for progressive, not revolutionary, change.

Debates between political economists and audience researchers have been responsible for many a heated argument and many a red or purple face in academic conferences, and they form the groundwork for many a polemic article, but audience research continued. Indeed, in the 1990s, numerous new paradigms for audience and fan research developed, paradigms that continue to today, several of which we survey in the remaining sections.

Television talk

Another critique leveled at post-Encoding/Decoding audience studies was that, as much as this work was sometimes dubbed "audience ethnography," the deep ethnographic method of anthropology had been replaced by short-focus groups or individual interviews, and hence by an over-reliance on the audience's ability to interpret itself. In part, this had been a conscious move, as anthropology as a discipline was at the time sustaining heavy fire from those who saw the individual anthropologist's claim to speak for an entire culture as troublesome and unacceptable. Renato Rosaldo makes this point in humorous fashion when recounting a story of visiting his fiancée's family and one morning jokingly offering an "ethnographic account" of the family's "ritual" act of having breakfast which sees "the women talk among themselves and designate one among them as the toast maker," while "the reigning patriach, as if in from the hunt," poaches eggs to the cooing, alternating approval of women and children.[51] Rosaldo's point was also made forcefully in a landmark collection called *Writing Culture*, in which a series of anthropologists (Rosaldo amongst them) analyzed the questionable politics of interpreting another culture and of speaking on its behalf. James Clifford's introduction to that collection notes that the ethnographer and his or her writing "is always caught up in the invention, not the representation, of cultures," and he writes of ethnographies as "systems, or economies, of truth. Power and history work through them, in ways their author cannot fully control."[52] Such work was matched in postcolonial studies by numerous writers who challenged the proclivity of the West to speak for others, and to reduce them to knowable, different, Other quantities through their personal interpretations that were prone to being colored by cultural biases.[53] Thus, the choice to solicit audiences' accounts of themselves was in part a political act, especially when the audiences in question had been systematically erased from many previous accounts of culture and cultural consumption, as with housewives, children, and racial and ethnic minorities.

Nevertheless, some researchers became increasingly uncomfortable with the degree to which they were studying audiences in artificial environments, asking them about a program that they watched in the researcher's lab, or talking about shows in a vocabulary and framework that did not match everyday experiences of TV talk. Hence, for instance, Morley attempted to watch families watching television for *Family Television*, and to ask them questions about it in their "natural" viewing environment. Similarly, in 1988, Janice Radway wrote a provocative article calling for a move to an ethnographic approach. She expressed concern with how, as a result of many audience studies examining reactions to single texts or genres, audiences "are cordoned off for study and therefore defined as particular kinds of subjects by virtue of their use not only of a single medium but of a single genre as well."[54] Audiences are not simply audiences of television, much less of a single television program or genre, she argued – they are "nomadic." Thus audience research would need to find a way to study their consumption habits more generally, and in relation to one another. As such, she pondered "whether it might not be more fruitful to start with the habits and practices of everyday life as they are actively, discontinuously, even contradictorily pieced together by historical subjects themselves as they move nomadically via disparate associations and relations through day-to-day existence."[55]

Radway's call, while sound, proved remarkably hard to answer, given that it would require a researcher, or a team of researchers, to engage in a longitudinal study stretched out over multiple years. Since audience work within television studies rarely asks seemingly "empirical" questions, and hence rarely gives firm answers based on the weight of statistical evidence, it has rarely attracted the same kind of research funding that audience work in the social science tradition has, and so studies such as those called for by Radway have regularly proved unfeasible. However, a rare exception can be found in the groundbreaking work of Marie Gillespie, published in *Television, Ethnicity, and Cultural Change*. In classic anthropological style, Gillespie moved to a suburb of London known for its large Punjabi population. She obtained work at a local high school teaching media literacy, and lived with a Punjabi family. Over three years, she proceeded to record countless conversations and overheard comments with the local teens about what they watched on television, how they watched, and why. Gillespie sought to record "TV talk" and did so by situating herself where such talk would continually be all around her. Thus, whereas, as Pertti Alasuutari notes, Stuart Hall's Encoding/Decoding model led to a generation of audience research "obsessed with 'determinate moments'" of encoding and decoding,[56] Gillespie was instead able to examine how programs took on meaning over time, and also how these programs interacted with each other in the ways in which the local teens discussed them. For instance, she found that the teens used ads as a way to situate themselves within British and western commercial culture, while also using video tapes of the devotional texts of Hinduism recorded off Indian television and purchased by their parents to negotiate a relationship with their "Indianness" or "Punjabiness." "TV talk is a crucial forum for experimentation with identities,"[57] she notes, and thus her study is as much an analysis of identity formation – in which television figures as a major object – as it is an analysis of television.

Gillespie's work shows the potential for audience research to discover the multiple *intertextual* links between programs, and for audience researchers to examine not simply how an audience is reacting to a specific program, but also how they contextualize and frame that program within their everyday lives and within other media consumption habits. It also allows us as analysts to shift focus from examining consumption as a "determinate moment" and as reactive to encouraging us to situate television as a resource in multiple people's lives, one with a wide variety of uses. Another rare study in this respect is Stewart Hoover, Lynn Schofield Clark, and Diane Alters's study of family viewing and discussion about it. Here, a team of interviewers probed numerous families regarding a wide variety of topics to do with media and family, resulting in transcripts that chart television talk in multiple modes and sites.[58] David Gauntlett, too, has conducted interesting work into audiences by asking participants to respond to his questions about the media by playing with Lego or drawing pictures, and then to discuss these with him. His methodology hoped to avoid the standard, and overly structured and structuring, question and answer format of much audience research, and instead to see how audience interaction works through play and creativity.[59] Or consider recent research by Helen Wood that involves videotaping participants while they view television in order to record their conversations during talk shows. Her methodology creates "texts" to read from the transcripts of the interaction between the viewer and the text, what she calls "texts-in-action," devised to capture talk at the moment of reception for close analysis.[60]

In her book, *The Audience in Everyday Life*, S. Elizabeth Bird – an anthropologist by training – similarly wrestled with ways to examine consumption as multi-sited. Adopting an experimental methodology for studying audiences' interactions with mediated stereotypes of Native Americans, for example, she formed numerous focus groups, each of which was asked to create a television show premise and characters, one of whom must be a Native American. She then left the room and filmed the groups, in an attempt to allow a freer flow of conversation unburdened by the immediate presence of the researcher. Bird found significant evidence of deeply rooted, media-centered stereotypes by charting the ways in which these Native American characters were penned in. Even those who tried to avoid stereotypes "essentially found themselves unable to draw on cultural knowledge that would help them imagine a fully developed Indian character," thereby showing the imprint of their various media consumption habits on their everyday attitudes.[61]

Bird's book, though published only eight years after Gillespie's, benefited considerably, as would all work attempting to situate television in everyday life, from the rise of the internet and from fan forums, listservs, and mailing lists. One of Bird's other chapters examines ways in which conversation flowed at a *Dr. Quinn, Medicine Woman* listserv. In particular, she notes how the fans that constituted the community did not simply discuss the television show; rather, they also discussed their private lives, illnesses, worries, and so forth. The fandom and the fan community surrounding this one television show, therefore, opened multiple channels for all sorts of other interactions and social purposes that an analysis in terms of encoding and decoding would likely ignore, and yet that gave the fans' relationship with the show much of its meaning. This supports Bird's opening assertion that the notion of a television or media audience has become deeply problematic: we "cannot really isolate the role of the media in culture, because the media are firmly anchored into the web of culture [. . .] The 'audience' is everywhere and nowhere."[62] Prior to the internet, Bird would have had to obtain access to a group that met physically, and would have had to dedicate hundreds of hours to meeting with them. But the online nature of her study allowed her the seeming anonymity of being just another person on the listserv, rather than the awkward prominence of being a researcher in the room madly scribbling down or recording what was being said, and potentially changing the entire nature of the conversation in doing so. It allowed her the ability to hit the "print" button rather than spend yet more hours upon hours transcribing her interviews and discussions. And quite simply, it also allowed her the ability to study television viewing and discussion as it occurs for many viewers – spread out over many weeks, fervidly and excitedly at some points and not at all or with apathy at other points. In short, the internet allowed Bird greater proximity to the audience in everyday life.

Internet research has arguably become the dominant mode of studying audiences now, following the early pioneering work by scholars such as Nancy Baym.[63] As fan groups moved online, in particular, and as all manner of sites sprout from *Television without Pity* to each show's official fan pages, viewers became easier to find online, and the process of being an audience became intrinsically linked to the internet in many cases too. At the same time, this trend to online research is not without its problems. Whereas Gillespie's ethnographic approach sought to contextualize individual comments or reactions within a subject's life and consumption practices as a whole, online forums for discussion limit the researcher to whatever context is online, and to whatever context is made available by the individual posters. It also limits the researcher to those who are online, thus excluding vast swathes of the population as possible research subjects, and risking that audience research becomes even more Eurocentric and middle class in its focus than it has already, justly, been accused of being. Ethical concerns are also magnified when online research allows one to "lurk" and make notes on a group who may not know they have an observer, and thus this can become a troublesome form of research for university boards entrusted with ensuring the ethical treatment of human subjects. Some critics add that online forums allow all sorts of extravagant performances of identity that may be fictional and put on, and, while these concerns dovetail with a general moral panic in the news media about Facebook or YouTube stalkers and prowlers, they ignore that performance and deception are no less a part of offline life. Indeed, Nicholas Abercrombie and Brian Longhurst offer a thoughtful discussion of audiences precisely as performative, and of the act of being an audience as always performative of identity too.[64] Online research may add new kinks to such theories, may present new challenges, and it is no panacea to all former problems, but its prospects for allowing access to a more richly contextualized account of media consumption experiences and performances as a whole are promising, especially as more internet users are seemingly becoming comfortable sharing many details of their lives online.

User-generated culture

As discussed further in chapter 4, the internet has also allowed television shows to "overflow" into web venues, some of which ask for the active contributions and participation of viewers. With this, being an "audience" is a practice that may involve productive acts such as creating a mash-up, posting to a fan board, taking part in an alternate reality game, setting foot into a program's fictional spaces, sharing fan art or fanvids, writing blog posts about one's viewing, or so forth. If such acts were once the province of groups of fans whose actions were marginalized and subcultural, increasingly these acts are mainstream and commonplace. Marking the shift, Henry Jenkins's *Convergence Culture* returns to many of the practices that Jenkins had examined 14 years earlier in *Textual Poachers*, now noting how central such acts have become to the business of television. Jenkins notes that television producers can no longer afford to exclude and ridicule fans, as a new "affective economy" sees them forced to hold onto audience members by providing significant added value.[65] Gone are the days when a network could expect a third of the viewing audience to watch any given program, and, instead, the new television economy requires broadcasters to woo their fans with multiple technologies, platforms, and extra materials.

With this change in the structuring logic of broadcasting, though, comes an increased interest on behalf of producers to incorporate, tame, and harness their fans. Whereas the fans that Jenkins and others studied in the late eighties and early nineties were often regarded as annoyances by producers, if pandered to occasionally, now that their productive practices are more widely accessible, and now that the industry hopes for more audiences to approach their texts with similar levels of affect, fan incorporation is more common. Fiske saw the active audience as that which *excorporates* material from mass culture, turning it into popular culture, but he acknowledged that the other side of this coin sees the industry trying to commodify, control, and *incorporate* this popular culture back into the fold. Thus, where Jenkins and some others have quite excitedly noted a "convergent" media age in which "user-generated content" realizes some of the dreams of participatory culture, many fans worry about the degree to which official fan clubs, sites, and fan production competitions effectively turn the fans into unpaid laborers who add value to the texts, but that industry only accepts certain fan work while excluding and marginalizing other fan responses in the process.

Accordingly, fan studies of recent years have seen a shift from examining audiences poaching off the producers' land to charting fan reactions to a more dynamic, messy relationship between producers and audiences wherein the former at times work with the latter, and at times become the poachers themselves.[66] An especially important intervention in fan studies, Matt Hills's *Fan Cultures*, even structures its chapters around governing binaries of former discussions of fans, as he attempts to theorize fan cultures as "between consumerism and resistance," "between community and hierarchy," and "between cult and culture," for instance. Studies of production, meanwhile, have become more sophisticated, reminding scholars of the need to study "producers" as a varied, often internally divided, lot. For example, as Viacom sued Google for allegedly encouraging and supporting piracy of its shows through YouTube, and as they sought several billion dollars in damages, ironically one of their more successful shows, *The Colbert Report*, regularly saw host Stephen Colbert encourage viewers to mash up scenes from his show. If we are in the age of the "produser," as Axel Bruns has dubbed it[67] – user and producer combined – the key task for audience studies may now be to eke out precisely what forms of production are allowed, how both fans and the industry deal with this new age or how they seek to fight it, and how "produsage" of television changes the nature of its programs and of our relationships to them.

In this respect, audience studies and production studies have begun to merge. This move is not without precedent, as Ien Ang's important book, *Desperately Seeking the Audience*, and an article by Eileen Meehan, "Why We Don't Count: The Commodity Audience," had earlier drawn attention to audiences not just as individuals or communities, but also as aggregated figures that are used toward various purposes by the television industry.[68] Philip Napoli helpfully distinguishes between the predicted audience (which is what the advertiser buys), the measured audience (regarding which Nielsen, the British Audience Research Board (BARB), and other ratings systems offer statistics), and the actual audience, and he notes how frequently industry and audience discourse dangerously elides the three. But the pursuing and selling of audiences is a complex industry. As Napoli notes, "In selling audiences, media firms essentially deal in human attention, and human attention represents a much more abstract, elusive, and intangible product than, say, steel, insurance, or legal services."[69] Audiences serve multiple discursive functions within the industry and are invoked intuitively,[70] as numbers, as communities, as individuals, as publics, as trends, and in multiple other ways. Thus knowing how they are constructed and *how* producers interact with them will remain an important task for television studies, all the more so as new technologies, measuring systems and programs, and developments in psychographic profiling change how audiences function within the business.

As Nielsen in particular moves toward measuring "television" audiences online and iPod or smart phone-bearing "television" viewers, and as these ratings companies, content creators, and networks battle over the degree to which DVR ratings or online click-through ratings actually count, we are at a point in time when what constitutes "the television audience" is a hotly debated topic. If the audience is a construct that is used for various purposes, given various price tags and valuations, and measured or tracked by different methods, it is proving a remarkably volatile entity in an era of converging media and technical platforms and hence all the more vital to study closely and continuously.

Global and diasporic audiences

Another looming frontier for audience studies has been to make sense of audiences worldwide. Given the strength of television studies in North America, western and northern Europe, and Australia, much of the canonical audience research in the field has examined western audiences' encounters with western programs. But if contemporary television is characterized on one hand by digital convergence and narrowcasting, it is also characterized on the other hand by its increasingly global nature. Many beloved shows either originated in other countries or have moved there, whether as is or as a format that is then domesticated and localized. Hence the UK's *Pop Idol* begat *American Idol, Canadian Idol, Australian Idol, Indian Idol*, and various other official or unofficial spin-offs around the globe; *CSI*'s popularity in America led not only to *CSI: Miami* and *CSI: New York* but also to the immense popularity of the franchise globally; and ownership of a satellite dish can provide one easy (if expensive) access to programming from pole to pole. Meanwhile, media is not alone in moving, as audiences are on the move too, meaning that diasporic audiences have become major markets that must be addressed, or viable secondary markets that must make do with what is on offer to the primary market. How audience studies respond to such moves will undoubtedly determine the relevance of the subfield in years to come.

Two early studies of global audiences centered around the eighties hit evening soap, *Dallas*. As noted above, Ien Ang, and Elihu Katz and Tamar Liebes, carried out studies of the show, with a particular eye towards examining claims of cultural imperialism in the case of the latter.[71] While some worried about *Dallas* tearing a path of Americanization through the world, Katz and Liebes found that some Arabs watching the show in Israel saw the show as supposed proof of America's decadence, while all five groups examined (Moroccan Jews, new Russian immigrants, second-generation Kibbutzim Israelis, and Arabs, all in Israel, and second-generation Americans in the USA) differed, at times markedly, in how they retold, regarded, and processed episodes. Ang, meanwhile, saw ample evidence of Dutch fans of the show playing with it, not simply learning from it as if it was a schoolteacher. These studies thus superimposed active audience theory on global power structures to insist that global audiences were neither as powerless, nor as uncritical and accepting of American culture, as concerns of cultural imperialism alleged. Grandiose rhetoric of the "McDonaldization" of the planet,[72] or of a ubiquitous Americanization process, frequently flatter American popular culture with being better, sexier, more interesting, and more exciting than anything the rest of the world has to offer, and such rhetoric can all too often metaphorically reduce non-American cultures to being thin and delicate trees about to be destroyed by a flood of American content. Ang's, and Katz and Liebes's work, challenges the simplicity of this rhetoric and demands a more nuanced, more *respectful* account of the world's cultures.

Nevertheless, some critics have pointed out that, while global audiences have powers to read against and to reject what is on offer, they have strictly limited powers to determine what is on the television in the first place. Toby Miller, Nitin Govil, John McMurria, Richard Maxwell, and Ting Wang, in their *Global Hollywood 2*, for instance, note that the sheer size and value of the American television audience allows many American television producers to regard the rest of the world as value-added. By the time they ship their shows overseas, in other words, their overheads have often already been paid, and they are already raking in profits from the United States, thereby allowing producers to price programs well below what it would cost a local producer to make a similar show.[73] Add to this the marked presence of an ownership imperialism, wherein the same American corporations that run Hollywood – Disney, Comcast/NBC Universal, Viacom, CBS, Time Warner, and News Corporation – have sizeable holdings outside the United States, and local stations or local content sometimes simply do not stand a chance. Audiences may "make do" and "poach" in such situations, but their choices have been vastly limited, and the economics of Hollywood ensure that the American landowner is ever present. Within this schema, then, audience studies must balance an interest in what is made available to audiences, with what is subsequently "done" with that content.

To talk of global audiences, though, is not simply to talk of American media in other countries. As much as we should be concerned about American television's encroachment across the globe, sometimes discussions of local television patronize and belittle other nations when they prove themselves incapable of moving beyond a "cultural imperialism" frame. If questions of television style or "televisuality" and of the relationships between television and culture can be asked in the UK or the US, so too can and must these questions be asked of other nations' television and television audiences. For example, recent scholarship examines the Chinese and Indian *Idol* clones to quite different ends. While both programs' audiences could, of course, be interrogated for evidence of cultural imperialism, instead Francis L. F. Lee and Li Cui consider Nick Couldry's thesis regarding media's naturalization of itself (discussed later in this chapter) in their consideration of *Super Girls' Voice*'s audience, while Aswin Punathambekar draws on research into *Indian Idol*'s audiences to discuss "mobile publics" and connections between politics, nationhood, regional and ethnic identity, and television.[74] Both papers, in other words, advance other ongoing debates in television studies by allowing their audiences to be something more than just victims of or rebels against cultural imperialism. Divya McMillin makes this argument explicit, arguing impassionedly in her book *International Media Studies* for a postcolonial and critical audience research that is able to ask a wider range of questions about international audiences.[75]

Finally, just as Marie Gillespie's work amongst Punjabi teens in Southall documented, audience studies can also be used to examine how migrants, multinational citizens, and other cosmopolitans use the media to help fashion a sense of identity. Homi Bhabha has drawn from post-modern geography, and from its separation of place and space, to suggest the existence of "third spaces" in which migrants live.[76] Thus, for example, a Nigerian-Briton may feel neither totally Nigerian nor totally British, and s/he may consequently try to fashion a lived environment that is in a "third space" between Nigeria and the UK. Such third spaces can become physical realities in the form of certain stores, nightclubs, restaurants, or neighborhoods, but the media have also proven successful in creating them. To sit in a British sitting-room watching Nigerian soaps on the television, or to watch Australian sitcoms downloaded to one's computer while living in New York, is to place oneself between Nigeria and the UK, or Australia and the USA, and to use the media to create, or at least to help negotiate, a third space existence. Not only might this be the case for Nigerian-British or Australian-Americans, for whom the program might play an important part in adding a Nigerian or Australian character to their lives in the UK or USA respectively, but non-Nigerians and non-Australians too might use the television profitably to explore the world beyond their own nation, and perhaps to establish points of contact outside it too. If, as Benedict Anderson noted, the nation can only ever be an "imagined community" – too large for its citizens to congregate, meet each other, and come to consensus physically – then television remains one of the most powerful forces, with arguably the widest reach, in presenting and hence creating images of the nation. The nation, as such, will "occur" at the level of the television audience, and so too will any third space or hybrid identity similarly "take root" on screen. As such, studying audiences has proven a key way to study trans-national identities and lived realities.[77]

The ritual uses of television

Several other lines of – at times – starkly different audience research stem in part from the work of Roger Silverstone, a key name in British media and television studies whose work at Brunel University, Sussex University, and the London School of Economics helped to make all three schools centers for the study of media in the UK. Much of Silverstone's more famous work was theoretical, not empirical, but his continuing legacy is seen in an interest in the role of *ritual* in media, and in the ways in which audiences and the media alike structure the relations between each other.[78] Silverstone wrote poetically of television as the primary storyteller and mythmaker of our current era and was interested in audiences' ritual uses for such stories and myths. Television, he noted, "accompanies us as we wake up, as we breakfast, as we have our tea and as we drink in bars. It comforts us when we are alone. It helps us sleep. It gives us pleasure, it bores us and sometimes it challenges us. It provides us with opportunities to be both sociable and solitary."[79] It is not simply something we look at when bored, but something that serves a whole range of quite intimate ritual purposes in our lives; or, rather, its many stories and genres serve such roles.

To make sense of some of these roles, Silverstone drew on sociologist Anthony Giddens's writings on "ontological security."[80] Giddens observed that contemporary society is replete with risk – as you read this, for instance, a gas leak could be threatening your life; a terrorist attack might be seconds away from affecting your city; the financial markets could be imploding, taking your and/or your parents' savings with them; and so forth. This risk society therefore requires coping mechanisms and requires us to find ways to feel okay, to feel safe. This feeling of safety and comfort is called "ontological security," or security in one's being. Silverstone regarded television and its stories as key ways by which we establish ontological security, as alluded to in his above-quoted list of waking, beginning the day, having a break, and sleeping with the medium. So, for instance, one might ease out of the hardships of the day by watching a late night talk show, or one might wake up with the idle, upbeat chatter of a morning show. One might find connection to others through watching sitcoms with "people like me" or use the news to otherwise situate oneself in time, space, and a community. Given these multiple ritual uses, television has also taken on a distinctly domestic feel, "a member of the family in a metaphorical sense but also in a literal sense insofar as it is integrated into the daily pattern of domestic social relations, and insofar as it is the focus of emotional or cognitive energy, releasing or containing tension for example, or providing comfort."[81] In the process, television has become central to how many of us construct an image of "home," a point that Morley and others have applied to television's role in constructing the *national* home,[82] and a remarkably important tool in our everyday lives.

Silverstone's work has already had a profound effect on a more recent wave of fan studies, as two more recent fan studies scholars, Matt Hills and Cornel Sandvoss, both of whom studied under Silverstone, have asked questions about fans and ritual. Hills continues Silverstone's interest in ontological security and expands upon Silverstone's use of child psychologist D. W. Winnicott's notion of "transitional objects."[83] A transitional object, to Winnicott, is any object that a child invests with feelings of the ontological security provided by the mother – think of a favorite blanket, teddy, or toy. Silverstone posed that much television can serve as a transitional object, not just for children as was Winnicott's interest in transitional objects, but for an entire population coping with a society replete with risk and danger. Hills then argues that the fan object may serve especially strong duty as a transitional object for an individual, or, in shared form, for a fan community. Fan cultures, he notes, are likely to form around texts that have served as transitional objects for members of that community, and hence when the object has been invested with meanings and qualities that differentiate it from other texts through inspiring nostalgia, warmth, and comfort. As such, owning fan memorabilia and merchandise might be ways of injecting the positive feelings and memories associated with the fan object into one's daily life, as might having the ring tone of one's favorite show programmed into one's mobile phone, and as might fan boards and other sites for fan interactions.[84]

Sandvoss's more suspicious approach to fan objects is similarly motivated by an interest with how we use the fan object. In Sandvoss's case, though, he expresses concern with the degree to which fans might make their beloved object mean *anything*. If earlier active audience work had relied upon the notion of a "polysemic" text that could mean many things, and whose meaning was never completely nailed down, Sandvoss poses that fan texts will often become "neutrosemic," or so radically open that in truth we might see them as meaning nothing. He offers the contrasting examples of *Star Wars* fans who see the films as anti-war by nature, and others who see them as pro-war by nature. In such a situation, Sandvoss argues that the fans have turned the fan object into a "mirror" of themselves, seeing their own likes, dislikes, life choices, and preferences reflected back at them in their beloved object.[85] For our purposes here, Hills's and Sandvoss's work illustrates two points in particular: first, they offer examples of another way in which audience uses for television can be studied, as serving deeper ritual and psychological purposes; second, they should show how fan and audience work has evolved, opening up to a wide variety of other questions about individuals, communities, and their interactions with television and with larger societal structures.[86] Writing with Jonathan Gray and C. Lee Harrington, Sandvoss would later insist that a key role of studying fans should be to better understand "how we form emotional bonds with ourselves and others in a modern, mediated world," using audience behavior and uses of television to allow us "to explore some of the key mechanisms through which we interact with the mediated world at the heart of our social, political, and cultural realities and identities."[87]

Another important figure in the study of the ritual value of television, whose work has similarly been motivated by a keenness to make sense of central processes and operating principles underlying society, is Nick Couldry. Couldry's first book, *The Place of Media Power: Pilgrims and*

Witnesses of the Media Age, drew from audience research with fans on the set of *Coronation Street* and with protesters discussing the nightly news' construction of their actions to examine how television lays claim to being at the center of society, and how audiences variously fall into this trap or struggle to free themselves from it.[88] Couldry dubs this "the myth of the mediated center," and, in his subsequent *Media Rituals*, he describes it as "the belief, or assumption, that there is a centre to the social world, and that, in some sense, the media speaks 'for' that centre."[89] In this latter book, Couldry studies a variety of other examples, ranging from competition reality shows to mediated self-disclosure on shows such as *The Jerry Springer Show*, with a particular eye as to how these and other "media rituals" reinforce, legitimate, and naturalize the supposed centrality of the media, and of television in particular. As with Silverstone, Couldry also discusses morals and ethics in relation to media, examining what audience behavior tells us about these. Thus, Silverstone's final book, *Media and Morality: On the Rise of the Mediapolis*, and Couldry's *Listening Beyond the Echoes: Media, Ethics, and Agency in an Uncertain World* both wrestle with how understanding and moral value is constructed within, and works through, television, and with how citizens live or might live ethically with and through the media.[90]

Working continuously since television studies' birth has also been John Hartley, who while not "Silverstonian," and while exploring very different ground than Couldry, Hills, or Sandvoss, has similarly taken a broad, philosophic approach to television and its uses. Hartley is not an audience researcher, but he has been a keen theorist of audience behavior. In particular, he has often returned to how television situates viewers as citizens in a democratic polity. In *The Uses of Television*, for instance, he discusses how television has become the foremost medium of "cross-demographic communication" that allows us to learn of others, and hence contributes to the ways in which we think of ourselves as members of any given society. Television, he continues, offers forms of "cultural" and "do-it-yourself citizenship." A purveyor of "democratainment," the medium offers the tools and resources for one to construct one's identity.[91] If generations of television's critics have scowled at the medium's plethora of entertainment, worrying that the lack of "serious," "hard" news would disable a democratic polity, Hartley has shown how democracy is sustained through a much wider range of genres than such critics allow, and he gestures toward the multiple important uses of television that might occur in the seemingly most banal of programs and genres.[92] If much audience research and theory cautioned critics away from hasty judgments regarding the meaning and effects of television, together the work of Silverstone, Hills, Sandvoss, Couldry, and Hartley mines especially deep territory to suggest how multifaceted the medium is, and how many varying uses – ritual, mythical, psychological, moral/ethical, and political – audiences might have for it.

What now and what next?

As audience research within the television studies tradition moves comfortably into its fourth decade, numerous frontiers remain, some already discussed above. Quite simply, and most importantly, though, more empirical audience research is required. Qualitative audience research takes time, often involves long and tedious hours of transcription, and has rarely received much institutional support in the form of grant funding. Admittedly, fans' and other audiences' move into online forums has made some audience research easier, but it also risks turning the act of lurking with a printer at the ready into the normative way of studying audiences. If the 1980s and early 1990s were characterized by a larger number of television studies scholars engaging in audience research projects, the field is once more due for a boom in studies.

These projects could continue to address the multiple issues and questions already discussed above, but we would be particularly eager to see projects that try to interrogate the borders of "the audience," just as Abercrombie and Longhurst did when they attempted to focus on audiences as performative, for instance, or as Radway, Gillespie, and Bird did in examining the position of being an audience member as situated in practices of everyday life, and as did numerous scholars who turned their attention to global audiences.

One such expansive turn involves the interrogation of dislike, hate, distaste, and discomfort in the process of being an audience. As explained above, audience studies' momentum began with a somewhat "redemptive" project in mind, attempting to explore the nuanced ways in which audiences made sense of texts that many regarded as debased. Early fan studies soon became a key offshoot of this project. Practically, too, studying fans and eager audiences was in some ways easier – fans self-identified, and cared enough about the text under discussion to volunteer to discuss it with researchers for no pay, and fans knew the text well enough to offer cogent and highly literate commentary on it. But what about those who don't particularly care for a text or genre, or the entire medium? What might we learn from examining their own affective responses to shows, and their own discussion about them? Certainly, if, as fan studies has often suggested, many fans are drawn to beloved programs either by a feeling that those programs offer something that others do not, or by the promise that such shows could be repurposed and "poached upon" to create something better and new, such a theory automatically presumes that fans dislike other programs, and find many other shows both unworthy of their time and attention, and unyielding as objects to be repurposed. Fandom, in other words, exists within a wider context of anti-fandom, and of textual apathy, dislike, and concern.

Future work that examines anti-fandom more closely, then, could shed significantly more light not only on the entire range of audience responses, but also on those responses that audience studies has traditionally examined with great success. We might also better understand the limit points of "resistance" if we were to expand our study of anti-fans. Minority audiences, for instance, may well be capable of resisting a program's mainstream, hegemonic push, and they might find creative ways to undercut it; but we should also examine the moments when they are unable or unwilling to do so, and thus when television fails them. Audience research needs not only examine processes of "making do"; it can also examine what happens when one refuses to make do, and what the resulting effects of such alienation or frustration are on individuals and communities. Such work would require audience researchers to talk to people about what bugs them about television, what they hate, what is annoying, and what offends them, and so forth. Some work on anti-fans already exists, as, for example, with Diane Alters's work stemming from the previously mentioned Hoover, Clark, and Alters study of families' uses of television. Here, Alters discusses how parents positioned themselves and their children against certain ideologies by directing their family away from certain programs.[93] Aniko Bodroghkozy analyzes letters, many of which were disapproving and angry, to NBC about *Julia* – one of the first sitcoms with an African-American lead – and notes the significant tension that surrounded the show, and how symbolically laden it was.[94] Melissa Click has studied the interplay between loving and hating Martha Stewart, and how audiences performed aspects of their identity through both fandom and anti-fandom.[95] And though studying film, not television, Martin Barker, Jane Arthurs, and Ramaswami Harindranath offer a fascinating study of the censorship campaign that surrounded the release of David Cronenberg's *Crash* in the UK, and especially of how the ensuing public distaste for the film shaped audiences' reactions to it.[96] Anti-fan research is thus alive in these and some other projects, but we would welcome more such work.

Another frontier for audience research that is starting to be explored is that of television audiences and Politics. In capitalizing Politics, we reflect on how frequently audience research and theory has, over its short history, cared a great deal about "micro" and personal politics, and certainly about identity politics. However, still very little work has been conducted into how audiences interact with the world of party and governmental Politics. Several notable exceptions exist. As noted above, for instance, John Hartley's work has continuously examined cultural and governmental politics. Liesbet van Zoonen has also asked numerous provocative questions about the possibility for fan communities to overlap with and inform political communities in her book *Entertaining the Citizen*. While scholars who have studied fandom and those who have studied citizenship have often been separated by research paradigms, inter-area squabbles, and departmental boundaries, Van Zoonen profitably and convincingly notes that fan passion, mobilization, and interests in fantasy and imagination might tell us a great deal about how such issues could work in the political realm.[97] Others, including Gray, Sandvoss, Jenkins, and numerous authors included in an edited collection by John Corner and Dick Pels, have approached ardent and active news viewers as *fans* in an attempt to break down a wall that too often exists between academic discussions of citizenship and of fandom.[98]

If fandom is so central to the lives of many individuals and communities living in the industrialized and heavily mediated world, how do fandom and anti-fandom lead to, inspire, restrict, and/or interact with constructions of Politics and our place within it? Such a question requires a more concerted line of inquiry and attack. At times, one might even believe that a secret decree was issued in the nineties that restricted many qualitative audience researchers from discussing the news. But especially as political television has merged so seamlessly with entertainment programming, with programs as diverse as *The Daily Show with Jon Stewart*, *The Colbert Report*, and *The Glenn Beck Program* uniting news, politics, and entertainment,[99] the former terms of the decree – though never satisfactory – have become all the more unsustainable. Television studies' promise was always its interdisciplinary nature, and its interest not in a medium per se but in that medium as a prism for understanding modern culture, and so it must find ways to defy the restricted scope placed upon it, and to ask more questions of how politics, Politics, news, entertainment, citizenship, and the television audience interact. Perhaps, then, the challenge lies in seeing fan and anti-fan studies as primarily examinations of *affect* and *mobilization*, understandings of which are absolutely central to an understanding of how politics work.

Certainly, a path forward for audience studies would be to use audience research and theory to better understand a wide range of broad societal structures and operating principles. As we have seen, audience studies in the television studies tradition began as a tool for understanding the interplay between structure and agency and for comprehending how ideology, power, and resistance might work in everyday, "micro" instances of television consumption. Over time, audience studies and theory increasingly turned to explorations of identity and community. This was both a welcome and a vital turn, as it greatly increased academic knowledge about what audiences do, and, as noted in this chapter, it often entailed framing the act of being an audience member as a common, everyday act, thereby moving far away from a model of television influence wherein television is seen as an intruding force that sits in isolation from the identities and communities that constitute everyday life. Nevertheless, to invoke everyday life and the audience's role in it is also to pose a wide set of questions about power and ideology. And while we by no means call for an ending to examinations of identities and communities, audience research and theory is now at a place where it can also reintegrate such work back into the original project of studying power relationships between television and its viewers. Unkindly, audience studies' critics have at times characterized it as all about agency yet blind to structure, and, while this allegation has rarely had merit, a renewed push at examining structure could definitively deflect the criticism.

3

Institutions

Given that most people's experiences of television are with its programs and of talk and discussion about them, television studies' interest in programs and audiences is only to be expected. For many of us, television programs just seem to be "there," created by an unknown "they," as in: "*They* cancelled my favorite program," "What new programs are *they* making?," "Why would *they* make a show about that?" But television programs do come from somewhere, and "they" have names and motivations that can be explored and connected with the programs ultimately produced. How does a program come to be created? What factors determine its time-slot, success, or demise? Who creates television? How is the industry arranged? What motivates television production? How has the industry changed over time? How do programs' politics and narratives stem from the dominant structures supporting their construction? These and many more questions cannot be answered by turning to programs and audiences alone. Instead, they require a third key area of television studies – the examination of institutions – which endeavors to examine how television gets "there" in the first place and to understand why it is the way it is. If viewers have long referred simply to an ominous "they" that might include the writers, the network, the schedulers, the producers, or others, television studies' examination of institutions aims to flesh out how "they" work.

This third area of television studies is often classified as institutional, production, or industry studies. Here we include studies of the processes and entities involved in making and distributing television as well as its related technologies. Institutions include the production studios that produce programs, the networks or channels that distribute them to viewers, the global conglomerates that own studios and networks, and the regulatory and governmental agencies that allocate government dollars and set rules and policies. Additionally, institutional studies often consider the practices of television production, distribution, and macroeconomic concerns that guide the television industry but are broader than a particular entity, such as a studio or network. Those studying television institutions have examined the production of particular series, the process by which networks select and schedule programs, histories of the regulatory agencies and governmental bodies that have shaped the television industry, and the textual consequences of governmental policies and international trade practices, among many other aspects of making and circulating television shows.

The contemporary study of television institutions takes diverse foci, utilizes an array of methods, and begins from a variety of theoretical presumptions. Studies of television institutions historically have been less common than text or audience studies, but this has been an area of considerable growth and dynamism in the last decade. Explaining the likely causes of this inattention is complicated and tied very much to the various theoretical traditions that we explore in the next section. Most basically, it likely has much to do with the challenges of access and uncertainty regarding how to conceptualize such research amidst feuding critical intellectual traditions.

Given the slower and sparser development of institutional studies, it is less clear that there is a distinction between "television studies" and something else – such as "institutional studies of television" – in the manner that organizes textual studies. The paucity of work has led scholars to freely borrow ideas and methods firmly rooted in sociology, anthropology, and economics, as well as influences more common to other aspects of television studies. Theoretically, a television studies approach draws from various intellectual traditions of political economy and cultural studies that have at times been quite adversarial and yield a complicated and varied range of foundational perspectives. Methodologically, researchers use statistical analyses, mine business and regulatory archives, interview industry workers, and observe the daily work performed in the multiplicity of tasks required in the creation and distribution of television. The primary disciplinary influences have come from the social sciences and cultural studies, as institutional work often places much less consideration on the television text itself, although television studies approaches most certainly do take actual texts into account. When those in humanities traditions, such as English, examine television, the work risks being shockingly ignorant of industrial considerations.[1] We would assert, however, that one distinction of a television studies approach to studying television institutions involves the inclusion of attention to specific texts, rather than speaking of television content through broad, unspecified generalities.

As was noted of textual and audience work in the two previous chapters, the current state of television studies institutional research is very much informed by the questions and approaches that have developed over the past fifty years of study and assumptions about media and society that predate television's existence. And again, in constructing this intellectual history, we draw from many early works that in no way were designed to be exemplary of an emerging subfield of television studies. A synthesis of various perspectives and concerns gave rise to studying television institutions and inform the current state of television studies work in this area. Television studies approaches to studying institutions may not exclusively focus on matters of industrial operation, but at least they exhibit awareness of the significant role industrial practices and conditions contribute to thoroughly understanding programs or audiences.

Perhaps more than in other chapters, context is particularly crucial to understanding the operation of television industries and variations in approach to their study. For most of television's existence, this context largely has been defined at the national level, as each country cultivated a national policy toward the development of television, typically carried over from radio. This first order of industrial consideration queries "What is the mandate, or the goal, of the television industry?" In some cases, it is to earn profits for private industry, as in the commercial model that has dominated in the United States since the broadcast industry's origins. Much of the rest of the world began with a public broadcasting model in which the television industry was primarily supported by a tax and charged with serving the citizens of the nation. Although a blending of commercial and public mandates now can be found in many places, some significant differences in the development of research about television industries in the US and the UK can be explained by the different mandates that governed the operation of television in its early years and the corresponding different relationship between industry and academia that resulted. Nevertheless, the core attribute of the underlying mandate of the various entities within the television system has proven crucial to understanding why both television institutions and scholarship about them has developed in particular ways.

Influences on television industry studies: 1950–1980

An area of intellectual inquiry that actually conceives of and defines itself as television industry studies has only emerged in the last decade or so, and the utility of narrowing into such a specialization is arguably of some debate. Jennifer Holt and Alisa Perren have proposed the existence of "media industry studies," but a sub-subfield of television industry studies seems at this point too narrow.[2] Indeed, in relation to the project of the book, what we outline here are the intellectual influences that have been important to analysis of television industries, whether a work focuses exclusively on industry or includes such analysis among attention to other aspects of television. What we seek to illustrate here is the variety of intellectual influences that bear upon the contemporary study of television industries, as the range of thought and somewhat contentious relations among camps have clearly imprinted themselves upon television industry scholarship. As in the other chapters, various specificities of the television system and the academy contributed to the distinctions in US and UK scholarship that remain distinctive despite growing conversations. These intellectual roots also provide a foundation for increasingly global considerations of the practices and workings of television institutions which were not characteristic of the early years of study.

US administrative research

One possible starting point for discussing television institutions, although not yet television studies, is what has been categorized as *administrative research*. This work, at least in the US, dates to television's earliest days and involves academic study of television often done in tandem with, or with the support of, the television industry itself. Importantly, the different mandates of the US and UK at this time led the nature of this research to differ significantly, and the distinction of "administrative" research seems particular to the US, as explained below.

Administrative research tends to answer a research question of practical significance to a media creator, such as "Is the language used on radio or in newspaper appropriate for the intended audience?" or "Is a promotional campaign successful in advancing its intended aim?" Paul Lazarsfeld, one of the founders of the US social science media research tradition and a significant practitioner of "administrative" media research in the 1940s and 1950s, distinguished these approaches by noting "critical media research supplies a 'broad, often historical context' . . . addresses the 'general role of our media of communication in the present social situation' . . . develops a 'theory of the prevailing social trends of our time,'" and "insists on 'ideas of basic human values according to which all actual or desired effects should be appraised.'"[3] Critical research was thus consistent with the research enterprise of most contemporary university-based researchers, while administrative research was devoid of these qualities. Administrative research did not address the broader historical and cultural context in its studies and tended to ignore the significant role media played in setting cultural norms and their consequences. Such studies, for example, one examining the "appropriateness of language," would likely be viewed as focus group research today – the terrain of commercial research companies – in that it aims to gather information that the industry can use to maximize the communication act with little consideration of the importance or consequences of the message itself. At its core, administrative research offers lessons *for the industry* on how to improve its product or otherwise answers questions of interest to the industry, rather than actually studying the industry itself.

Administrative research is thus a paradoxical start for this discussion because it derives its importance not from examining the industry so much as for creating a site of interaction between academics and industry workers. As television first launched and faced skepticism and derision, some US television networks were eager to connect with the research reputations of academic institutions that might confer legitimacy upon television or at least dispel assumptions of its deleterious effects.[4] Thus, in television's first years, there was much more interaction between the industry and academics than would become the norm – at least in the US. Administrative research bears little in common with the other scholarly traditions noted here and has had scant influence on the study of television industries within television studies. Nevertheless, we begin tracing the intellectual roots of studying television industries here because these first encounters between industry and academia – and their differences in various media systems – are relevant to how academics subsequently came to think about these industries once they began to study them.

Administrative research supported by the television industry quickly waned in the US after television's establishment. With television's widescale adoption and availability in US homes, the television industry lost its interest in academic perspectives as its immense profitability proved the only legitimacy it needed, and as networks created their own research divisions internally. Likewise, the return to a strong effects model as the orthodoxy within the social sciences in the 1960s put industry- and government-funded researchers in opposition over questions about the effects of television violence, which made these relationships more adversarial than cooperative. Further, variations of Marxist thought also took hold in universities at this time and led those studying media to approach its institutions with much more critical regard – especially given the social tumult common by the late 1960s. Critical media scholars were confronted with instances in which media institutions seemed to stymie social change and approached media industries with skepticism and concern. Scholars working from the theoretical tradition of political economy began asking questions about the organization and practices of the television industry, and considered how these industrial and operational characteristics might shape the content produced – particularly in relation to the production of news.

Arguably, a corollary to US administrative research can be identified in early British academic research of British television institutions; however, this work is distinguished by the public mandate of the country's broadcasting system. Because the British television system was built on public service rather than commercial profit, the idea of academic involvement in studying the performance and behavior of television institutions – primarily the BBC at the time – has a different outlook and significance than US scholars' involvement with the commercial networks. It was more reasonable to envision aiding the BBC as contributing to the advancement of important social or national goals – even in being critical – than was the case of doing such work for institutions such as NBC or CBS that aimed primarily at corporate profits. Elihu Katz noted in his mid-1970s survey of British research on broadcasting, which notably was done *for* the BBC, "In Britain, I believe, there is much more mutual interest, and much more direct contact, between academics and broadcasters."[5] These early relationships have been important to the subsequent work developed in both national contexts.

Critical traditions of television industry study

The intellectual starting point for many taking a critical approach to studying all sorts of media industries is a now-classic essay by Theodor Adorno and Max Horkheimer, two German-Jewish emigrants who came to the US during World War II. Adorno and Horkheimer were part of the influential "Frankfurt School" of critical theorists, and their essay, "The Culture Industry: Enlightenment as Mass Deception," warned of how mass media commodified culture to the detriment of art and authentic culture while depoliticizing the populace.[6] For example, they write:

> Under monopoly all mass culture is identical, and the lines of its artificial framework begin to show through. The people at the top are no longer so interested in concealing monopoly: as its violence becomes more open, so its power grows. Movies and radio need no longer pretend to be art. The truth that they are just business is made into an ideology in order to justify the rubbish they deliberately produce.[7]

In particular, Adorno and Horkheimer charged that once culture was rendered an industry, it would follow the prerogative of profit, not of enlightenment, and thus that past successes would be replicated repeatedly as the industry attempted to "standardize" its products rather than forever strive to create bold, new, challenging fare that would be too risky for the industry. If art required innovation and offered fertile soil for radical politics, industry required a stagnant familiarity and was barren to all but the status quo. Written before television in 1944, the essay primarily took aim at the film and radio industries; however, its warnings were quickly applied to television – particularly the commercial model that took hold in the US.

From the theoretical vantage point of the early twenty-first century, the impact of "The Culture Industry" essay is substantially reduced in contemporary applications. Refinements in thinking about audience activity and meaning-making, as well as reconsideration of the distinction of elite art and the denigration of the popular made by Adorno and Horkheimer, have adjusted the salience of their claims and the direct influence of their work, particularly for those who locate themselves within cultural studies. Their perspective, however, was foundational to the origins of critical study of media, and despite its limitations, their naming of the tools of production and identification of industry as originator of content were important steps in recognizing institutions as sites of analysis.

Until recently, a chapter focused on industrial aspects of television might likely be titled "political economy." As David Hesmondhalgh suggests, "political economy" has been "used as a rather lazy synonym for 'studies of media production' (or media industries)."[8] This categorization of nearly all studies of production or industry as "political economy" has obscured significant variations in theories, methods, and premises across a broad array of scholarship that might all be considered "critical," but that understand this concept in different ways. Some, like Douglas Kellner, define political economy broadly, as in: "political economy calls attention to the fact that the production, distribution, and reception of culture take place within a specific economic and political system, constituted by relations between the state, the economy, social institutions and practices, culture, and organizations such as the media."[9] Studies of media industries following Kellner's definition – who draws from cultural studies' perspectives – are less formulaic in mandating a certain emphasis on any one aspect of the factors constituting the political economy of television, such as the state or economic institutions. Most drawing from this perspective do not only study traditional political and economic entities, but are likely to also include specific consideration of texts, specific contexts of production, and other cultural aspects. Such a project might, for instance, examine how pressure from a network to change characters or plotlines was accepted or negotiated by a series' creative staff and then analyze how ideological components of the text changed as a result.

In practice, though, political economy has been more often defined by a far more narrow approach, in line with that described by Vincent Mosco as "the study of the social relations, particularly the power relations, that mutually constitute the production, distribution, and consumption of resources, including communication resources."[10] Here it is not only an emphasis on power relations but specifically the power relation of base and superstructure theorized through a Marxist framework that stresses macro-level power relations such as media ownership. An example of such a project would be one that examines shifting ownership patterns of contemporary media, as does Ben Bagdikian in *The New Media Monopoly* in which he catalogs the ever-decreasing number of media companies that control most of the global media.[11]

North American and British political economy scholars have taken varied emphases, and the British version, explored below, has been more influential for television studies. Nonetheless, a few words on the development of the North American political economy approach to media is warranted, given that many of the questions central to the investigations of television studies scholars have been driven by the omissions in this work.[12] The tradition of North American political economy is most closely associated with Herbert Schiller and Dallas Smythe. Both trained as economists but came to predominantly study media industries, with Smythe working in media regulation early in his career. Vincent Mosco notes that, "One of the chief influences on the development of a political economy approach was the transformation of the press, electronic media and telecommunications from modest, often individual or family-owned enterprises, to the large, multidivisional organizations that marked the twentieth-century industrial order."[13] Much of this transition occurred after World War II, and concern regarding this macro-level ownership transition is clearly imprinted upon the research of the era. Schiller and Smythe applied critical Marxist perspectives to understanding media institutions and their role in society and produced field-charting work that theorized the role of media in imperialism and the audience as commodity in commercial media. Their work tended to focus on news and informational media to the near-complete exclusion of entertainment and relied on methods largely divorced from assessing the actual media products created by media industries.

Although Schiller and Smythe trained students who have continued to examine a macro-level conceptualization of power, theories such as cultural imperialism have not withstood subsequent developments, and even failed empirical testing early on.[14] This type of political economy introduces the importance of ownership on the operation of the television industries that continues to animate analyses, for example in the writings of Robert McChesney and Ben Bagdikian, particularly as the processes of conglomeration Schiller and Smythe considered expanded in the deregulatory environment beginning in the 1980s.[15] And while critical scholars uniformly agree with the idea that who owns media is important, little empirical research explains *how* ownership matters or what consequences it has – particularly in work that links these matters with analysis of actual texts.

The distinction of the original mandate of US television as a commercial enterprise and the public service mandate of Britain and most of the rest of the world required that the focus of political economy on broadcasting outside the US be more on the relationship between television and the state than private business.[16] Perspectives toward media industries are hardly uniform among the intellectual genealogies emerging from Britain, but attention to industry was crucial among both political economists' and early cultural studies adherents' thinking. Studies of media industries developed from a variety of media research facilities in Britain – each with a slightly different focus. As in the US, early research developed through relationships with the television industry, although the terminology of "administrative" research does not appear. In the British case, the Independent Television Authority (ITA) funded early media studies centers, originally with a mandate that they examine television's impact on society and particularly young people; however, this mandate was broadened to support more critical research from a political economy perspective.[17] Such funding was crucial to the establishment of the Centre for Mass Communication Research at the University of Leicester (under the direction of James Halloran) as well as the CCCS (first directed by Richard Hoggart) and the Centre for Television Research at Leeds (under the direction of Jay Blumler).[18]

Philip Lodge acknowledges that the Centre for Mass Communication Research at the University of Leicester under Halloran "defined 'mass communication' in a way which allowed them to develop a thoroughgoing critique of the 'professionals' whilst relying on funding which in part may have been influenced by the same professionals."[19] Leicester was home to two key figures of British critical political economy, Peter Golding and Graham Murdock. But as Lodge notes, those at Leicester did not develop into as cohesive a unit as was the case at other centers – such that he cites Golding as noting, "there never was a 'Leicester School' . . . in nearly the same sense that one can speak of a Birmingham School."[20] Murdock's theorization of the distinction between operational and allocative control was designed to address media industries in general but has been particularly helpful to television studies researchers who have sought to explore how owners may allocate funding but that this allows for creative work to happen in a range of ways at an operational level.[21]

Those at the University of Westminster – led by Nicholas Garnham – participated in media policy debates and developed a related British approach to examining media industries; they also had perspectives informed by Marxism *and* literary studies, which James Curran notes as the central distinction from those at Leicester, and provided some of the closest attention to the television industry. The Polytechnic of Central London – Westminster's predecessor – offered Britain's first media studies degree in 1975 and many of those who trained or taught in that program developed a particular approach to studying media industries that Curran names the Westminster School. Many of those among the "Westminster pioneers" most relevant to studies of television, such as Garnham, Curran, Steven Barnett, Jean Seaton, Paddy Scannell, and David Cardiff, had a comprehensive profile of personal experience that led them to understand media industry operation as more complex than other models allowed. Curran notes that many had studied English literature, so were well versed in humanities perspectives, and were affected by the radicalization of the late 1960s and early 1970s, which led to a particular political bent. Many also had previous media industry experience and more than half taught applied courses related to working in media industries, which anchored their criticism to the realities of the actual operation of media industries in a manner that significantly differentiated them from most North American political economists. As a result of this profile, Curran notes it is "difficult to explain" why the Westminster School parted company with those at the CCCS in Birmingham who "were also strongly influenced by Marxism and literary studies."[22]

The other significant site of study at this time, then, was at the CCCS. Industry research is not as readily associated with the work developed at this time; however, connecting industrial conditions with the production of cultural forms was always central to the cultural studies project. With its influences of theoretical Marxism, combined with textual analysis and notions of active audiences, cultural studies was more commonly linked with scholarship on audiences and textual criticism during the 1980s and 1990s. Yet the industrial dimensions of media creation were part of early works and often present throughout the later years as well. Hoggart attended to the concentration of press ownership and the production process of media texts in *The Uses of Literacy*, industrial and technological aspects figured centrally in Raymond Williams's consideration of technology and the role of culture in determining its use and meaning in *Television: Technology and Cultural Form*; production was

one half of Stuart Hall's widely regarded Encoding/Decoding model and
deliberately included in circuit of cultural production frameworks offered
by Richard Johnson and Paul du Gay et al.; and Angela McRobbie, an
early CCCS student, would go on to conduct close analysis of industry
operations in later work on fashion.[23] It is clear that industrial aspects
were always intended as central to the cultural studies project, despite
detractors' tendency to ignore such work. It is fair to say that industrial
aspects were often not as central to some cultural studies' analyses, particularly the version of cultural studies that took root in the United States
and as typically practiced in literature departments; however, the recent
emphasis on industrial work in television studies – outlined later –
derives its foundations from the critical perspectives of these cultural
studies theorists.

Researchers based in sociology departments – the origin for much of
the research of the television industry performed before the coherence of
an entity identifiable as television studies – produced a wealth of studies
about certain television institutions in the late 1970s, much of which
focused upon news organizations, utilized sociological methods of interview and direct observation, and much was done in Britain. These
scholars – and colleagues in anthropology – brought disciplinary tools
and methods, such as the interview and workplace observation, that
offered considerable depth to the macro-level economic analyses otherwise common. The well-known *Bad News* study by the Glasgow University Media Group made preliminary efforts toward production study
due to limited access, but made key contributions in textual analysis
while laying the groundwork for subsequent studies of journalists and
newsroom operations.[24] Tom Burns published *The BBC: Public Institution and Private World* in 1977, which provided a broad sociological
examination of this national broadcasting institution and its changes
from the mid 1960s to mid 1970s.[25] Most other research focused specifically on the institutional processes involved in the creation of news,
drawing on the already fertile critical textual analysis of news.[26] In
Making News, Gaye Tuchman used years of participant observation and
interviews in both television and newspaper newsrooms to explore how
news frames were established.[27] Although her analytic focus is on the
construction of news rather than television in particular, her study was
among the first that sought to examine the sociology of media creation
and drew from the budding social science communication research in the
US, as well as the political economy work emerging from Britain. That
same year, Philip Schlesinger published *Putting "Reality" Together*,
which endeavors to understand the process of news construction through
fieldwork done in the national newsrooms of the BBC.[28] Schlesinger also
used a combination of direct observation and interviews to expand on

the research being done by other British political economists. The sociology of the newsroom emerged as a topic of considerable interest as scholarship sought to link industrial structures and organizational practices with the common content of news, also evident in the work of Herbert Gans and Jeremy Turnstall, among others.[29] In a few cases, researchers moved beyond news creation to consider the industrial processes involved in the production of entertainment programming, notably Philip Elliott's 1972 *The Making of a Television Series*.[30] Elliott's study did not stray too far from the genre of news by studying a documentary series, *The Nature of Prejudice*, but did include an exploratory audience study and textual analysis. Others, including Manuel Alvarado and Edward Buscombe, John Tulloch and Alvarado, Tulloch and Albert Moran, and Todd Gitlin, would consider entertainment television in coming years (discussed below), but the overwhelming emphasis of industrial studies of television before the 1980s attended to news.[31]

In the US during this time, the figure of the producer provided the focus of research that examined the creation of fictional television. Sociologist Muriel Cantor, who conducted interviews with television producers for her 1972 book, *The Hollywood TV Producer*, authored one of the earliest significant studies.[32] The producer became a central object of study for those wishing to understand more about the practices that led to the production of television texts. In addition to the social scientific approaches of sociologists and anthropologists, Horace Newcomb and Robert Alley also examined the role of producers with a more humanities-inflected focus – emphasizing the creative process and offering up interviews with leading producers of the time.[33] These studies of producers – with whom central creative authority lies in the US industry – drew some inspiration from the film studies' tradition of auteur study and were an important initial step toward understanding the behind-the-scenes aspects of commercial television production, but only captured a single component of a much broader process. The artistic significance of the producer is undeniable; however, these accounts offer only the slightest perspective on the expansive industrial dynamics and power relations of networks, advertisers, government regulators, and media conglomerates.

At the same time that this preliminary research on producers appeared, journalists such as Les Brown, Sally Bedell, and Ken Auletta, who covered the industry for trade publications, produced another important branch of "research" about television institutions.[34] Brown offers a detailed and insightful explanation of the range of microprocesses involved in running a commercial television network, while Auletta captures the complexity of a key moment of ownership change and the shifting business strategies involved. The quotation marks around "research" are not meant to denigrate this work, as in fact it is some of the most well-informed writing about the actual operation of US television studios and networks. What we mean to acknowledge is the distinction of this work. Although some political economists might question whether the work of Cantor and Newcomb and Alley should be categorized as "critical" because of their emphasis on individuals and aspects of culture rather than traditional political economic institutions such as the state and industry, it is more the case that many of the books about the television industry written by journalists were explicitly not critical. The journalists, nevertheless, offered exceptional detail and had years of access to industry decision-makers and thus often produced accounts of the functioning of the industry that far exceeded the academic work in its detail. What the journalistic accounts tended not to do, however, was to connect these practices with their larger social and cultural significance and consequences. Many remain valuable secondary sources – full of concrete examples for critical application – to this day.

Industry research within television studies and its contemporary strands

Todd Gitlin's 1983 *Inside Prime Time* and his journal publications previous to and drawn from this research are key works exemplifying industrially rooted studies of television, and arguably provided the most sophisticated understanding of the operation of the network-era US television industry available – especially its production of entertainment programming.[35] Gitlin brought together interview and observation methods, previously more the terrain of the industry journalists, with critical Marxist training. He spent seven months interviewing 200 people working in the US television industry in Los Angeles in 1981 and recounts the information he gleaned through an accessible narrative style rooted in specifics. For example, Gitlin explains the industrial processes and personalities involved in the development of particular programs and includes firsthand accounts of how and why the programs were viewed as successes or failures. His extensive chapter on *Hill Street Blues* blends textual analysis with insights drawn from both the network and the production team to present a richly informed explanation of the commercial and artistic tensions at the core of much US entertainment television. Notably, Gitlin avoids obvious Marxist analysis in the pages of *Inside Prime Time*, which disappointed some in the academic audience who likely expected a work comparable to his analysis of the news portrayal of 1960s social movements in *The Whole World is Watching*.[36] Gitlin had also offered a compelling analysis of the hegemonic operation of entertainment television informed largely through textual analysis in his "Prime Time Ideology" essay.

Gitlin trained as a sociologist, yet drew from emerging cultural studies theories and Marxist and neo-Marxist political economy theories while quite critical of the social science tradition in the United States that drew from Lazarsfeld. Julie D'Acci notes that

> Gitlin's influential 'Dominant Paradigm' article of 1978 played a major part in priming the American pump for a flood of scholarship from England and Australia that would channel the energies of critical US scholars desperate for an alternative to the administrative/effects model, and for a critical approach that would deal with television programs and viewers as well as television industries.[37]

In this essay, Gitlin critiques the dominant paradigm of media sociology based upon Lazarsfeld's behaviorist examination of effects that organized much of the research thinking in the US.

D'Acci's quotation suggests the complex interplay of ideas and traditions that took place during the 1980s and that would become characteristic of television studies' considerations of industry. Following *Inside Prime Time*, the influence of British cultural studies – particularly Hall's "Encoding/Decoding" manuscript – became increasingly evident in the work of the rising generation of television scholars. As D'Acci notes, James Curran, Michael Gurevitch, and Janet Woollacott's *Mass Communication and Society* valuably brought together British political economists, cultural studies innovators from the UK, and media scholars from the US to influence "a particular brand of American cultural studies – a brand dedicated to analyzing the interworkings of industries, programming, and everyday life."[38] Although textual and then audience analyses seemed to dominate the writing of the 1980s and 1990s, many incorporated some industry analysis while others addressed the importance of attention to production in models of study. James Carey and Joli Jensen authored important works that attempted to bridge the divide in the US between the North American political economy tradition and those who sought to study culture and incorporate attention to the institutions that create it.[39] D'Acci acknowledges that, "James Carey's work had begun to direct US scholars to a type of cultural analysis, but it was the British and Australian scholarship that, in my opinion, fully ignited a widespread cultural studies approach."[40]

This "cultural studies approach" comes to define what we distinguish as television studies. Strategies for blending this array of influences appears in a rich confluence of studies researched in the mid to late 1980s and published in the early 1990s that became characteristic of a television studies approach that incorporates analysis of the industry with considerations of texts and, in some cases, audiences. Many of these works were historical examinations, yet nearly all exhibited an awareness of the importance of industrial aspects to the textual or cultural considerations they offered. The publication of books by Christopher Anderson, William Boddy, Michael Curtin, Michele Hilmes, Julie D'Acci, and Lynn Spigel in the early 1990s marked a watershed moment and began establishing television studies in the US as an approach to the study of television informed by humanities, social science, and cultural studies traditions that included attention to industrial matters.[41] In this work, approaches to political economy and culture common in Britain met with US scholars trained in film departments that emphasized textual analysis to create some of the most elaborate assessments of the intersection of the television industry and culture available to date. Nearly all took historical objects of study, and we consider some of these works in more detail in chapter 4.

Despite the valuable synthesis of contextual, textual, and industrial factors and the sophisticated method and theory of these books that are still largely regarded as examples of the best television scholarship, the industrial aspects of these works were overshadowed – at least in the near term – by political economists and cultural studies adherents engaging in the intellectual equivalent of coming to blows in the early 1990s. The conflict began as an acrimonious conference panel at the 1993 meeting of the International Communication Association in Washington, DC, which was then extended into a 1995 Colloquy published in *Critical Studies in Mass Communication*. Even fifteen years removed, it is impossible to valorize either position – both sides took advantage of the breadth of political economy and cultural studies work to make claims that were surely true of at least some instances but hardly true of these approaches in their entirety. Central points of argument involved the degree to which some political economists adhered to economic determinist positions and the increasing tendency of some in cultural studies to focus excessively on "resistance" and oppositional readings.

Robert Babe, who offers considerable background on the intellectual genealogies of political economy and cultural studies as well as a detailed analysis of the Colloquy debate, asserts that at the core of the debate were resolvable issues about which the camps were not as opposed as it seemed.[42] He identifies the core disputes as about varying understandings of the notion of false consciousness, disagreement over whether production or reception should be prioritized, and whether economic factors are determinant in culture. The more difficult issue, he asserts, had to do with a split emerging within cultural studies regarding the incorporation of post-structuralist critiques of concepts such as authenticity and truth relative to cultural materialism, issues that remain unresolved in cultural studies.

The reasonable substance of what could have been a productive intellectual consideration of the textual turn and depoliticized nature of cultural studies as it came to the US and was absorbed by many humanities fields was lost in grandstanding and overheated exchanges. Scholars could have agreed to look critically upon how some fields took the active audience theory as an excuse to completely disregard the industry, suggesting, justifiably, that author intention did not define the meaning, but also, more problematically, that the mode of production was irrelevant. Nevertheless, one of the consequences was that many began to presume that cultural studies did not attend to industry research and those interested in cultural texts and industry were often compelled to "pick sides," especially those studying at institutions employing key voices on both sides of the debate. Not all cultural studies and political economist adherents *asked* for their graduate students to pick sides, but many students nevertheless did, thereby solidifying the acrimonious divide.

Perhaps the significance of this dispute remains overstated. For instance, some in the US colloquially discuss "The Battles of Vilas Hall," a reference to the theoretical dispute of the time between John Fiske, then a Professor of Communication Arts and a leading name of the cultural studies approach, and Robert McChesney, then a Professor of Journalism and Mass Communication and a leading name of political economy, both at University of Wisconsin-Madison, on the sixth and fifth floors of the Vilas Hall building respectively. Fiske, however, insists that many romanticized and overstated the extent of the "battle" or "rivalry."[43] Yet it unquestionably affected much of the scholarship produced over the following decade and influenced, in some way, multiple generations of television industry study. It was also significant as it marked a trans-Atlantic and multidisciplinary conversation about the methods and theory involved in studying media institutions.

Indeed, this was not an exclusively television studies-based debate and not all of the scholars involved would likely be categorized at the time or subsequently as television scholars. The ensuing intellectual debate was germane to the establishment of television studies largely because the various polemics in and in response to the colloquy established fault lines circumscribing the terrain of political economy versus cultural studies during the time in which a distinct entity that could be considered television studies emerged and television scholars increasingly attended to industry in their research. This debate continued in multiple published collections and very much can be characterized as a dominant intellectual discourse through the end of the decade.[44] The conflict explains the tensions in the field that remain even today among approaches to studying media industries. Those part of the emerging television studies in the late 1990s and 2000s who wished to include analysis of industrial considerations faced a challenge in locating their theoretical foundation, as political economy used the early 1990s dispute to establish itself as the de facto critical approach to media industry study.

Before turning to more recent television studies' examinations of television industries, let's pause to stress the particular theoretical and methodological influences that currently distinguish this work. Television studies scholars claim their work is equivalently "critical" to that of political economists, although often to political economists' considerable objection, and follows more from Kellner's conception of political economy. Many conceptualize power through neo-Marxist or Foucauldian frameworks and attend to smaller practices and processes such as the agency of individuals working within media industries, although not exclusively so.[45] Television studies scholars also tend to draw much more from the methodologies of sociology and anthropology and root the empirical basis of their work in more micro-level questions and objects of analysis than is characteristic of the methodological approach of North American political economists.

Contemporary television industry studies

Despite the tensions, various work began moving beyond the seemingly insurmountable caricatures of political economy and cultural studies as some became more invested in advancing thinking than in extending debate. Particularly key were empirically based efforts that systematically countered and even disproved some of the broad theoretical assertions of North American political economists, such as Schiller's cultural imperialism thesis. By the late 1990s, work emerging primarily from Australian scholars, including Stuart Cunningham, Elizabeth Jacka, John Sinclair, Tom O'Regan, and Albert Moran, managed to disregard the political economy/cultural studies dustup and offered grounded studies of television industry operation conceptualized around global flows of content. Cunningham and Jacka emphasized the need for "middle-range methodology, which steers a course between the 'total' explanations of political-economic theories and the narrow 'micro-institutional' audience analysis informed by ethnography."[46]

The Australian work and its efforts to negotiate a middle methodological and theoretical way proved particularly valuable to the next generation of scholars who sought to engage questions of television industry operation but struggled for a theoretical language amidst the complicated aftermath of the political economy/cultural studies debates.

In a 2009 article, Timothy Havens, Amanda Lotz, and Serra Tinic proposed an approach to media industry study distinguished as *critical
media industry studies*.[47] Although labeled to include the breadth of
media studies rather than just television, the authors work primarily in
television studies and their publications illustrate some of the research
that is part of the burgeoning industrial perspective in television studies.
The distinction of critical media industry studies (CMIS) grew out of the
authors' frustration with the lack of a language or established perspective
within which to place their culturally informed industry studies and the
frequency with which they defined their work primarily through dis-
avowal as examining media institutions, but "not political economy,"
because of the orthodox hold the North American political economists
maintained on the term in many quarters. The authors instead claim their
approach to industry study is rooted in cultural studies' theories that
examine power as it operates within media organizations and allows for
the agency of those workers that is negotiated with the macro-level
structures of capitalism and the relations of power it creates. The CMIS
approach provides a theoretical framework in which scholars can explore
and explain the differentiation within media texts that some political
economy approaches gloss over or presume not to exist. The CMIS
approach is largely consistent with what Holt and Perren call for as a
subfield of "media industry studies."[48]

Although Havens, Lotz, and Tinic have only recently attempted to
identify a distinct approach, many television scholars have produced
work consistent with the CMIS intellectual framework, as their article
names an approach already in existence. Such research often seeks to
explain a particular phenomenon evident in television programming
through interrogation of the industrial conditions in which it is located.
Such studies might examine broad shifts in programming patterns, as
evident in Chad Raphael's explanation of the growing prevalence of
"reality" or unscripted television on US network schedules in the 2000s.[49]
He explores how the cost containment provided by reality programming
helped networks negotiate shrinking audiences and related decreases in
advertising revenue for prime-time network television at the same time
other genres experienced rapidly rising costs that left the networks des-
perate for the lower programming costs that unscripted programs
provide. Other studies identify shifts in representational trends and relate
them to changes in television's industrial norms. Ron Becker links the
rise in gay-themed programming in the 1990s with networks' efforts to
cater to more affluent and socially liberal audiences.[50] Or Lotz explains
the emergence and prevalence of female-centered dramas in the mid-
through-late-1990s by enumerating the industrial conditions that led the
practice of narrowcasting to a distinctly female audience to become an

economically viable programming strategy. Notably, Becker's and Lotz's studies are not solely industrial, as they also make use of textual analysis, but here we see a strength of contemporary CMIS work, when it uses the industry and the program to make sense of one another.[51]

Much of the current growth in television industry studies takes a non-US or -UK focus and builds upon the work of those such as Cunningham and Jacka in revising the once-dominant cultural imperialism thesis of political economists by theorizing the sophistication of international media flows. Havens's explorations of US-produced comedies with black casts, which have considered reception as well as how and why these shows are sold in various contexts, reveal how dynamics of racial power operate across international boundaries.[52] Similarly, the research of Moran and others on the sale of television formats explores this increasingly dominant form of television sale.[53] Rather than the sale of complete programs (usually from the US), much of the international marketplace has shifted to the sale of formats – typically, but not exclusively, of reality shows – that provide a tested template for a program that is then remade with local participants and the possibility of incorporating local perspectives.

Other work seeks to build richer understandings of television and culture outside the US or UK, such as Yeidy Rivero's work linking textual analysis of the construction of blackness in Puerto Rican television to interviews with production personnel to better understand the perpetuation of discourses of race in Puerto Rican culture.[54] Or Marwan Kraidy explores the role reality television plays in Arab politics by including analysis of production conditions with analysis of shows to assess how they contribute to discussions of modernity, publics, and public life.[55] Similarly, Aswin Punathambekar considers how *Indian Idol* and the act of viewers voting for favorite performers enacts and raises regional tensions; and Shanti Kumar examines the influence of cable and satellite channels in India on the construction of national identity in India's postcolonial period.[56] Others offer rich accounts of understudied national contexts, such as Tinic's exploration of the Canadian television industry, which weaves together the distinctive regional aspects that emerge in funding as well as the particularities of a country with a public system geographically connected to the commercial content of the US through porous broadcast borders and as a site for "runaway production."[57]

As with Tinic's work, another focus of recent scholarship has blended questions of trade policy with the economics of production and distribution for contemporary television industries. Several scholars have explored how international trade policies, in concert with the changing economics of television, have led to increased international co-productions on one hand, and/or to the marked presence of another country's production core on the other. Toby Miller, Nitin Govil, John McMurria, Richard Maxwell, and Ting Wang in particular, in their *Global Hollywood 2*, move beyond a crude notion of cultural imperialism, but nevertheless depict a system of media production that sees Hollywood exploit many other countries' labor – through what they dub "The New International Division of Cultural Labor" – and diversify production globally in ways that maintain control but that simultaneously dodge all sorts of tax and regulatory obstacles in the process. For instance, they note how Hollywood's runaway productions have often pitted countries' and states' labor and politicians against each other, both within countries and transnationally, in a race to the smallest paychecks for labor and the smallest tax burden for multinational media corporations; on this point their work is echoed by several other scholars' accounts of runaway production.[58] Hollywood has also developed its savvy, they note, at engaging in format exchanges and other forms of co-production that allow them to break through legal barriers put in place by governments to protect local production. And lest we take Hollywood at their word when they claim to be fond of the "freedom" or "deregulation," Miller et al. note how American multinational media corporations have been remarkably successful at pressuring the State Department to push for international intellectual copyright laws that ease their march through foreign markets and increase the revenues of said march.[59]

Such work offers clear information regarding the business behind global media flows.[60] It also considers how the economic requirement of transnational circulation leads to particular textual outcomes that vary in relation to the nature of the co-production or whether the producer simply seeks for vibrant international sales.[61] For example, Jeanette Steemers examines government and industry initiatives, in a particular historical context and in relation to particular shows, to offer greater understanding of the dynamics of British television exports, while Michele Hilmes steps back to chart the long history of television and radio trade between the UK and the US.[62] Much other work aims to expand the detail of our knowledge of the non-western television industries.[63] A recent project of Michael Curtin engages in an innovative analysis of "media capitals," and of how media circulate around the world through a limited number of hubs, such as Los Angeles, New York, London, Hong Kong, Lagos, and Mumbai.

An emerging area for television industry research has considered the consequences of notable institutional adjustments, such as those wrought by digitization and globalization on traditional practices of industrial operation. Lotz charts how the shifts in production, distribution, technology, and financing of television during the two-decade multi-channel transition of the mid 1980s through the mid 2000s changed the competitive environment and textual products of the US industry.[64] Likewise, many authors collected in Graeme Turner and Jinna Tay's *Television Studies after Television* and Lynn Spigel and Jan Olsson's *Television after TV: Essays on a Medium in Transition* provide yet other analyses of shifting industrial norms, often in other national contexts or in relation to specific technologies.[65] Lotz's edited collection, *Beyond Prime Time: Television Programming in the Post-Network Era*, brings together assessments of the consequences that new industrial norms have for nonprime-time series US television.[66]

Another related approach to television studies' industrial examinations specifically categorizes its approach as *production studies*, although the distinction between critical media industry studies and production studies remains somewhat vague, and production studies has a longer history of use, including works done by UK and Australian scholars in the 1980s. To some extent, it seems those recently categorizing work as production studies often take a particular site of production as the object of analysis, such as talk shows or reality television casting, and draw heavily from sociological and anthropological methods of ethnography, observation, and interviewing to produce studies that examine how the practices involved in the making of television programs connect with broader social power relations. As such, these studies offer in-depth insight – described in the anthropological parlance as "thick description" – of the processes involved in making particular media. In subtle distinction, critical media industry studies have looked at broader practices, such as distribution or co-production, which provide a less bounded object of analysis. But again, as both these terminological distinctions have developed or reemerged recently and simultaneously, hard and fast characteristics remain uncertain and considerable overlap and conversation productively exists.

Much of the method and theory for recent developments in production studies roots itself in the teaching and writings of John Thornton Caldwell who draws heavily from a background in film studies and as a filmmaker in his thinking about the operation of power in the making of media texts.[67] Caldwell has helpfully created a vocabulary for identifying many of the sites more available to researchers, such as "cultivation rituals," and has emphasized the importance of moving beyond studying those at the top of industrial hierarchies to construct broader knowledge about the ways in which many practices and workers that are obscured by top-down approaches to the industry play a significant role in the production process. This interest in grounded knowledge identified in specific practices that are deemed meaningful is central to much television studies research of industries.

Some examples of recent production studies exploring television include Laura Grindstaff's analyses of the talk show, which relied on her work on the set of numerous talk shows as part of her research. Blending grounded methods and critical theory, Grindstaff reveals how the producers elicit certain textual conventions, such as creating an environment that would produce an emotional outburst of tears or anger, and then connects those displays of self with perceptions of class and power perpetuated by the shows.[68] Grindstaff has recently used these research methods to investigate various reality television programs, including MTV's *Sorority Life*, which filmed on her campus.[69] Likewise, Vicki Mayer has used these tools to examine the practices of casting reality television series to examine the continued relevance of the Marxist concept of alienation.[70] Carolina Acosta-Alzuru examines the context of the production of telenovelas in Venezuela in order to examine the genre's representation of women and feminist ideas.[71] Georgina Born uses these sociological and anthropological tools to examine the operation of a vast broadcast institution in *Uncertain Vision: Birt, Dyke and the Reinvention of the BBC*. Access to meetings and 220 interviews with those working in and contracting for the BBC over eight years yields a richly informed examination of the interworkings of the BBC.[72]

Another major area of television studies' industrial examinations explores questions of *cultural policy*. Traditionally, policy was a subfield far removed from humanities, with research of trade figures and analysis of the relationship between cultural products and Gross Domestic Product devoid of consideration of the actual texts viewers encountered. But just as the business motivations of multinational conglomerates and public service mandates of national broadcast institutions are an essential component of understanding why television looks a certain way, so too is it necessary to explore the history of regulations and how their shifts have yielded textual consequences. The work in this area often aligns more closely with political economy approaches, yet recent publications indicate greater embrace of aspects of culture and texts that suggests affinity with the approach to studying television that we delineate.

Some key figures, such as Tony Bennett, have not studied television particularly, but helped to establish a central role for policy within cultural studies.[73] Many of television studies' policy examinations have taken a historical focus. Early examples include William Boddy's examination of the Federal Communications Commission during the 1950s that connects the regulatory decisions at the time with the way in which television became available to the US populace and the particular ways it was thus integrated into the culture.[74] Michele Hilmes examines how the establishment of a commercial mandate through regulatory machinations in radio also determined key features of the relationship between broadcasting and the film industry.[75] Likewise, Thomas Streeter's account of the development of US cable policy, Laurie Ouellette's examination of the establishment of the US Public Broadcasting System, as well as Megan Mullen's exploration of the development of the cable industry offer analyses of broad structures that organize the contemporary television system.[76]

Television studies policy work with a more contemporary focus includes Jennifer Holt's examination of self-dealing and conglomerate practice in the wake of US deregulation and the phase out of the Fin Syn rules, or John McMurria's account of how shifting competitive norms, globalization, and international trade policy affected the content and quantity of long-form television.[77] Or consider Mayer's examination of the *Girls Gone Wild* soft-core pornography enterprise, which she analyses by bringing together regulatory analysis, industrial data, ethnographic interviews and trade accounts.[78]

Given the difference between the US commercial television systems and the public systems that have dominated or at least structured the television of much of the rest of the world, questions about and approaches to cultural policy have varied by national context and been much more vibrant outside of the US where cultural policy has been more robust. Policy has remained a central concern of British television scholars, and in that context often attends to the complicated present environment of mixed commercial and public mandates now common. Many British scholars, including David Hesmondhalgh, Sarah Baker, David Lee, Anna Zoellner, and Richard Paterson and Gillian Doyle, attend to questions and research related to the viability of independent production and related policies.[79] Des Freedman and, within the larger framework of media policy in general, Aeron Davis have offered significant work that charts, theorizes, and historicizes currents in British and foreign policy.[80] Some new work categorized as "creative industries" attempts to bring more humanistic and cultural studies theoretical perspectives and methods to bear on questions of policy. Such work has been particularly robust in Australia where academics have embedded themselves in policy and production strategies and research.[81] This approach has also generated significant controversy and debate that remains unresolved among media scholars.

Emerging trends

Perhaps by the time you read this, industry studies will be as common as textual or audience studies of television among contemporary work. At this point, many rich opportunities – both historical and those that consider the quickly changing present – exist for expanding our

understanding of the significance of industrial aspects on the texts produced and circulated by television. Given how recently much of this
research on television institutions has been published, it is somewhat
more difficult to clearly map this area of research than others that offer
greater historical distance for both gauging the influence of varied work
and perceiving how and where it fits within a broader intellectual project.
Intellectual debates in this area in recent years have suggested some
thawing of the political economy/cultural studies standoff, and studies
of television industries continue to be influenced by a range of intellectual
traditions that yield hybridity that further confounds efforts to demar-
cate clear boundaries.[82]

But at a minimum, we'd assert that a key discrepancy between general
industrial studies of television and television studies' analyses of industry
involves the manner in which the text is considered. One of the biggest
limitations of macro-level political economy study is that its breadth
makes attention to actual television programs quite difficult. Thus, one
of the central critiques cultural studies levies against this work is that it
takes a simplistic view of the text, often assuming broad commonalities
that those who actually view content find wanting. Analyses based on
economic or ownership determinism tell us important things about
media industries but don't explain the contestation and difference that
those who deeply engage the medium see. Television studies consistently
incorporates consideration of actual television texts – not "television"
in the abstract – in its analyses. It seeks to "ground" its theory in actual
cases connecting industrial practices with the texts they create.

It is not our intention to strictly police the boundaries of various
approaches to industry studies and those most relevant to television
studies. As in the other chapters, considerable overlap exists between
industrial studies of television and television studies' analyses of industry. Here again, our primary concern is to productively establish an
entity of television studies that has existed but been uncertainly defined
to date. We don't mean to suggest that television studies work is any
better than others we don't include; the politics of classifying perhaps
becomes particularly contentious here, given the history of acrimony
between cultural studies and political economy. After years of pointed
barbs and ignoring those outside one's paradigm, the significant disrup-
tions in long-entrenched industrial operations by forces such as post-
Fordism, globalization, and digitization have created great need for
intellectual conversations and studies that cross beyond a single scope
and framework of study. We don't need less of any one type of study, so
much as more studies and conversations among them.

Recent scholarship has productively pushed the boundaries of what
many have traditionally included within the realm of the television indus-

try. Work by Toby Miller and Vicki Mayer looks not at the making of television programs but the making and disposing of televisions, exploring how those televisions arrive in our living rooms and where they go when we replace them.[83] This has opened up new areas for exploring political and economic consequences related to the environmental ramifications of our many screened environments. Television studies needs to continue to push the boundaries of what television "production" or television "industry" entails.

An area of clear growth involves the intersections of television, technology, and industry. Although "convergence" appears the buzzword *du jour*, the changing technological realm of television and video content cannot be avoided, and scholarship in this area is primarily considered in chapter 4. As the screens upon which audiences view "television" evolve, the relevance of broadcast networks and cable channels decreases, and audience behaviors adjust accordingly, we'll need much more work that examines the role of distributors and seeks to re-explain and analyze the process of getting video content to viewers. Similarly, it is likely that such shifts in the technologies we use and how we access television will also bear consequences for the production process and require reconsideration of our existing knowledge and assumptions about the making of television content. Finally, despite the decades-long trend toward conglomeration and consolidation in media industries, very little analysis of these issues exists that uses methodological tools more refined than that of macro economics to understand the behavior of these entities and the consequences of these ownership structures on media texts. Indeed, in broaching the topic of ownership conglomeration, we necessarily move beyond "television" studies, as television ownership is mostly blended with ownership of other media entities.

This returns us to the phenomenon of convergence and the difficulty of cordoning off television studies just as we attempt to define it. All of these adjustments bear significant implications for television's established economic relations that continue to result in varied outcomes dependent on the mandate of the system. It also remains the case that much of the regulatory policy for television was established for an era of broadcasting. These frameworks are already outdated and the processes of policy creation and their outcomes will yield rich opportunities for new scholarship as more appropriate regulatory structures are developed.

4

Contexts

As we have argued till now, the program, the audience, and the industry are three key sites for analysis of television. The tangibility of these entities provide obvious objects of analysis, whether it be as images on television, a DVD box set that one can hold in one's hand, one or more people watching or talking about television, or production studios and office buildings filled with people engaged in some aspect of production. However, television studies' richness can also come from studying less tangible objects, forces, and processes. Program, audience, and industry are all situated, of course, historically, spatially, and in relation to one another, and thus a proper study of television programs, audiences, and industries requires that we inquire into the many contexts that surround these other agents, that give them meaning, and that play a key role in creating and nurturing them. To offer an analogy, if one were to try to make sense of a particular building, one would hopefully not just study its blueprints and its construction, look at who lives in it, and examine the construction company that made it – one could gain a much richer understanding of that building and its place in society by examining the time, and place it is in, its history, how it compares and contrasts to other buildings, and how its look and functions are related to other buildings around it. In short, one would need to *contextualize* the building. So too with television. A wide range of forces determines how programs, audiences, and industries work, while further determining how and why television matters. Though these forces are less tangible than the "holy trinity" of program, audience, and industry, and thus, while a chapter that addresses them risks appearing like a grab bag of "other things that we find important," they are vitally important.

To begin with, we will discuss medium theory, as one of the earliest attempts within media and communication studies to explain an entity such as television. Rallying around Marshall McLuhan's famous dictum that "the medium is the message," medium theorists treat television or other media as entire ecosystems, believing a medium determines the environment in which program, audience, and industry will operate, or that technologies possess their own meanings and effects, independent of the specific agents or elements within them.[1] However, while there is merit in thinking oneself out of the specificities of program, audience, and industry, medium theory flirts with being technologically determin-istic and with ill-advisedly reducing those specificities to irrelevance. Television studies was developed in part to move beyond such determin-ism, and we will explore how contextual work within television studies insists on the medium being socially produced, and thus always open to change. The types of change that might occur form the subject matter of this chapter.

After discussing medium theory, then, we turn first to what has been a strong vein of television studies work, namely historical analyses that situate television's role within its time period and that, in some cases, chart its changing roles over time. To say that television is situated by the culture around it, though, is also to reflect on how television affects itself, given that television is such an obvious mainstay of contemporary culture. Consequently, much of the remainder of the chapter turns to ways in which we can contextualize programs and their audiences' knowledge, expectations, and interpretive strategies in terms of other programs that have been watched, that surround the program in ques-tion, or that otherwise color one's understanding of the program in question. First, we discuss genre analysis, wherein programs' meanings are seen as related to other supposedly similar programs. Second, we examine what Raymond Williams dubbed "flow," and how programs next to each other in sequence will change each other's meanings.[2] Third, we examine a specific form of flow, "intertextuality," that crisscrosses time and place, yet that similarly affects meaning in important ways. Finally, before closing the chapter, we again discuss potential future routes for contextual analysis. We discuss the intertextual control exerted by the considerable world of hype, promos, fan creativity, and other elements that surround and refer to a program. And since some of these elements challenge notions of what the text is in the first place, and of whether the television program is truly central, this leads us to a discus-sion of "convergence" and of transmedia products that place television within a larger network of technologies, platforms, and meanings.

Medium theory

Some of the earliest work on television was contextual, interested less in any program, audience community, or system of industrial organization, and more in the technology itself. Medium theory proved a dead end and never integrated into television studies, but it dominated a moment in time prior to television studies' arrival and development. Yet reviewing this false start helps distinguish what does shape television studies and reveals the accomplishment of the contextual studies that follow. Over time, this school of work became known as "medium theory" or "media ecology," as it sought to make sense of what any given medium makes possible, impossible, and more or less likely, and hence of how any medium changes and governs its environment. This school can be traced back to the work of four figures in particular – Harold Innis, Walter Ong, Marshall McLuhan, and Neil Postman – and thus a brief discussion of these figures serves as a brief introduction to the field.

Harold Innis was a political economist whose work proved influential to some studying media industries, but his broader academic mission followed his fascination with how history had been directed by different media of communication. In *The Bias of Communication* and *Empire and Communications*, he considered and speculated as to how various empires had grown from the powers allotted them by their careful management and control of the dominant media of the time, through what he called "monopolies of knowledge."[3] Innis's interests, in other words, examined how power stemmed from, was made possible by, and was flavored by, technology. Less interested in power per se, Walter Ong was still interested in how media shaped culture. In his key book, *Orality and Literacy*, he discussed humankind's move from orality to literacy and then to print media, seeing each shift as profound. For instance, he argued that literacy allowed both history, since linearity was now possible and allowed documentation and evidence to replace myth and legend, and science, with its emphasis on verifiability and the ability to build upon others' experiments that was only truly possible once records could be kept. Both writers saw technology as setting the ground rules for what was, respectively, politically or culturally possible.[4]

By far the most famous medium theorist, though, and the most renowned for his work on television specifically, was Marshall McLuhan. McLuhan became something of the patron saint of new media, celebrated in popular media – including a cameo in Woody Allen's *Annie Hall*, and an interview in *Playboy* – and still quoted to this day for coining the term "global village" and his dictum that "the medium is the message," and embraced as one of media studies' very few public intellectuals.[5] McLuhan's broad, rather spacey, philosophic writing style and penchant for sound bite-style observations of the media attracted a generation trying to make sense of the televised era in which they found themselves. For instance, he noted obliquely that "the TV Child cannot see ahead because he wants involvement, and he cannot accept a fragmentary and merely visualized goal or destiny in learning or in life."[6] He also famously distinguished between "hot" and "cool" media, the former being those that did all the interpretive work for their audience, the latter that left something to the imagination – as do sunglasses, he noted. He therefore analyzed the Kennedy–Nixon debates as damaging to Nixon in the "cool" environment of television that "rejects the sharp personality and favors the presentation of processes rather than products,"[7] yet complimentary to the preeminently cool Kennedy, while radio listeners had supposedly favored Nixon because Kennedy's cool facade played poorly on this hot medium.

Media ecology's fourth key figure, and the one who would institutionalize the field in a graduate program at New York University in 1971, was Neil Postman. Postman's *Amusing Ourselves to Death* remains one of the best-selling books about television. An excoriating broadside on the medium in total, he attacked it for dumbing down its audience by automatically privileging quick, visual "arguments" rather than careful deliberation and rational discussion, as he claimed a previous "literate mind" had once done. The television viewer, he alleged, ends up "knowing *of* lots of things, not knowing *about* them"[8] and lacks critical context. Television is a spectacle, a "world without much coherence or sense; a world that does not ask us, indeed, does not permit us to do anything; a world that is, like the child's game of peek-a-boo, entirely self-contained. But like peek-a-boo, it is also endlessly entertaining."[9] Everything on television to Postman, therefore, is entertainment, and nothing asks for our serious attention since it will all be replaced by another image, another snippet of entertainment, in a few seconds or minutes.

In attempting to take a big picture view of television and other media, though, media ecology ran up against television studies as it was developing along the lines discussed so far in this book. Television studies was keen to examine specifics – differences between texts and genres, audiences, and industries – while media ecology either downplayed or outright ignored the importance of such specifics in favor of grand, sweeping commentary. These broad predictions about television had a magnetic attraction for those confused and worried about the new environment around them, whereas television studies' attention to smaller details lacks their neatness in comparison. But at its worse, media ecology can wax wholly unempirical and can be deeply reductive. Take, for instance, McLuhan's unsubstantiated above-noted observation about "the TV child," or his equally odd pronouncement that "most TV stars are men, that is, 'cool characters,' while most movie stars are women, since they can be presented as 'hot' characters."[10] Or take Postman's thumbnail sketch of the golden age of the "literate mind," which – ironically, given his critique of television's supposed reductiveness – is largely ahistorical. Postman contrasted television's sound bite-style politics to the Lincoln – Douglas debates and the crowd's supposed endurance and eagerness to stay for four hours of rational deliberation. Media historian Michael Schudson, though, has noted that the debates were accompanied by revelry and play, and that their lack of amplification left many in the crowd as restless and distracted as Postman sees the modern television audience.[11] Statements that the medium is the message or Postman's reductive assertion that television never allows us time to think also erase and render irrelevant vast differences between programs, audiences, and industries in an indefensible manner – *Meet the Press* becomes no different from *The Jerry Springer Show*, *Iron Chef*, or *The Wire*, fan communities and first-time watchers are equated to one another, and FOX, BBC, or Malawi's Television One are flattened into the same thing.[12]

Medium theory risks freezing television in time and place, making any one of its iterations seem natural and inherent. Television in the US in the 1980s – when Postman was writing – is not "television" in general, though; not only is it significantly different now in the US, but it was also different in the US at other moments in the past, and it is often fundamentally different in other nations. Some television is hot, some cool, some warm, just as some is wholly rational and deliberative, while some is mindless. Medium theory still offered a great deal by asking that scholars not get lost in the minutiae of any given program, audience, or industry, that they attend to issues that might be germane to the entire medium, and that they think about the ground rules that structure television, or which television sets for society. But its dead end was significant, given that it shows the importance of studying historical and geographic specificities. Admittedly, some media ecologists have admirably attended to such specifics, and others have, wisely, been more careful about making grand, unempirical observations. But television studies' own engagement with technology needed to grow in different ways.

Histories of television

From the field's early days, a vibrant area of television studies has been historical work that aims either to situate the medium culturally and chart its social role at a specific point in time, or to chart the changes and continuities of the medium, a genre, or an industrial practice over a span of time. Such work mixes medium theory's fascination with how technologies affect society with an empirically guided refusal to see those effects as in any way permanent or inherent. To properly discuss this work, though, somewhat clashes with this book's chapter organization. After all, many television histories can be neatly categorized in one of the preceding chapters as historical examples of analyzing television's programs, audiences, or industries. However, a great many book-length studies of television history transcend these imposed classifications so flagrantly as to embody a category all their own by depicting the environment around programs, audiences, and industries, not just their details.

The earliest works of television history tend to be more traditional approaches to technological or industrial history. To this day, Erik Barnouw's three-part volume tracing the history of US broadcasting remains one of the most detailed accounts, although Barnouw's vantage point was that of a practitioner, having worked in radio. Barnouw's project details the industrial aspects of how and why broadcasting developed – who was involved, when it happened.[13] In the UK, James Curran and Jean Seaton's *Power Without Responsibility*, now in its seventh edition, served as a key history of the BBC and hence of the early days of British television.[14] Both provide a rich secondary source for subsequent scholars, although historical studies of television that would lay the groundwork for television studies were considerably more multidimensional and influenced by cultural studies. Detailed social histories of broadcasting began appearing in the 1990s, often rooted in radio. For example, Paddy Scannell and David Cardiff's *A Social History of British Broadcasting* presents a narrative account of the establishment of broadcasting in Britain up to 1939 – thus just covering the earliest beginnings of television – while Scannell's *Radio, Television and Modern Life* takes a phenomenological approach to texts, exploring how they work for audiences and emphasizing their ordinariness and their role in daily life.[15] Writing about the US context, Michele Hilmes's *Hollywood and Broadcasting* and *Radio Voices* and Susan Douglas's *Inventing American Broadcasting: 1899–1922* blended archival research of government and corporate entities with social history and analysis of the content of radio broadcasts where possible – mainly in the later years of radio covered in *Radio Voices*.[16] Such work provided an important foundation, both methodologically and in grounding the prehistory of television, which drew considerably upon radio's industrial and textual foundations.

The first contextual histories of television largely emerged from those trained in film studies and generally focused more on the nexus of television and culture than did work such as Barnouw's. As discussed earlier, what might be argued to be the first generation of television scholars completed doctoral work in the mid to late 1980s amidst a heady mix of theoretical and methodological ferment largely related to the infiltration of British cultural studies. The importance afforded to mass culture central to British cultural studies provided a theoretical foundation for those wishing to locate a focus outside of film. Perhaps by chance, perhaps as a hedge against continued concern about the legitimacy of television as an object of study, many in this cohort chose historical intellectual projects.

No single formula unites books such as Lynn Spigel's *Make Room for TV: Television and the Family Ideal in Postwar America*, William Boddy's *Fifties Television: The Industry and Its Critics*, Christopher Anderson's *Hollywood TV: The Studio System in the Fifties*, and Michael Curtin's *Redeeming the Wasteland: Television Documentary and Cold War Politics*,[17] but common methodological practices can be found among them and all operate with a consistent serious engagement with a combination of television's industrial, cultural, and textual practices that had heretofore been absent. All were clearly influenced by the work done at the CCCS over the previous decade, although the work of the British scholars remained consistently focused on the present. Perhaps what we continue to find most significant about these books is their perspective about or attitude toward television which grows in appreciation alongside recognition of how challenging it must have been at the time to take such a stance. These books are neither overly defensive nor reactionary in their tone, despite willfully defying established traditions in the social sciences and humanities in their methods or objects of analysis. Instead, each implicitly makes the case for the importance of its subject matter by providing broadly researched claims and meticulous analysis. There is no overarching "Television" in their books, but rather a set of possibilities, paths taken and not taken, and richly textured attention to how the aspect of focus came to be.

To draw down to a few specifics, consider Boddy's book, which can be described as an industrial history of the Federal Communications Commission in the 1950s – and yet it is so much more. Boddy breaks from the dominant historiographic design of policy history by charting the key decisions of the dominant US regulatory body and actions of television set/program makers – as at this time they were largely one and the same – while engaging critical discourses about the programming produced within the industrial conditions of this time, particularly nostalgic assertions of this as some kind of Golden Age of television content. Unlike the great majority of existing and subsequent institutional research, Boddy analyzes business documents, regulatory records, and trade press, as well as television programs. In his book, we see one of the first models for a television studies' approach to studying television industries in that he seeks to connect the cultural texts of television with the conditions of their production – a rarity in political economy or other approaches to industry dominant at the time.

Or, in another case, Spigel's examination of the introduction of television into the American home provides a foundational model of a media-related social history through its methodological rigor infused with a sophisticated understanding of social theories of media and consideration of its shows. Spigel draws from a rich array of cultural texts – in this case mainly magazines – to examine how television was talked about and presented, particularly to the American housewife. Yet she also provides industrial analysis of the advertising practices of this era and consideration of the fictional avatars of 1950s' families depicted dealing with television on television. Although Boddy's book could reasonably be considered an example of multidimensional industrial analysis, Spigel's book is resistant to the classification scheme used to organize this book as it so thoroughly integrates a range of sites of analysis. *Make Room for TV* also invites comparisons with medium theory, for, while Spigel notes the degree to which television becomes a domestic, feminized medium, she never regards this as inherent. To the contrary, through empirical, archival research, Spigel looks at how women's magazines and other aspects of popular culture in the US *made* television domestic, and hence the book is an examination of how the medium was *given* a societal role. Spigel draws on advertisements and publications from the 1950s to explore how television was alternately represented as a force that might bring together or divide the inhabitants of the family home. Advertisements emphasized television's unifying properties while popular pundits instilled worry about the medium's deleterious effects. And women were particularly entrusted with the role of making television an acceptable member of the family. If many still regard television as a domestic medium, both attuned to and constitutive of the rhythms of everyday domesticity, Spigel shows how the television/domesticity link was actively constructed in the US over several years, and how women in particular were asked from an early date in the US to play a very specific, mediating role for the medium.[18] Mary Beth Haralovich's article on "Sit-coms and Suburbs: Positioning the 1950s Homemaker" provides a rich illustration of how such contextualized television history might be contained in an article-length investigation.[19]

Many among the first self-identified generation of television studies scholars – several of whom were trained at the University of Wisconsin-Madison by Spigel, Hilmes, and Julie D'Acci, alongside John Fiske – have written analyses that explore television during particular moments in television history, often focusing on how a specific theme or entity appeared on television in a blend of cultural history, institutional context, and textual analysis. Aniko Bodroghkozy, for example, examines US television in the 1960s and the tensions that the commercial medium faced in addressing the youth revolt and counterculture of this time.[20] She traces not only commercial television, but also the efforts of the counterculture to harness television's powerful ability of visual storytelling. In *Wallowing in Sex: The New Sexual Culture of 1970s American Television*, Elana Levine examines how tensions regarding changing sexual attitudes were manifest on television in content ranging from daytime television, to advertisements, to made-for-television movies.[21] And although Jason Mittell's book provides a substantial contribution to theorizing genre and strategies of genre analysis – described below – it too is profoundly historical in its approach to the topic, making historiography a central tool for analyzing and understanding genre.[22] In addition to these and other monographs, a variety of edited collections have provided more focused historical considerations of various aspects of television.[23]

Another common approach for conducting historical research in television studies is to track a process across time. Mittell's research on cartoons offers a good illustration of this, as he walks through the ways in which the genre gradually became seen as one for children, but then later, with the advent of *The Simpsons* and a subsequent wave of prime-time animation, it ceased to be seen solely as something to be watched by children on Saturday mornings.[24] Or, at book length, Derek Kompare provides an engaging history of the syndicated series in American television. He examines the initial stigma against replaying television; the structural and industrial determinants that led to its eventual use, not only originally, but then again as a method of channel-branding in the age of cable channel expansion; the cultural impact of series syndicated long after production that became surrounded by nostalgia and were seen as a national historian of sorts; and a wide range of other shifts in the relationship between US television, syndication, its audience, the industry, and the changing discourses of value that accompanied these shifts.[25]

Another branch of work can arguably be categorized as histories of the present. John Thornton Caldwell's *Televisuality: Style, Crisis and Authority in American Television* studies television style in the 1980s and early 1990s.[26] Caldwell looks at the technological and industrial innovations and the greater attention to visual style they allowed. For example, he notes the simultaneous arrival of more "videographic imagery" related to the increasing availability of affordable home video recorders and the aesthetics of shows such as *America's Funniest Home Videos* at the same time as increasingly cinematographic visuals appeared as shifts in technology enabled television to utilize visual qualities and techniques previously specific to film. Amanda Lotz's *The Television Will*

Be Revolutionized similarly mines the present and immediate past to contextualize how shifting industrial practices adjusted the content produced in prime-time US programming.[27] This work is mirrored by several accounts in James Bennett and Tom Brown's edited collection, *Film and Television after DVDs*, and in another edited collection by Bennett and Niki Strange, *Television as Digital Media*,[28] both of which similarly study the current moment's textual, audience, and industrial contexts. Or, illustrating the porous boundaries of television studies, Derek Johnson's account of the rise of television and film franchises begins with historical context by examining how the logic of the franchise infiltrated Hollywood, and also offers a richly detailed account of what the contemporary franchise is, as an industrial entity, for the audiences who follow franchises and engage with them, and as a storytelling platform.[29]

Admittedly, some of these works' "histories" are of the present day. Whether examining the 1950s or 2010, though, what they bear in common is an attention to the context of television: its historical placement, the temporal environment, and the sociocultural moment in which texts, audiences, and industries find themselves. Geography and spatial environment, of course, are also hugely important, though less work has focused on this, and thus we return to it at chapter's end when discussing new directions for television studies.

At the risk of stating the obvious, historical studies also prove vital for an appreciation of the present moment. If scholars have questions about the radical or conservative potential of any given text, audience behavior, or industrial practice, a knowledge of history can contextualize the degree to which the object under study truly is significant, while also offering information on how similar texts, audience behaviors, or industrial practices fared elsewhere in time and why. Historical work on policy, for example, tells us what strategies activists have used in the past, how industries met and resisted them, and the success of these strategies. Or, as we will argue at the chapter's end, situating the convergence culture of 2010 within its historical precedents might help us move beyond crude utopian or dystopian prognostications toward a historically informed sense of how to evaluate our current moment. History situates television and tells us what it is, what it was, and what it is becoming, but it is also television studies' "case law," setting importance precedents to be analyzed carefully.

Contextual program analysis

If context is about temporal and spatial placement, though, television studies must look not only at social history and at the world outside television but also at textual history and at textual placement. We always encounter television in a specific setting, next to or alongside other programs. Moreover, as we attempt to make sense of programs, we will always do so in part with structures learned through previous programs and experiences. Sometimes these previous programs and experiences will be immediate, as in the case of two programs watched back to back, and at other times, they will be distanced by time and space, but nevertheless regarded as helpful interpretive tools. Much of the remainder of this chapter turns to these contexts and to what we could call contextual program analysis. If close reading asks us to find meaning inside any given program, contextual program analysis invites us to find ways in which meaning is established *between* texts, and to search for ways in which any given program's meaning is prefigured by that which comes before it, or changed after the fact by subsequent programs. Contextual program analysis regards television as its own thriving society and culture, populated by countless programs, audiences, and industries, and it attends to the relationships between these inhabitants, and to how these relationships affect one another.

Genres

Genre provides a simple mechanism by which meaning is constructed across and between texts. Many actions, characters, and plot developments have radically different meanings in different programs, based largely on our understanding of the show's genre. A misunderstanding between two characters, for instance, may be cause for concern for a viewer watching a drama, whereas in a comedy it might cause pleasure over the anticipation of humor that will arise from the situation. In such instances, other programs and what they have told us and prepared us for are just as responsible for creating meaning. A genre frames our understanding, and in doing so it should remind us that frames are vital in interpretation. As in all contextual program analysis, genre analysis challenges the analyst to realize the multiple levels of "text" that exist; the text of the single program has already been discussed in chapter 1, but the text of the genre is another.

Genres are industrial constructs, in that the industry will quite often think of itself as creating a specific *type* of program, and often have vastly different personnel entrusted with developing these different genres. Genres are also meaningful for audiences, as audiences arrange their viewing accordingly; for example, saying they feel like watching a comedy, a procedural, or a game show at a certain moment or refusing to watch anything that isn't news or "quality drama" at other times.

And genres are textual entities, having meanings themselves and beyond the specifics of any single program within the genre. A genre leads to certain expectations – whether the episode will end happily or not, whether bad characters are dangerously so, whether we can expect change or just the status quo, and so forth – and the "effects" or messages of any given text within the genre may be all the stronger through reinforcement across that genre. Consequently, many projects within television studies have not taken a singular program as their object of analysis, but rather a family of shows, and the similarities and differences within it. The method here often borrows a great deal from textual analysis since indeed the genre is being analyzed as a text, albeit a considerably larger one.

To take a recent example, Laurie Ouellette and James Hay's *Better Living Through Reality TV: Television and Post-Welfare Citizenship* examines how multiple reality shows have come to take the place of a welfare society. They argue that a wide range of reality television, from makeover shows, to parenting programs, weight-loss competitions, addiction interventions, and various competitions, posit the individual as the proper locus for change, so that "The citizen is now conceived of as an individual whose most pressing obligation to society is to empower her or himself privately. TV assists by acting as a visible component of a dispersed network of supporting technologies geared to self-help and self-actualization."[30] Thus, they note, "At a time when privatization, personal responsibility, and consumer choice are promoted as the best way to govern liberal capitalist democracies,"[31] reality TV lights a path forward for the individual and for society, and it is no surprise that thousands of Americans apply directly to reality television programs to meet their basic needs, rather than (or in addition to) soliciting help from governmental sources.[32] Whether it is *Nanny 911*, *Supernanny*, or *Wife Swap* telling parents, and especially mothers, how to be better, or *What Not to Wear* requiring us all to have a decent style, and subjecting us to surveillance and ridicule should we not comply, or whether it is multiple competition reality shows such as *The Apprentice* or *Big Brother* asking us to reflect on how we act in business and leisure settings, reality television often echoes the call to take a good, long hard look at oneself. It thereby contributes to a "reinvention of government [that] assumes, encourages, and increasingly requires that citizens assess and manage their own risks."[33]

While close analysis of any given reality TV program could reveal this message, and while their book contains many sections with single textual analyses, Ouellette and Hay illustrate how valuable close textual analysis can be when it is assembled with other similar analyses of similar programs. Any given genre is composed of a variety of requirements for relations between individuals, individuals and institutions, and individuals and viewers, all of which render a genre as rich a text for analysis as any single program. The resulting analysis is also given more immediate relevance through being attached to an entire family of programs, not simply one program, as with Ouellette and Hay's examination of arguably the most pervasive genre in television of the first decade of the twenty-first century.

As with textual analysis, genre analysis can focus on a wide variety of elements in the individual texts. Thus, for instance, Ouellette and Hay focus predominantly on plot and dialogue. Elsewhere, though, Mark Andrejevic also examines reality television but by focusing more closely on its visual style, and hence on how it borrows from closed circuit television and "fly on the wall" documentary style to invite audiences to look at and surveil its characters. He concludes that the genre works to normalize widespread surveillance in society, even making it look pleasurable.[34] Or Kompare looks at resemblances between the traditional family sitcom and the reality show *The Osbournes* to see how the latter show still works within a rather conservative frame that is common to the traditional family sitcom as genre.[35] Indeed, numerous writers, from David Marc to Michael Tueth, Ella Taylor to Brett Mills and Gerard Jones, have examined a large number of sitcoms and have charted a strong family resemblance in the form of a genre that may appear to have radical potential, and that occasionally may take advantage of that potential, but that largely conforms to and sells the status quo in terms of gender, family, and societal relations.[36] Other genre analyses by other scholars include Catherine Johnson's discussion of science fiction and fantasy, Glen Creeber's analysis of serial drama, Elayne Rapping's treatment of law and order shows, Robert C. Allen's work on soap operas, Kevin Glynn's examination of low-budget, spectacularizing reality television, and the collected essays in books on *Satire TV*, *Reality TV*, *Teen TV*, to name but a few.[37]

If we have until now presented genre analysis as primarily textual by nature, this need not be the case. Instead, several of the above-listed projects, and many others, are just as interested in the genre as an industrial entity, and in what logic lies behind their continuation. For example, in chapter 3, we referenced Chad Raphael's explanation of the industrial causes of the proliferation of reality television. Or chapters examining the changing industrial dynamics of producing made-for-television movies, sports, soap operas, and talk shows among others in *Beyond Prime Time* can also be considered as genre analysis.[38] Likewise, audience studies often focus on the viewing of a particular genre, seen most clearly in research on soap opera viewing. Contextualized genre analysis will often require a significant component of industry and/or audience analysis, or at least audience consideration, as the industry's and audience's relationship to and use of the genre become an important part of the picture.

Recent work on genre has moved away from defining genre through textual similarities to argue that they are discursively constructed; in other words, they are created in and by the discussion of them, as well as by a variety of extra-textual sources and that they come to mean different things at different times. In his book on genre and television, Jason Mittell examines the various sites of the discursive construction of genres, from the industry and from reporting on the industry, to fan discussion, to marketing and related materials that surround them, to regulation and policy. Mittell's work convincingly argues that close reading of genres can only tell us so much. He argues, "television genre is best understood as a process of categorization that is not found within media texts, but operates across the cultural realms of media industries, audiences, policy, critics, and historical contexts."[39] Yet because audiences may regard any given program through the lens of its stated or assumed genre, it follows that this wide range of forces will affect any given text, making careful genre analysis a potentially vital step in the analysis of any program.

Flow

Genres are born and change over time. But for a more immediate form of context, we can look at what Raymond Williams calls "flow." In his early book on television, Williams noted that the medium does not simply provide us with distinct programs, but with a flow of material; hence, an opening credit sequence leads into Act One, leads into a series of ads, with station-identification material embedded, to more of the show, and so forth. As such, for most of television's early years, one could not watch a show without seeing it as part of a greater whole, and "these sequences together compose the real flow, the real broadcasting."[40] Moreover, those working in the television industry were deeply aware of the potential for viewers to keep watching, and they frequently made programming decisions based around the attempt to keep the audience for a popular show by offering them more of the same, or by beginning shows "in medias res" with a "cold start" in the hopes of hooking them before they had time to turn away from the previous show. Television executives' jobs relied on convincing audiences to watch a programming block, not single shows. Consequently, Williams posed that analysis could and should move beyond the level of the show to contemplate how the meanings in advertising breaks rubbed off on the shows' meanings, how one show affected the show before or after it, and so forth. To break the experience of flow into smaller units, he stated, "is understandable but often misleading," for the "real" program offered is often a sequence.[41]

Williams reminded us, in other words, that the audience's "text" may be larger than the individual program. Showrunners for cancelled shows have long blamed their time-slots, and while such responses always carry an element of blaming the tennis racket for a missed shot, at times they have significant merit. Some shows are great tonal fits for each other, while others clash. Some cancelled shows have even sought refuge on other channels, on the rationale that they would be a better "fit" with the programs to be found there. Or from its perch as a hugely successful show, *Seinfeld* included an episode ("The Butter Shave") in 1997 that featured a second-rate standup comedian – Kenny Bania – benefiting from always following Jerry Seinfeld's superior routines, thereby taking a dig at parent network NBC's habit of scheduling second-rate sitcoms after *Seinfeld* in order to benefit from the casual, fun atmosphere that *Seinfeld* created. In these and many other ways, flow is operational and is a text to be read and interpreted in its own right.

Interestingly, though Williams's call is oft cited, as close to canon as one finds in television studies, and though the idea of flow has significant intuitive purchase, very few scholars took Williams up on his call.[42] This may be in part because of the idiosyncrasies of flow: two viewers watching the "same" show in different cities will likely experience different flow, as will two viewers in different countries all the more so, or even the same viewer watching the same show later in rerun. Would-be studies of flow were also quickly affected by the very technologies that could have made studying flow all the more common – VCRs and DVDs. As television producers began to realize the vast amounts of money they could make through rereleasing entire episodes of series, television sections of bulk sellers, such as Virgin Megastore or Barnes and Noble, grew in size over the course of the nineties from a single rack to a sizeable portion of the floor space. Viewers could now watch the live broadcast, or on VCR or DVD, with ads removed, and stripped from the particular place in the programming flow, time, and space that Williams had argued was so important.

A consideration of flow renders abundantly clear the need for audience analysis, to chart the contexts in which viewing actually occurs. It also signals how profoundly new media and technologies have fragmented the television text into many different versions. To use contemporary media to further illustrate this point, one can consider the experience of watching a television show live, at its scheduled time, with ads, with computer open, as one's friends on Twitter respond to it, and once a week for an entire season or six, and compare this to the experience of watching the "same" show three or four years on, straight through over the course of a week or two, on DVD, without ads, and divorced from the context in which many others are experiencing this at the same time. Here we see how hard it is becoming to analyze flow, and hence to know which text of television to study, when each and every show can have so many different versions, and can be situated in so many different flow streams.

At the same time, though, television scholars have often been too timid in the face of such fragmentation and too overwhelmed by the prospect of divergent flows. After all, while audience analysis may be required to chart exactly how texts multiply, and while such analysis may seemingly prove the futility or at least idiosyncrasy of analysis of any given version, flow can still work in predictable ways. To play with the metaphor, we might note that sedimentary layers, canyons, and damp soil can all help to predict where bodies of water will flow over time. Similarly, certain combinations of texts and images can be predicted. To take a simple example, Williams notes the interweaving of ads and shows, and so we might ask how the structures of feeling that are sold and invoked by ads carry into the show or vice versa. In times of national tragedy, as after the terrorist attacks of 9/11, for instance, it is common to cut or vastly reduce advertising, on the rationale that peppy spokespeople encouraging one to brush with this or that toothpaste or to treat one's pimples with this or that lotion reads as tasteless when cut to or from scenes of people dying. We might also imagine how many advertisers would rather advertise on feel-good shows than on dark, sinister shows – unless their product favored the latter. Here, then, we see evidence of the interplay between juxtaposed segments of television. Learning from this effect, more close analysis that considers both ads and shows may suggest ways in which they change each other, even if we know that some viewers are not watching the ads. Now that television is available online, too, we may ask how such varying contexts of delivery might affect an understanding of the show. Also, new advertising technologies aim to offer different advertisements to different homes, based on geography and other demographic features. Such developments further personalize context in a way to make its study exceedingly challenging.

Some have also begun to realize the importance of channel branding.[43] Most channels give up a significant amount of advertising space not only to advertise their other programs but also simply to advertise the channel itself. In a multi-channel environment, having an identity has proven important for many cable channels, and after FOX arrived in the US, branding itself as the hip, young, and edgy alternative, even long-familiar broadcast networks needed an identity. This identity is expressed in which shows are commissioned or purchased and in how they are sold, pointing on one hand to the utility of a channel's marquee shows for trying to frame others in the lineup – being the channel of *The Simpsons*, *In Living Color*, and *Married . . . with Children* did a lot for FOX, as did being the channel of *ER*, *The West Wing*, and *Seinfeld* for NBC, or being a channel that plays *Baywatch* and *CSI* reruns for Channel Five in the UK. A lineup tells one what to expect, thereby inviting viewing strategies and either creating or squelching anticipation. A channel's identity, though, is also communicated through its channel identity ads, through branding taglines, through its choice and use of spokespeople, through its website design, and so forth. All of these elements help to create flow from known quantities – whether other shows or a channel-brand identity – to unknown ones, such as a new show at hand.

Intertextuality

Another way to predict certain forms of textual interaction – or "intertextuality" – would be to examine shows or segments that explicitly invoke other shows or segments. An obvious example is parody. As Jonathan Gray observes in *Watching with* The Simpsons: *Television, Parody, and Intertextuality*, *The Simpsons* frequently bases its humor on discussions of other genres. Thus, when we laugh at such jokes, we are being asked to contemplate and perhaps even change our understanding of those other genres. Krusty the Klown's endless egregious examples of selling out beg us to reconsider stars' involvement in product placement and sponsorship deals, the inane ads that the Simpsons family watch criticize ads and often pull back the curtains on the inane techniques used by advertisers, Kent Brockman's news reports teach a form of media literacy in preparing viewers for the news' own questionable techniques, and in each and every episode, the writers once more critique the structure and generic formula of the situation comedy.[44] Nor is *The Simpsons* alone, as *The Daily Show with Jon Stewart* pans the news, *The Colbert Report* is an extended attack on *The O'Reilly Factor* and other pundit shows within its vein. Many other shows engage in either continued and unrelenting or momentary parodic, intertextual attacks on their televisual neighbors. As with genre, in other words, some other streams of "flow" jolt across time and televisual space, and, while we cannot be sure that any given audience member will experience this flow, we are nevertheless presented with a form of flow that surely will be active for some viewers.

Intertextuality, and parody in particular, frequently rely upon the audience's understanding of various genres and of how they work. Above, for instance, it was noted that *The Simpsons* regularly toys with the rules and generic formula of sitcoms. So too do several contemporary comedies, such as *Modern Family* or *South Park*. Thus, much of the humor only exists in the first place because it plays upon the expectations that viewers have generated of a genre based on their previous encounters with it. For instance, in the *Simpsons* episode "Miracle on Evergreen Terrace," the family's presents are all burned at Christmas, resulting in Marge declaring that this may have been a blessing in disguise, since it reminds them all of what really matters at Christmas – namely, family – but Bart and Lisa interject that if the presents hadn't burned, they would have had both presents *and* family, making it all the better. The joke is largely funny because it relies upon viewers' well-worn expectations of Christmas episodes ending with a similarly saccharine, schmaltzy moral, and hence it is funny precisely because it speaks back to the show's generic predecessors. Or, for another example, the sitcom *How I Met Your Mother* frequently plays with unreliable narration, as its voice-over narrator will at times backtrack or otherwise revise his storytelling, requiring the scene that plays out in front of us to change too. The notion that someone telling a story may get things wrong is wholly unremarkable, and hardly funny in itself, yet, in *HIMYM*, the humor stems from the show playing with our generic and formal expectation of a narrator *on* TV, specifically, that they are entirely trustworthy. These examples are mundane but they point to how much of a show's form and structure borrows from, builds upon, edits, speaks back to, and/or revisits form and structure from elsewhere, and how often meaning is established through such intertextual links.

To study a text's intertextual links is thus another way of analyzing it in depth. At the same time, though, intertextuality thoroughly challenges the division between text and context. To be clear, we repeat this division in our chapter structure solely because television studies has often replicated it, and thus because it has discursive weight and history. But in truth, no text operates in and of itself. Rather, as the great intertextual theorist Mikhail Bakhtin noted, "Any utterance is a link in a very complexly organized chain of other utterances" for "any speaker is himself a respondent to a greater or lesser degree. He is not, after all, the first speaker, the one who disturbs the eternal silence of the universe."[45] Bakhtin, Julia Kristeva, Roland Barthes, and other intertextual theorists have thus argued that it is literally impossible to read a single text without reading others, or to understand the meaning of anything without doing so in context. Any text, writes Kristeva, "is constructed as a mosaic of quotations; any text is the absorption and transformation of another," and, evoking Jacques Derrida's discussion of the eternal deferral of meaning to other sources, she notes that "The word as minimal textual unit thus turns out to occupy the status of *mediator*,

linking structural models to cultural (historical) environment," an observation which applies all the more to any given text as a collection of
thousands of words and images.[46] And if the text only comes to mean
anything, only comes into existence, because it draws on and builds upon
other texts, this poses a way for textual analysis to situate any given
show within a history of shows. Intertextual analysis bring genealogy
and chemistry into textual analysis, asking questions of what a show
says to and about other shows, and asking how shows interact with each
other.

Intertextuality can also help us to better appreciate a show's messages
regarding gender, race, nation, class, sexuality, politics, or any other
topic. Often, for instance, a program's representations will be especially
meaningful to society – or perhaps not – in part because of how they
differ from or conform to those of other current and past programs.
Being the first show to say something, or the only one to say it, is meaningful in and of itself. Other messages may be created in seemingly subtle
ways by playing with the expected norms of a genre, channel, or other
grouping. Thus, making the lead character in *Prime Suspect* a woman
may to some seem innocuous enough, but when one considers how
overwhelmingly male the detective genre has been, especially prior to
Prime Suspect's premiere in 1991, having a middle-aged woman at its
center then becomes more significant. Intertextuality matters a great deal
to the industry as it decides which shows to greenlight and how to sell
them within frames of the already known, and to audiences in their
evaluation of shows. Therefore, intertextuality must matter to the analyst.

To invoke audiences' interactions with programs and the industry's
commissioning of them is to invoke another intertextual entity of significant importance to both fans and the industry, that of the star or celebrity. Casting, after all, is never simply an act of matching a character to
an actor; it is also, for better or worse, a marketing decision. Questions
abound about what an actor will "bring to" a role, and yet what they
bring is much more than acting skills or lack thereof: it is also an intertextual history in other roles, and it is a public persona with its own
meanings that in turn color our interactions with their character. Think
of how quickly audiences could accept Lauren Graham as the hip young
mother in *Parenthood* after she had played that role for many years on
Gilmore Girls. Or of the disjunctures brought about by against-type
casting, as when *The Wonder Years*' beloved Fred Savage appears as a
physically abusive boyfriend in the movie of the week *No One Would
Tell* – abusing a girlfriend played by *Full House*'s DJ Tanner, Candace
Cameron, no less! – or when *Cheers*' loveable if simple bartender, Ted
Danson, appears as a selfish corporate tycoon on *Damages*. Parody can
also be created intertextually, as when *Full House*'s seemingly perfect dad

figure, Bob Saget, appears playing a drug-addicted, midget-porn-obsessed star of a family sitcom in the short-lived Showtime drama *Huff*, or when Jon Hamm appears on *Saturday Night Live* or *30 Rock* in roles that play with his identity as *über* male, established in *Mad Men*. And of course anything that happens in a cast member's life can bleed into his or her roles. When episodes of *8 Simple Rules for Dating my Daughter* and *Last of the Summer Wine* mourned the death of central characters whose screen deaths were necessitated by the actors dying, both were significantly more profound since they dealt with audiences' relationships to the two stars, John Ritter and Bill Owen, not simply with the passing of two characters. Or we might note the built-in air of tough street smarts that Ice T and LL Cool J's characters enjoy in *Law and Order: SVU* and *NCIS: Los Angeles* respectively, due to their actors' history as rappers. Celebrity images cut across shows but always flavor the characters within them. With this in mind, a small number of television studies scholars have examined celebrity culture and the meanings that travel with these celebrities, sometimes outside of any specific program, sometimes superimposed upon it intertextually.[47]

Paratextuality

Yet another vital part of television that both surrounds programs, audiences, and industries, as the bedding in which they all lie, and cuts across them, is the paratext. This term derives from Gérard Genette, a literary theorist who coined it to describe all those things that surround a work of literature that are not traditionally thought of as the work itself. Thus, a book's cover is an obvious paratext, and one that, as the famous indiction to "not judge a book by its cover" reflects, holds significant power to shape our expectations and interpretations of the work. Similarly, typeface, prefaces, interviews with the author, paper quality, and reviews are all paratexts. Genette writes of them as the "thresholds on interpretation," acknowledging that since we will always experience many of them before reaching the work, they will always begin the process of interpretation.[48]

More recently, Jonathan Gray has applied the concept to film and television. In his book *Show Sold Separately*, he argues not only that paratexts begin interpretation and hence in a real sense could be seen as creating the text, but also that a whole host of other paratexts regularly intervene in our viewing and interpretive process along the way and over time. Thus, on one hand, television paratexts include "entryway" paratexts that get to us before a program does – think of opening credit sequences, posters, promos, articles in the entertainment press about forthcoming shows, or within shows' "Next week on" segments. But on the other hand they include "in medias res" paratexts that might change the course of our interpretation after first encountering the program, or otherwise direct us toward specific interpretations – think of DVD bonus materials and commentary tracks, podcasts by production personnel, the wide world of fan discussion and creativity, licensed merchandise and games, interviews with stars and writers, and "previously on" segments. As Gray argues, such entities are pervasive in our media culture, and not the mere add-ons or "secondary" entities that they have long been considered to be.[49]

Paratexts work as do intertexts. Indeed, paratextuality can be seen as a subset of intertextuality, the interaction and co-creation of meaning between program and surrounding material, rather than between program and program. As with intertexts, we can rarely assume that any given paratext will be known to all audiences, thereby making it impossible to see it as part of the text *for everyone*. But for those who are aware of the paratext, their version and understanding of "the text" will necessarily include that paratext. To parse out all paratexts, whether industrially created as promos and hype, or designed by audiences in response to and in anticipation of the program, from entities such as *CSI*, *The Simpsons*, or any program for that matter, is conceivable, yet an analytic exercise alone, and one that moves away from the audience's experience of the program with each subtraction. The paratext is an intrinsic part of the text. While "textual" analysis may continue to extricate paratexts for the sake of a more easily manageable "close reading," and, while we do not necessarily criticize this choice, one must always remember the damage that is being done to the text-as-experienced by engaging in such analysis. Studying paratexts alongside their shows, by contrast, offers the promise of a richer understanding of our object of study.

We can also regard paratexts as game-pieces in a game of interpretation. Many industry-created paratexts try to set limits for interpretation around a program, inviting audiences to look at the program in a certain way. And even within industry-created paratexts, we may see several players jockeying for power – a network's marketing team may choose to highlight certain aspects of a show and to sell it as one entity, while the showrunner or stars may subsequently use DVD commentary tracks, podcasts, and interviews to highlight different aspects of the show, and to insist on other interpretations. Audiences are then able to play this game themselves. When a fan, for instance, writes fan fiction that toggles, underplays, or amplifies certain dynamics in either a show or its industry-created paratexts, the fan makes his or her moves in the game of interpretation. Several privileged, tastemaker – or would-be tastemaker –

audiences, such as critics and academics, can also add further paratexts in the form of reviews or essays that do yet more to frame and color interpretation. As chapter 2 noted, interpretation is always open and up for grabs; within this "game," though, paratexts can play a key role in shifting a program one way or the other.

For an example, consider the various discourses that surround *Mad Men*. Some discourses lay claim to the show's artistry and membership in an elite club of "quality television." Some regard it as elitist garbage, boring viewers to tears with supposed, yet ultimately lacking, meaning. Some focus on its visual style, sometimes dotingly and approvingly, sometimes critically, regarding the show as nothing but style. Some situate the show as an important and revealing analysis of gender. But how do these discourses circulate in the first place? Paratexts are key here, bringing interpretations from one to many. Some will take the simple form of discussion, whereas others are more elaborate, whether reviews, playful mash-ups, entire essays, AMC promo spots, sketches on *Saturday Night Live*, posters on transit systems, Banana Republic co-sponsorship campaigns, or so forth. Each tries to push or pull us toward certain interpretations of the show, and thus much of the show's place in popular culture is due not only to the show itself, but to the many paratexts that surround it.

As should be evident here, through paratextuality, the study of "television" often requires the study of many other media, and the critical analysis of television's programs in particular requires the critical analysis of its paratexts and their own construction of "common sense" across media. Spigel's above-noted study of television, for example, used the paratexts of ads and articles in women's magazines to make sense of television as a whole. Or other scholars may be studying television through analyzing licensed video games, online discussion groups, print, radio, or internet ad campaigns, or merchandise.

Overflow and convergence

The range of texts and objects of focus this discussion of intertexts and paratexts suggests reveals the necessary broadening of television studies to a focus on a matrix of other media. Recently, numerous scholars in television studies, and in media studies more generally, have sought to unfix television as the supposed center, starting point, and endpoint of analysis, and instead examine the entire matrix, attending at some point to the varied texts, industries, and audiences involved. Two complementary metaphors for this current situation come to us in the form of "overflow" and "convergence."

In an essay on *Dawson's Creek*, Will Brooker noted that the show was "overflowing" from the boundaries of the television show, with a website offering one access to "Dawson's Desktop" and to his private emails, with American Eagle and J. Crew selling the wardrobe of the characters, and so forth. Such overflow seemingly allowed audiences to set foot within the world of the show – into its "diegesis" – or variously, to bring that world into their own. It also went beyond using multiple media platforms to advertise the show and started to author the show, and to offer details about its world not otherwise available in the show, at its paratextual outskirts. In such a situation, the logic of a central show and "peripheral" "extratextuals" is somewhat challenged, since the text of *Dawson's Creek* is continuing in those other sites, having "overflowed" into them.[50] When Brooker first wrote his essay, such a technique was still relatively rare, but we now see such a strategy in a wide variety of television shows. *Heroes* had an online comic book that expanded upon its world, penned by the show's writers, as well as a mobile media game, a novel (*Saving Charlie*) that told a whole side story in the life of one of the show's time-traveling characters, and numerous websites set in the world's diegesis. *Lost* also had spin-off novels and websites, and fans could sign up to join the diegetic, nefarious Dharma Initiative in between seasons. *Gossip Girl* offered a Second Life version of its world in which fans could interact. *24* had a licensed video game set between Seasons Two and Three, written by *24* staff and offering yet more information about the characters, and also had published *The House Special Subcommittee's Findings at CTU* which discusses the action of Season One, while adding extra information, all in diegetic frame.[51] Numerous web shorts and an interactive game, that allows viewers to sign up to "work" at the fictional Dunder Mifflin paper company, surround *The Office*, and so on. Increasingly, most shows are no longer just television shows.

Henry Jenkins reverses Brooker's metaphor, and, instead of posing this situation as one of a television show overflowing, a model that centralizes the original text, he writes of various media and platforms "converging." In this model, the text is formed by the coming together of various platforms and media. He offers *American Idol* as a prominent example. This series can only work because of its phone-voting system and its purpose would also seem to be the creation of an "idol" who will live on in radio, CD sales, and iTunes downloads. Along the way, it invites fan mobilization over the internet. And to create extra revenue, it has a touring concert off season. *American Idol*, therefore, cannot truly be regarded as a television show: it is a convergent media entity that brings together radio, television, the internet, CDs, the mobile phone, and live concerts.[52]

What follows from Brooker's and Jenkins's work is not simply the contextual reminder that television is part of a larger system but also that television studies must therefore be part of a larger system of media studies. Studying television increasingly requires scholars to work with and through a variety of media. If shows, their audiences, and the industries that create them have been analyzed to date, overflowing, convergent media demand that we also analyze entire meaning systems, how audiences respond to and act across media platforms, and how industries manage such intricate systems. And television studies has responded. As their titles suggest, Sharon Ross's *Beyond the Box: Television and the Internet* and Jennifer Gillan's *Television and New Media: Must-Click TV* concentrate on television's life off television, and on the degree to which the internet in particular is now a key site of television, and hence for television analysis. And the various chapters in Denise Mann's edited collection on *Wired TV* similarly pay close attention to how producers manage and create in such overflowing or convergent spaces. Given the hot-button nature of this topic, we are sure that many more books, articles, and chapters are currently working their way through academic presses.[53]

If such work asks us to de-center television, though, this leaves the field of television studies, and by extension this book, with a looming question: namely, is it time to be done with television studies? We therefore conclude this book by discussing that question. But, first, we wish to examine other frontiers for contextual analysis in television studies.

What now and what next?

While earlier in this chapter we argued that temporal and spatial contextualization enriches the study of television, we feel compelled to note that the field has a great deal more work to do in terms of *spatial* constructions. Or, rather, a proportionately small amount of global space has been covered by the bulk of television studies. As such, the field can say a great deal about different ages and moments of television in the US and the UK, but the rest of the world beckons. A key concern here regards the geographically static nature of the major US and UK television studies conferences, where scholars meet, hatch plans for future work together, and learn about each other's research. Dominant academic organizations tend to be more national than international, which has prevented more international collaboration and idea sharing. Television has also been a fairly domestic enterprise, and given its long form – not to mention linguistic barriers – it is difficult for scholars to be deeply familiar with a wide range of national television production.

These factors on one hand limit the amount of international and/or comparative work that is conducted, and on the other hand limit the degree to which such work is shared and widely read when it is conducted.

That said, the rest of the world isn't just waiting for US and UK scholars to act, and television studies has witnessed growth both in multiple regions of the world, and in scholarship regarding more of the world. In 2010, therefore, leading journals in television studies included publications by scholars examining a range of national contexts in, for instance, New Zealand, Japan, China, Cuba, Canada, India, Slovenia, Thailand, Mexico, South Africa, Nigeria, and Norway. Meanwhile, many departments of late have realized the importance of offering classes and developing scholarship that analyzes various international contexts. As such, it is with cautious optimism that we look forward to a future in which television studies can offer a much wider range of international contexts than at present, thereby offering a much wider range of global televisions.

To speed this process, television studies would be wise to learn especially from some of the work being conducted in anthropology. As many anthropologists abandoned the idea that their task was to examine the "primitive," "pre-modernized" cultures of the world, their ensuing deep ethnography has often involved close attention to television's contexts around the globe. This literature is highly relevant to audience studies scholars around the world, but also to those interested in differing institutional histories. Thus, for instance, to offer two solitary examples, Brian Larkin's work on broadcasting and videotape in Nigeria offers a fascinating picture of the contexts in which such media consumption occurs, while Katrien Pype's multiple articles on teleserials in the Democratic Republic of the Congo similarly offer themselves as highly relevant to a television studies scholar, written from outside the field, yet offering a great deal to those within it who hope to expand an understanding of television beyond Anglo-American contexts.[54]

Comparative work would also be warmly welcome, as Divya McMillin calls for.[55] Even the much discussed British and American television systems have inspired remarkably few comparative analyses, with Ien Ang's early examination of television systems in the US, UK, and the Netherlands, and Michele Hilmes's recent historical analysis of the interactions, trade, and verbal jousting between US and UK broadcasters being two rare exceptions.[56] If some of the excesses of medium theory generalizations about what "Television" is and is not in total have continued, television studies will more definitively destroy the idea of the world sharing anything like the same "Television" when it can offer a compendium of work on the world's varying televisions. But we would also like to see work that considers regions rather than accepting the nation as always the most appropriate context for television. These regions may be supranational or subdivisions within nations. In the case of the latter, for example, though television history is full of lore regarding profound differences between rural and urban Americans, more work that examines different regional contexts of viewing could perhaps turn lore into something more tangible.

We imagine that such work would, as a bonus, lead to careful studies of technology as a contextualizing force. Often different places around the world experience a different television due to a host of technological specifications, and thus to open television studies up to more of the globe would by nature be to produce better work on technology as context. Larkin's above-cited work, for instance, not only tells us about broadcasting in northern Nigeria, but also contributes to a better understanding of how videotape works and how it colors the experience of television, as does Moradewun Adejunmobi's own work on "Nollywood" video.[57] Or Lisa Parks's continuing macro/global work on satellites around the world tells us a great deal about the varying meanings that satellites take on, and hence about the meanings of satellite television more generally, just as does Charlotte Brunsdon's more micro/local level analysis of satellites as markers of low and/or foreign interests in certain areas of England.[58] This work often reminds us that television is not simply one technology or medium; it is nearly always accompanied by others, by antennae or satellite dishes or cable, by iPods or computer screens, by high-definition sets with surround sound systems[59] or by old rickety tubes playing in mono, and by DVDs, DVRs, Slingboxes, and countless other technologies. As Daniel Chamberlain asserts, we must also attend to issues of television *interface* – to how we search for programs through our service provider's built-in systems, and to the apparatus that surrounds the many different windows through which we watch.[60] And as Max Dawson insists, when industry, popular, and academic discussions so often turn with great interest to the new digital gadgets and their users, contextual scholarship must also attend to how such technologies change the contexts of viewing for those without digital bells, whistles, and killer apps.[61] As earlier noted, television studies has little use for grand statements about what any item of technology "is" and unequivocally always is, but we have considerable need for work that addresses the vital context that is technology and interface.

Another development that we welcome and of which we would like to see more, is the historicization of technological change, and particularly of the "convergence culture" that stems in part from technological convergence. Intertextuality as a theory had its heyday when postmodernism was all the rage in the 1980s and 1990s, and calls for analyses of paratexts and convergence have been more recent still. The risk, though, is that intertextuality, paratextuality, and convergence appear to be recent phenomena, ushered in by Steve Jobs, Larry Page, and Sergey Brin. A corrective is thus required. The beginnings of this corrective can be seen in the historical work collected in Janet Staiger and Sabine Hake's *Convergence Media History* and in some of Avi Santo's analyses of the paratextual entourage and strategy surrounding *The Green Hornet* and *The Lone Ranger*.[62] The continuation of such work, though, will face the significant challenge of the fickleness of archives – if toys, merchandise, and other paratexts now seem important, the continued development of such work relies on the hope that archivists considered them worth collecting in the first place. As with international work that usually requires higher research funding and the time to conduct it, here the future of work on television's contexts will be limited by what is possible and by the institutional support or lack thereof made available to scholars.

Ultimately, though, almost everything is potentially important context. Thus, we fully expect to see contextual analysis continue to extend into all sorts of areas. As noted at the chapter's beginning, contexts tend to be intangible. A few exceptions exist – paratexts among them – but their lack of tangibility has often rendered them invisible or only partially visible, reduced in stature behind the big, obvious three of program, audience, and industry. Television studies, though, is at its best when it remembers that context is key, and as such the primary hope we have for the future of contextual analysis is that those who analyze programs, audiences, and industries feel always compelled to contextualize.

Conclusion

This book has endeavored to offer the novice reader an introduction to television studies by charting its intellectual history, roughly demarcating its porous edges, and highlighting some of its most notable scholarship. In doing so, we have called into existence an entity called television studies that has otherwise been uncertainly defined. Prescribing television studies in any way undoubtedly does some violence to its edges – perhaps shoring off some topics and approaches or including others who never considered such a designation. And though we aimed to be exhaustive, some sizeable omissions unquestionably will be found.

We've argued that television studies is distinguished from studies of television primarily by a concern for context and breadth; that television studies may at times focus primarily on only one of the triumvirate of institutions, programs, and audiences, but that it will always at least be mindful of, open to, and acknowledge the context provided by the other two and by any number of other contexts discussed in chapter 4. We've offered chapters focused on each of these areas and highlighted some of the best and most insightful research that we could incorporate but also attempted to place that research within a narrative about the creation and development of television studies that would provide readers with a meaningful sense of how we arrived at a "field" with the particular contours we identify.

This intellectual history is drawn from revisiting many of the field's first publications, from reports on early conferences – when possible – and conversations with those who took part. It is not a rigorously investigated history – that remains an important and necessary task – but, in introducing television studies, we found it imperative not simply to describe what it has been but to pose a suggestion as to why it has taken this form. Given the nature of an introductory book, our mention of specific scholarship is at times superficial; there is still much to mine from the early publications of the field and more systematic and rigorous interviews to be conducted to construct a deeper and more specialized history. Rich stories remain to be told by charting the evolution of editions of key collections in the field, such as Newcomb's *Television: The Critical View* or Curran, Gurevitch, and Woollacott's *Mass Communication in Society*, for what they reveal about transitions in topics, theories, and methodologies.[1] And more sustained examination of key institutional developments are needed, such as timelines of the creation of degree-granting programs – particularly if anything such as a set of departments of television studies should ever come into existence. We've already detailed paths forward in each of the areas in previous chapters, so we close by clarifying our arguments and making more general calls and inquiries.

Have we made television studies impossible?

It became exceedingly clear, as we endeavored to be as exhaustive as possible in acknowledging the range of ways that scholars have considered television's programs, audiences, industries, and contexts, that the possible demands of breadth and depth of contemporary television studies are quite daunting. The previous chapters recount calls to be expansive in analysis of what is watched, by whom, how it was created, and the sociohistorical conditions of its creation. But, at the same time, we've also recounted adjustments since the establishment of television studies that involve not only the creation of far more programs – and thus audiences and so on – but also the process of scholars expanding how they delimit the text, and a digital era that has led to an ever-proliferating array of intertexts, paratexts, and so forth.

We do not intend the breadth of our efforts to provide a prescription for what the successful television studies project must engage. We quite intentionally make the distinction of being mindful and aware of the other areas, as no single rule could ever be workable. Scope ultimately must be driven by the researcher's question – and the researcher can never hope to speak of "television," but only ever the piece that the study actually investigates. The point of the emergence of a coherent "field" or area of study is that it involves a community of inquiry in which an array of voices contribute pieces of the puzzle of the whole that build on what has come before or that others do coterminously.

That being said, to require "mindfulness" places a burden on the television studies scholar to, as the term suggests, fill one's mind, to read widely, and at least to be aware of the breadth of possibilities and the lines of investigation not taken – and in some cases, to explain such decisions. The preceding chapters should call to mind a hundred different possible projects – conceivably about the same show – and it is a crucial task not only to select a line of inquiry, but deliberately to not select others. Choosing to examine a program and industrial process, but not audience, or to limit a study to a particular genre, historical period, or single text in all its extensions, can only be done intelligently if the researcher first entertains what is lost in not making other selections. Television studies is a broad field but in truth it remains considerably smaller than many others; thus this breadth of familiarity, with its many intellectual enterprises, is not an especially burdensome expectation.

Despite our allowances that one work can only do so much, we do wish to highlight Julie D'Acci's *Defining Women: Television and the Case of 'Cagney & Lacey'* because it remains such an exceptional prototype of the possibilities of ambitious television studies research.[2] D'Acci's book takes a single show as its case study but analyzes aspects of the program and audience response through letters written to producers, and examines its conditions of production. D'Acci carefully contextualizes the particularities of this series – which was notable for featuring two female characters at the center of the narrative and for achieving surprising popular success. Thus, while only about a single show, D'Acci's book is able to offer important perspectives about interactions between a production studio and network, the audience and network, and the program and its audience. Certainly D'Acci's task was in some ways made easier by the network era industrial context, but her book is also a testament to the importance of careful topic selection, as the richness of insight she provided could not have been achieved with any program, even with the use of her multi-sited methodology.

In considering some of the broadest work in the last chapter's assessment of contextual analysis, we posed the possibility that perhaps all of the "overflow" or convergence might suggest that it is time to be done with television studies. Although we maintain the caveats we identified in our first pages – that it is foolishly medium-specific at its basic level of denotation and a particularly US construct – we remain convinced of the remarkable centrality of television. New technologies may enable many new program forms and experiences and may be eroding past norms of centralization and common experience, but television remains intact, at least for now. Mobisodes, paratexts, and the many other related textual forms are still supported by the tentpoles of conventional, broadcast/cablecast television shows. Coming years will undoubtedly offer new cases that counter this dominance and that require us to revise this assertion, but transitions are often slower than expected, and we remain comfortable in our embrace of television.

Without doubt, "television studies" is an identifier with its fair share of limitations. As veterans of terminology debates over postfeminism and postcolonialism, though, we are well aware of the imperfection of language and of the ultimate pointlessness of spending a disproportionate amount of time hand-wringing about what to call something when it derails a ready conversation about something the term clearly signifies. We hope the breadth of content explored on the preceding pages illustrates the understood amorphousness and wide possibilities of television studies. Related, this should not be read as a call to "television studies" as the one true way. We've often appreciated scholarship – perhaps a close, yet completely uncontextualized reading – that has served as a useful secondary source or helped us think about a phenomenon of study in a new way. Just as the texts created as television series remain the tentpoles from which many new texts now expand, and we've written of television studies taking a "big tent" approach to its identity, we would encourage its practitioners to continue to venture outside its confines and perhaps return with the new tools and perspectives that have led to such a vibrant short history.

In closing, we'd also like to encourage television studies' practitioners to keep experimenting with format and audience. The quick-moving, "flowing" medium of television has been saddled with a very slow form of sharing ideas about television studies for much of its history. Events conclude, research is conducted, written up, submitted to a journal or press, critiqued, revised, resubmitted, proofread, typeset, sent to press, and finally released, and quite often three or more years have passed in the meantime. We pose that television studies must have a second gear. In saying this, we do not mean to suggest that research should be rushed, or that the processes by which work is improved through peer evaluation should be curtailed. Some projects need time, deserve time, and must continue to be given time. But a thriving television studies must be one in which scholars can also discuss the here and now in the here and now, not just three or more years in the future.

As such, we would like to acknowledge the continued innovation evident in television studies in recent years, whereby some television studies scholars have endeavored to create new spaces for developing and sharing their ideas with greater speed. Indeed, the digital era and "new media" enable many of these, explaining their recent development. *Flow: A Critical Forum on Television and Media Culture* (www.flowtv.org), created at the University of Texas at Austin, began as an online publication meant to help television scholars address an endlessly changing object of study with greater timeliness than traditional academic venues allowed. The digital publication quickly expanded to include a deliberately unconventionally structured biennial conference. *In Media Res* (mediacommons.futureofthebook.org/imr/) then developed to take advantage of the new possibilities of efficiently sharing digital images and featuring daily videos, often organized around a weekly theme, which scholars who explain the significance of the video artifact curate in brief statements. The University of Wisconsin-Madison found a third distinctive way for television studies to make use of the age of digital publishing with its blog *Antenna: Responses to Media and Culture* (blog.commarts. wisc.edu/) that provides brief and timely musings by a wide variety of television scholars and often robust discussions. Others have slaved over personal blogs, continually offering content and analysis on contemporary developments in the field. And all these venues are accessible by a broader public, at times explicitly speaking to and with that public, and thus experimenting with a television studies that engages more than just other academics.

Others have attempted greater bridge-building between academia, industry, and/or policy-makers in efforts to make television studies scholarship more relevant. Voices familiar to television studies are being heard by broader audiences – whether the efforts of John Hartley and others in Australia connecting television studies scholarship to governmental economic initiatives under the auspices of creative industries work, or Henry Jenkins, who has been a rare media scholar from the humanities tradition called to testify before Congress about video games and who is increasingly positioned as a public intellectual. While we'd acknowledge that engaging larger constituencies is not without its downsides, to date it seems that broadening the conversation beyond a small, insular intellectual pool by and large outweighs them.

Ultimately, in closing this book about television studies, we'd like to remind scholars that television studies need not only exist in its pages, nor in its classrooms, as absolutely important as those sites are. Television programs remain broadly shared pieces of culture that challenge, entertain, anger, and inform us, and the ideas within them continue to maintain a pervasive hold on how we imagine our worlds. It may be the case that a greater variety of worlds may be on offer, but this is all the more reason to dig in deeply and seek to understand the many roles and reasons that television endures.

Notes

Introduction: Why Television Studies? Why Now?

1 Marshall McLuhan, *Understanding Media: The Extensions of Man* (Cambridge, MA: MIT Press, 1994 [1964]).
2 John Hartley, "Housing Television: Textual Traditions in Television and Cultural Studies," in Christine Geraghty and David Lusted (eds), *The Television Studies Book* (London: Hodder Arnold, 1998), p. 33.
3 In a history of broadcasting research developed by Elihu Katz for the BBC in 1977, he dates the origins of broadcasting research to the mid 1930s in the US and that of the earliest experimental studies in the UK to the late 1930s. Elihu Katz, *Social Research on Broadcasting: Proposals for Further Development* (London: BBC, 1977), p. 22.
4 Of many works, consider Paul Lazarsfeld, *Radio and the Printed Page* (New York: Duell, Sloan and Pearce, 1940); Harold Lasswell, "The Structure and Function of Communication in Society," in Lymon Bryson (ed.), *The Communication of Ideas*, (New York: Institute for Religious and Social Studies, 1948), pp. 37–51.
5 Katz, *Social Research*, p. 24.
6 Katz, *Social Research*, p. 22.
7 Katz, *Social Research*, p. 23.
8 Katz, *Social Research*, p. 25.
9 Katz, *Social Research*, p. 26.
10 Philip Lodge, "Towards an Institutional and Intellectual History of British Communication Studies," paper presented at the 2008 International Communication Association Conference, Montreal, Quebec, Canada, 10. Available at www.allacademic.com/meta/p231837_index.html, accessed February 2011.

11 Glasgow University Research Group, *Bad News* (London: Routledge and Kegan Paul, 1976).

12 Horace Newcomb, "American Television Criticism: 1970–1985," *Critical Studies in Mass Communication* 3 (1986): 217–28, 226; John Fiske, "Television and Popular Culture: Reflections on British and Australian Critical Practice," *Critical Studies in Mass Communication* 3 (1986): 200–16, 202.

13 Katz, *Social Research*, p. 27.

14 Matthew Arnold, "Culture and Anarchy," in *Selected Poems and Prose* (London: J. M. Dent and Sons, 1978), pp. 212–26.

15 Neil Postman, *Amusing Ourselves to Death: Public Discourse in the Age of Show Business* (New York: Penguin, 1985).

16 Horace Newcomb, *TV: The Most Popular Art* (New York: Anchor Books, 1974); Raymond Williams, *Television: Technology and Cultural Form* (London: Collins, 1974); John Fiske and John Hartley, *Reading Television* (London: Methuen, 1978).

17 Richard Hoggart's *Uses of Literacy: Changing Patterns in English Mass Culture* (Fair Lawn, NJ: Essential Books, 1957); Raymond Williams, *Culture and Society: 1780–1950* (London: Chatto & Windus, 1958); E. P. Thompson, *The Making of the English Working Class* (New York: Vintage Books, 1963).

18 Stuart Hall, "Encoding/Decoding," in Stuart Hall et al. (ed.), *Culture, Media, Language: Working Papers in Cultural Studies, 1972–1979* (London: Routledge, 1991), pp. 107–16.

19 See David Morley and Charlotte Brunsdon, *The Nationwide Television Studies* (New York: Routledge, 1999).

20 Charlotte Brunsdon, "*Crossroads*: Notes on Soap Opera," *Screen* 22(4) (1981): 32–7; Dorothy Hobson, *Crossroads: The Drama of a Soap Opera* (London: Methuen, 1982).

21 Angela McRobbie, *Feminism and Youth Culture: From Jackie to Just Seventeen* (Houndmills, Basingstoke, Hampshire: Macmillan, 1991); Dick Hebdige, *Subculture, The Meaning of Style* (London: Methuen, 1979).

22 David Morley, "Introduction," in Ann Gray, Jan Campbell, Mark Erickson, Stuart Hansen, and Helen Wood (eds), *CCCS Selected Working Papers*, vol. 2 (London: Routledge, 2007), p. 259.

23 Lynn Spigel, "My TV Studies . . . Now Playing on a You Tube Site Near You," *Television & New Media* 10(1) (2009): 149–53, 150.

24 Charlotte Brunsdon, "What is the 'Television' of Television Studies?" in Christine Geraghty and David Lusted (eds), *The Television Studies Book* (London: Arnold, 1998), pp. 95–113 (p. 96).

25 Newcomb, "American Television Criticism," p. 220; Fiske, "Television and Popular Culture," p. 202.

26 Robert C. Allen, "Frequently Asked Questions: A General Introduction to the Reader," in Robert C. Allen and Annette Hill (eds), *The Television Studies Reader* (New York: Routledge, 2004), pp. 1–26.

27 Allen, "Frequently Asked Questions," p. 5.

28 Allen, "Frequently Asked Questions," p. 5.

29 See publications from the conferences: Douglass Cater and Richard Adler, *Television as a Social Force: New Approaches to TV Criticism* (New York: Praeger, 1976) and Douglass Cater and Richard Adler, *Television as Cultural Force* (New York: Praeger, 1977).
30 Horace Newcomb (ed.), *Television: The Critical View* (New York: Oxford University Press, 1976). Subsequent (and largely revised) editions were published in 1979, 1982, 1987, 1994, 2000, and 2007.
31 Newcomb, "American Television Criticism," p. 222; Todd Gitlin, *Inside Prime Time* (New York: Pantheon, 1983); David Marc, *Demographic Vistas* (Philadelphia: University of Pennsylvania Press, 1984); Michael Intintoli, *Taking Soaps Seriously* (New York: Praeger, 1985); Hal Himmelstein, *Television Myth and the American Mind* (New York: Praeger, 1984); Robert C. Allen, *Speaking of Soap Operas* (Chapel Hill: University of North Carolina Press, 1985); E. Ann Kaplan (ed.), *Regarding Television* (Los Angeles: University Publishers of America, 1984); John E. O'Connor (ed.), *American History/American Television: Interpreting the Video Past* (New York: Frederick Ungar, 1983); Willard Rowland and Bruce Watkins (eds), *Interpreting Television* (Beverly Hills: Sage, 1985); Jane Feuer, Paul Kerr, and Tise Vahamagi (eds), *MTM: Quality Television* (London: BFI, 1985); Patricia Mellencamp (ed.), *Logics of Television: Essays in Cultural Criticism* (Bloomington: Indiana University Press, 1990).
32 Fiske and Hartley, *Reading Television*; Hobson, *Crossroads*; Roger Silverstone, *The Message of Television: Myth and Narrative in Contemporary Culture* (London: Heinemann, 1981); Charlotte Brunsdon and David Morley, *Everyday Television: "Nationwide"* (London: BFI, 1978); and David Buckingham, *Public Secrets: EastEnders and Its Audience* (London: BFI, 1987).
33 Phillip Drummond and Richard Paterson (eds), *Television and Its Audience: International Research Perspectives* (London: BFI, 1988).
34 Horace Newcomb, "Television and the Present Climate of Criticism," in Horace Newcomb (ed.), *Television: The Critical View*, 5th edn, (New York: Oxford University Press, 1994), pp. 3–13 (p. 4).
35 Charlotte Brunsdon, "What is the 'Television' of Television Studies?" in Christine Geraghty and David Lusted (eds), *The Television Studies Book* (London: Arnold, 1998), pp. 95–113 (p. 96).
36 Michele Hilmes, *Hollywood and Broadcasting: From Radio to Cable* (Urbana: University of Illinois Press, 1990); Lynn Spigel, *Make Room for TV: Television and the Family Ideal in Postwar America* (Chicago: University of Chicago Press, 1992); William Boddy, *Fifties Television: The Industry and Its Critics* (Champaign: University of Illinois Press, 1993); Christopher Anderson, *Hollywood TV: The Studio System in the Fifties* (Austin: University of Texas Press, 1994); Julie D'Acci, *Defining Women: Television and the Case of Cagney & Lacey* (Chapel Hill: University of North Carolina Press, 1994); and Michael Curtin, *Redeeming the Wasteland: Television Documentary and Cold War Politics* (New Brunswick: Rutgers University Press, 1995).
37 David Morley, *Family Television: Cultural Power and Domestic Leisure* (London: Comedia, 1988) and *Television, Audiences and Cultural Studies*

(New York: Routledge, 1992); Charlotte Brunsdon, *Screen Tastes: Soap Opera to Satellite Dishes* (New York: Routledge, 1997); David Buckingham, *Children Talking Television: The Making of Television Literacy* (London: Taylor and Francis, 1993); Roger Silverstone, *Television and Everyday Life* (New York: Routledge, 1994); Ann Gray, *Video Playtime: The Gendering of a Leisure Technology* (New York: Routledge, 1992); Justin Lewis, *The Ideological Octopus: An Exploration of Television and Its Audience* (New York: Routledge, 1991).

38 Robert C. Allen (ed.), *Channels of Discourse, Reassembled: Television and Contemporary Criticism*, 2nd edn (Chapel Hill: University of North Carolina Press, 1992).

39 Lynn Spigel, "Television Studies for 'Mature' Audiences," *International Journal of Cultural Studies*, 3(3) (2000): 407–20, 407.

40 The closest to regular television studies conferences have been the more long-standing "Console-ing Passions" and the younger "Flow"; however, neither conference maintains a membership structure.

41 Charlotte Brunsdon, "What is the 'Television' of Television Studies?" in Christine Geraghty and David Lusted (eds), *The Television Studies Book* (London: Arnold, 1998), pp. 95–113 (p. 95).

42 Lynn Spigel, "Introduction," in Lynn Spigel and Jan Olsson (eds), *Television after TV: Essays on a Medium in Transition* (Durham: Duke University Press, 2004), pp. 1–40 (p. 2).

43 Julie D'Acci, "Cultural Studies, Television Studies, and the Crisis in the Humanities," in Lynn Spigel and Jan Olsson (eds), *Television after TV: Essays on a Medium in Transition* (Durham: Duke University Press, 2004), pp. 418–46 (p. 432).

44 The internal battle required for the Society for Cinema Studies to become the Society for Cinema and Media Studies is a vivid illustration of this.

Chapter 1   Programs

1 Jerry Mander, *Four Arguments for the Elimination of Television* (London: Harper Perennial, 1978).

2 John Crowe Ransom, *The New Criticism* (Westport, CT: Greenwood, 1979 [1941]); Cleanth Brooks, *The Well Wrought Urn: Studies in the Structure of Poetry* (New York: Harcourt Brace and Company, 1947).

3 I. A. Richards, *The Principles of Literary Criticism* (London: Kegan Paul, Trench, Trubner, 1924), *Practical Criticism* (London: Kegan Paul, Trench, Trubner, 1929); F. R. Leavis, *The Common Pursuit* (London: Chatto and Windus, 1952).

4 See Matthew Arnold, "Culture and Anarchy," in *Selected Poems and Prose* (London: J. M. Dent and Sons, 1978), 212–26.

5 Jeremy G. Butler, *Television Style* (New York: Routledge, 2009).

6 See Lloyd F. Bitzer and Edwin Black (eds), *The Prospect for Rhetoric: Report of the National Development Project* (Englewood Cliffs, NJ: Prentice-Hall, 1971).

7 Laura Mulvey, "Visual Pleasure and Narrative Cinema," *Screen* 16(3) (1975): 6–18.
8 Ferdinand de Saussure, *Course in General Linguistics* (New York: Open Court Press, 2000 [1916]); Charles Peirce, *Collected Papers: Volume V. Pragmatism and Pragmaticism* (Cambridge, MA: Harvard University Press, 1934); Charles Morris, *Writings on the General Theory of Signs* (The Hague: Mouton, 1971).
9 http://slayageonline.com/
10 See Karl Marx, "Preface," *A Contribution to the Critique of Political Economy*, trans. N. I. Stone (Charleston, SC: Forgotten, 2010); Louis Althusser, *Ideology and Ideological State Apparatuses* (London: Verso, 1971); Antonio Gramsci, *Selections from the Prison Notebooks*, trans. Quintin Hoare and Geoffrey Nowell Smith (New York: International, 1971).
11 Roland Barthes, *Mythologies*, trans. Annette Lavers (St Albans: Paladin, 1973).
12 See, for instance, Claude Lévi-Strauss, *The Raw and the Cooked: Mythologiques, Volume 1*, trans. John and Doreen Weightman (Chicago: University of Chicago Press, 1983); Clifford Geertz, *The Interpretation of Cultures* (New York: Basic Books, 1977); Victor Turner, *Dramas, Fields, and Metaphors: Symbolic Action in Human Society* (Ithaca, NY: Cornell University Press, 1975).
13 See James W. Carey, *Communication as Culture* (New York: Routledge, 1989); James W. Carey (ed.), *Media, Myths, and Narratives: Television and the Press* (Newbury Park, CA: Sage, 1988); Roger Silverstone, *The Message of Television: Myth and Narrative in Contemporary Culture* (London: Heinemann, 1981).
14 Jacques Derrida, *Of Grammatology*, trans. Gayatri Chakravorty Spivak (Baltimore: Johns Hopkins Press, 1976).
15 See, for example, Michel Foucault, *Discipline and Punish: The Birth of the Prison*, trans. Alan Sheridan Smith (New York: Vintage, 1995 [1977]), *The Archaeology of Knowledge and Discourse on Language*, trans. Alan Sheridan Smith (New York: Pantheon, 1982 [1972]).
16 See especially Stuart Hall, "The Question of Cultural Identity," in Stuart Hall, David Held, and Tony McGrew (eds), *Modernity and Its Futures* (London: Polity, 1992).
17 Horace Newcomb, *Television: The Most Popular Art* (Norwell, MA: Anchor, 1974); Horace Newcomb, "Reflections on *TV: The Most Popular Art*," in Gary Edgerton and Brian Rose (eds), *Thinking Outside the Box: A Contemporary Television Genre Reader* (Lexington: University of Kentucky Press, 2008), pp. 17–36 (p. 25).
18 Newcomb, "Reflections on *TV: The Most Popular Art*," p. 34.
19 Christine Geraghty, "Origins of Television Studies," Society for Cinema and Media Studies Conference, Los Angeles, CA, March 10, 2010.
20 John Hartley, *The Uses of Television* (New York: Routledge, 1999), p. 199.
21 Hartley, *The Uses of Television*, p. 200.
22 John Fiske and John Hartley, *Reading Television* (London: Methuen, 1978).

23 Fiske and Hartley, *Reading Television*, p. 14.
24 Fiske and Hartley, *Reading Television*, p. 17.
25 Horace Newcomb and Paul Hirsch, "Television as a Cultural Forum," reprinted in Horace Newcomb (ed.), *Television: The Critical View*, 5th edn (New York: Oxford University Press, 1994), pp. 503–15 (p. 505). Originally published as "Television as a Cultural Forum: Implications for Research," *Quarterly Review of Film Studies* (Summer 1983) 8(3): 561–73.
26 Newcomb and Hirsch, "Television as a Cultural Forum," p. 503.
27 Newcomb and Hirsch, "Television as a Cultural Forum," p. 506.
28 Roland Barthes, *S/Z*, trans. Richard Miller (Oxford: Basil Blackwell, 1990), p. 4.
29 Roland Barthes, "From Work to Text," in *Image Music Text*, trans. Stephen Heath (Glasgow: Fontana Collins, 1977), pp. 163, 157.
30 John Fiske, *Television Culture* (London: Methuen, 1987).
31 John Fiske, "Moments of Television: Neither the Text Nor the Audience," in Ellen Seiter, Hans Borchers, Gabriele Kreutzner, and Eva-Maria Warth (eds), *Remote Control: Television, Audiences, and Cultural Power* (New York: Routledge, 1989), p. 59.
32 Charlotte Brunsdon, "What is the 'Television' of Television Studies?" in Christine Geraghty and David Lusted (eds), *The Television Studies Book* (London: Arnold, 1998), pp. 95–113 (p. 101); Horace Newcomb, "Television and Present Climate of Criticism," in Horace Newcomb (ed.), *Television: The Critical View*, 7th edn (New York: Oxford University Press, 2006), pp. 1–10 (p. 5).
33 Patricia Mellencamp, "Situation Comedy, Feminism, and Freud: Discourses of Gracie and Lucy," in Tania Modleski (ed.), *Studies in Entertainment: Critical Approaches to Mass Culture*, (Bloomington: Indiana University Press, 1986), pp. 80–95.
34 Kathleen Rowe, *The Unruly Woman: Gender and Genres of Laughter* (Austin: University of Texas Press, 1995), pp. 1–19.
35 Mary Beth Haralovich, "Sit-coms and Suburbs: Positioning the 1950s Homemaker," in Lynn Spigel and Denise Mann (eds), *Private Screenings: Television and the Female Consumer*, (Minneapolis: University of Minnesota Press, 1992), pp. 111–41.
36 Judith Mayne, "*L.A. Law* and Prime-Time Feminism," in Charlotte Brunsdon, Julie D'Acci, and Lynn Spigel (eds), *Feminist Television Criticism: A Reader* (New York: Oxford University Press, 1997), pp. 84–97 (p. 87).
37 Danae Clark, "*Cagney & Lacey*: Feminist Strategies of Detection," in Mary Ellen Brown (ed.), *Television and Women's Culture: The Politics of the Popular* (London: Sage Publications Ltd., 1990), pp. 117–33.
38 Clark, "*Cagney & Lacey*: Feminist Strategies of Detection," pp. 118, 124, 128.
39 Jeremy Butler, "Redesigning Discourse: Feminism, the Sitcom and *Designing Women*," *Journal of Film and Video* 45(1) (1993): 13–26; Lauren Rabinovitz, "Sitcoms and Single Moms: Representations of Feminism on American TV," *Cinema Journal* 29 (1989): 3–19.

40 Bonnie Dow, *Prime Time Feminism: Television, Media Culture, and the Women's Movement Since 1970* (Philadelphia: University of Pennsylvania Press, 1996).

41 Dow, p. xvi.

42 Amanda D. Lotz, *Redesigning Women: Television after the Network Era* (Urbana: University of Illinois Press, 2006).

43 Tania Modleski, "The Search for Tomorrow in Today's Soap Operas: Notes on a Feminine Narrative Form," *Film Quarterly* 33, no. 1 (1979): 12–21.

44 Charlotte Brunsdon, "Feminism, Post-feminism, Martha, Martha, and Nigella," *Cinema Journal* 44(2) (2005): 110–16.

45 Charlotte Brunsdon and David Morley, *Everyday Television: "Nationwide"* (London: BFI, 1978), p. 8.

46 Brunsdon and Morley, *Everyday Television*, p. 86.

47 Stuart Hall, "Which Public? Whose Service?" in Wilf Stevenson (ed.), *All Our Futures: The Changing Role and Purpose of the BBC* (London: BFI, 1993), pp. 23–38.

48 Victoria E. Johnson, *Heartland TV: Prime Time Television and the Struggle for US Identity* (New York: New York University Press, 2008).

49 Darrell Y. Hamamoto, *Monitored Peril: Asian Americans and the Politics of TV Representation* (Minneapolis: University of Minnesota Press, 1994).

50 J. Fred MacDonald, *Blacks and White TV: African Americans in Television since 1948* (Chicago: Nelson-Hall, 1992); Donald Bogle, *Primetime Blues: African Americans on Network Television* (New York: Farrar, Strauss, and Giroux, 2001).

51 Kristal Brent Zook, *Color by Fox: The Fox Network and the Revolution in Black Television* (New York: Oxford University Press, 1999).

52 Bambi Haggins, *Laughing Mad: The Black Comic Persona in Post-Soul America* (New Brunswick: Rutgers University Press, 2007).

53 Jimmie L. Reeves and Richard Campbell, *Cracked Coverage: Television News, the Anti-Cocaine Crusade and the Reagan Legacy* (Durham: Duke University Press, 1994).

54 John Fiske, *Media Matters: Race and Gender in US Politics* (Minneapolis: University of Minnesota Press, 1996).

55 See, for example, Kathleen Battles and Wendy Hilton-Morrow, "Gay Characters in Conventional Spaces: *Will and Grace* and the Situation Comedy Genre," *Critical Studies in Media Communication* 19(1) (2002): 87–106; Bonnie J. Dow, "*Ellen*, Television, and the Politics of Gay and Lesbian Visibility," *Critical Studies in Media Communication* 18(2) (2001): 123–41.

56 Ron Becker, *Gay TV and Straight America* (New Brunswick: Rutgers University Press, 2006).

57 Glyn Davis and Gary Needham (eds), *Queer TV: Theories, Histories, Politics* (London: Routledge, 2009).

58 John Corner, *Television Form and Public Address* (London: Edward Arnold, 1995).

59 Jeffrey P. Jones, *Entertaining Politics: New Political Television and Civic Culture* (Lanham, MD: Rowman and Littlefield, 2004), *Entertaining Politics:*

Satiric Television and Political Engagement (Lanham, MD: Rowman and Littlefield, 2009).

60 Some recent work clearly and explicitly engages the debate of "good" television, as is especially evident in a special issue of *Journal of British Cinema and Television* (3(1), 2006), and in Jason Mittell's "*Lost in a Great Story*: Evaluation in Narrative Television (and Television Studies)" in Roberta E. Pearson (ed.), *Reading Lost: Perspectives on a Hit Television Show* (London: IB Tauris, 2008). However, it is still rare to find discussions of quality and aesthetics that takes the concepts seriously while still problematizing the notion of objective quality, as Jason Jacobs's rather Arnoldian reinstatement of rhetorics of quality in the former illustrates.

61 John Ellis, *Visible Fictions: Cinema: Television: Video* (New York: Routledge, 1993), p. 116.

62 Frances Bonner, *Ordinary Television: Analyzing Popular TV* (Thousand Oaks, CA: Sage, 2003).

63 Fiske, *Television Culture* and *Understanding Popular Culture* (London: Routledge, 1989).

64 Kevin Glynn, *Tabloid Culture: Trash Taste, Popular Power, and the Transformation of American Television* (Durham, NC: Duke University Press, 2000).

65 Derek Kompare, *Rerun Nation: How Repeats Invented American Television* (New York: Routledge, 2004).

66 See Amanda Lotz (ed.), *Beyond Prime Time: Television Programming in the Post-Network Era* (New York: Routledge, 2009).

67 See Heather Hendershot, *Shaking for World for Jesus: Media and Conservative Evangelical Culture* (Chicago: University of Chicago Press, 2004).

68 For a recent welcome exception, see Melissa Aronczyk and Devon Powers (eds), *Blowing up the Brand: Critical Perspectives on Promotional Culture* (New York: Peter Lang, 2010).

69 See Corner, *Television Form*; Brunsdon and Morley, *Everyday Television*; Justin Lewis, *The Ideological Octopus: An Exploration of Television and Its Audience* (New York: Routledge, 1991).

Chapter 2   Audiences

1 Charles Winick, "Tendency Systems and the Effects of a Movie Dealing with a Social Problem" [1964], in Will Brooker and Deborah Jermyn (eds), *The Audience Studies Reader* (New York: Routledge, 2003), pp. 37–49.

2 Eunice Cooper and Helen Dinerman, "Analysis of the Film *Don't Be a Sucker*: A Study in Communication" [1951], in Will Brooker and Deborah Jermyn (eds), *The Audience Studies Reader* (New York: Routledge, 2003), pp. 27–36.

3 Stuart Hall, "Encoding/Decoding," in Stuart Hall, Dorothy Hobson, Andrew Lowe, and Paul Willis (eds), *Culture, Media, Language: Working Papers in Cultural Studies, 1972–79* (London: Routledge, 1991), pp. 107–16.

4 Antonio Gramsci, *Selections from The Prison Notebooks*, trans. Quintin Hoare and Geoffrey Nowell Smith (New York: International Publishers, 1974).

5 Dick Hebdige, *Subculture: The Meaning of Style* (London: Methuen, 1979).

6 Angela McRobbie, *Feminism and Youth Culture: From Jackie to Just Seventeen* (London: Unwin Hyman, 1991) and *In the Culture Society: Art, Fashion and Popular Music* (New York: Routledge, 1999).

7 See the collected work in David Morley and Charlotte Brunsdon, *The Nationwide Television Studies* (New York: Routledge, 1999), and retrospective commentary and analysis in David Morley, *Television, Audiences and Cultural Studies* (New York: Routledge, 1992).

8 Morley, *Television, Audiences and Cultural Studies*, p. 97.

9 Morley and Brunsdon, *The Nationwide Television Studies*, p. 2.

10 Morley, *Television, Audiences and Cultural Studies*, p. 82.

11 David Morley, *Family Television: Cultural Power and Domestic Leisure* (London: Comedia, 1988).

12 Hermann Bausinger, "Media, Technology and Daily Life," in *Media, Culture and Society* 6(4) (October 1984): 349.

13 James Lull, *Inside Family Viewing* (London: Comedia, 1990).

14 See David Morley and Roger Silverstone, "Domestic Communication: Technologies and Meanings," *Media, Culture and Society* 12(1)(1990): 31–55; Roger Silverstone, David Morley and Eric Hirsch, "Listening to a Long Conversation: An Ethnographic Approach to the Study of Information and Communication Technologies in the Home," *Cultural Studies* 5(2) (1991): 204–27; Roger Silverstone and Eric Hirsch (eds), *Consuming Technologies: Media and Information in Domestic Spaces* (New York: Routledge, 1992).

15 Ann Gray, *Video Playtime: The Gendering of a Leisure Technology* (New York: Routledge, 1992).

16 David Morley, personal interview with Jonathan Gray, August 30, 2009.

17 See some of her articles on these issues in Charlotte Brunsdon, *Screen Tastes: Soap Opera to Satellite Dishes* (New York: Routledge, 1997).

18 Janice A. Radway, *Reading the Romance: Women, Patriarchy, and Popular Literature* (Chapel Hill, NC: University of North Carolina Press, 1984).

19 Dorothy Hobson, "Housewives and the Mass Media," in Stuart Hall, Dorothy Hobson, Andrew Lowe, and Paul Willis (eds), *Culture, Media, Language: Working Papers in Cultural Studies, 1972–79* (London: Routledge, 1991), pp. 107–16; see also Dorothy Hobson, *Soap Opera* (Cambridge: Polity, 2003).

20 Ien Ang, *Watching Dallas: Soap Opera and the Melodramatic Imagination* (London: Routledge, 1985), pp. 83, 17; Elihu Katz and Tamar Liebes, *The Export of Meaning: Cross-Cultural Readings of Dallas* (Oxford: Oxford University Press, 1990).

21 See, for instance, Robert C. Allen, "Bursting Bubbles: 'Soap Opera,' Audiences, and the Limits of Genre," pp. 44–55, and Ellen Seiter, Hans Borchers, Gabriele Kreutzner, and Eva-Maria Warth, " 'Don't Treat us Like We're so Stupid and Naïve': Towards an Ethnography of Soap Opera Viewers," pp. 223–46, both in Ellen Seiter, Hans Borchers, Gabriele Kreutzner, and

Eva-Maria Warth (eds), *Remote Control: Television, Audiences, and Cultural Power* (New York: Routledge, 1989).

22 David Buckingham, *Public Secrets: EastEnders and Its Audience* (London: BFI, 1987), p. 5.

23 Buckingham, *Public Secrets*, pp. 177, 180.

24 Justin Lewis, *The Ideological Octopus: An Exploration of Television and Its Audience* (New York: Routledge, 1991), pp. 32, 34.

25 Lewis, *The Ideological Octopus*, p. 49.

26 Lewis, *The Ideological Octopus*, p. 54.

27 John Fiske, *Understanding Popular Culture* (London: Routledge, 1989), p. 23.

28 See Fiske, *Understanding Popular Culture*; John Fiske, *Television Culture* (London: Methuen, 1987) and *Reading Popular Culture* (London: Routledge, 1989).

29 Fiske, *Understanding Popular Culture*, p. 23.

30 See Michel de Certeau, *The Practice of Everyday Life*, trans. Stephen F. Rendall (Berkeley: University of California Press, 1984).

31 Fiske, *Understanding Popular Culture*, pp. 14, 15.

32 Pierre Bourdieu, *Distinction: A Social Critique of the Judgement of Taste*, trans. Richard Nice (London: Routledge, 1984), p. 7.

33 Henry Jenkins, *Textual Poachers: Television Fans and Participatory Culture* (New York: Routledge, 1992), p. 27.

34 Jenkins, *Textual Poachers*, p. 18.

35 Jenkins, *Textual Poachers*, p. 114.

36 See Camille Bacon-Smith, *Enterprising Women: Television Fandom and the Creation of Popular Myth* (Philadelphia: University of Pennsylvania Press, 1992); Constance Penley, "Feminism, Psychoanalysis, and the Study of Popular Culture," in Lawrence Grossberg, Cary Nelson, and Paula Treichler (eds), *Cultural Studies* (New York: Routledge, 1992), pp. 479–500.

37 Jenkins, *Textual Poachers*, p. 162.

38 Constance Penley, *NASA/TREK: Popular Science and Sex in America* (London: Verso, 1997), p. 3.

39 John Fiske, "The Cultural Economy of Fandom," in Lisa Lewis (ed.), *The Adoring Audience: Fan Culture and Popular Media* (New York: Routledge, 1992), pp. 30–49.

40 Fiske, *Understanding Popular Culture*, p. 35.

41 William R. Seaman, "Active Audience Theory: Pointless Populism," *Media, Culture and Society* 14 (April 1992): 301–11; Meaghan Morris, "Banality in Cultural Studies," in Patricia Mellencamp (ed.), *Logics of Television: Essays in Cultural Criticism* (London: BFI, 1990), pp. 14–43.

42 Seaman, "Active Audience Theory," p. 306.

43 Seaman, "Active Audience Theory," p. 304.

44 Seaman, "Active Audience Theory," p. 309.

45 David Miller and Greg Philo, "The Active Audience and Wrong Turns in Media Studies: Rescuing Media Power," *Soundscapes: Journal on Media Culture* 4 (September 2001), www.icce.rug.nl/~soundscapes/VOLUME04/Active_audience.shtml

46 Celeste Michelle Condit, "The Rhetorical Limits of Polysemy," *Critical Studies in Mass Communication* 6(2) (June 1989): 103–22.

47 Morris, "Banality in Cultural Studies."

48 Jenkins, *Textual Poachers*, p. 104.

49 David Morley, "Theoretical Orthodoxies: Textualism, Constructivism, and the 'New Ethnography' in Cultural Studies," in Marjorie Ferguson and Peter Golding (eds), *Cultural Studies in Question* (London: Sage, 1997), p. 125.

50 See James Curran, "The New Revisionism in Mass Communications Research: A Reappraisal," pp. 256–78, and David Morley, "Populism, Revisionism, and the 'New' Audience Research," p. 280, both in James Curran, David Morley, and Valerie Walkerdine (eds), *Cultural Studies and Communications* (London: Arnold, 1996).

51 Renato Rosaldo, "After Objectivism," in Simon During (ed.), *The Cultural Studies Reader* (London: Routledge, 1993), p. 105.

52 James Clifford, "Introduction: Partial Truths," in James Clifford and George E. Marcus (eds), *Writing Culture: The Poetics and Politics of Ethnography* (Berkeley: University of California Press, 1986), pp. 2, 7.

53 See, for instance, Edward W. Said, *Orientalism* (New York: Vintage, 1979); Gayatri Chakravorty Spivak, "Can the Subaltern Speak?" in Cary Nelson and Lawrence Grossberg (eds), *Marxism and the Interpretation of Culture* (Champaign, IL: University of Illinois Press, 1988), pp. 271–315.

54 Janice A. Radway, "Reception Study: Ethnography and the Problems of Dispersed Audiences and Nomadic Subjects," *Cultural Studies* 2 (October 1988): 363.

55 Radway, "Reception Study": 366.

56 Pertti Alasuutari, "Introduction: Three Phases of Reception Studies," in Alasuutari (ed.), *Rethinking the Media Audience: The New Agenda* (London: Sage, 1999), p. 4.

57 Marie Gillespie, *Television, Ethnicity and Cultural Change* (London: Routledge, 1995), p. 25.

58 Stewart M. Hoover, Lynn Schofield Clark, and Diane F. Alters, with Joseph G. Champ and Lee Hood, *Media, Home, and Family* (New York: Routledge, 2003).

59 David Gauntlett, *Creative Explorations: New Approaches to Identities and Audiences* (New York: Routledge, 2007).

60 Helen Wood, *Talking with Television: Women, Talk Shows, and Modern Self-Reflexivity* (Urbana: University of Illinois Press, 2009).

61 S. Elizabeth Bird, *The Audience in Everyday Life: Living in a Media World* (New York: Routledge, 2003), p. 99.

62 Bird, *The Audience in Everyday Life*, p. 3.

63 Nancy Baym, *Tune In, Log On: Soaps, Fandom, and Online Community* (London: Sage, 2000).

64 Nicholas Abercrombie and Brian Longhurst, *Audiences: A Sociological Theory of Performance and Imagination* (London: Sage, 1998).

65 Henry Jenkins, *Convergence Culture: When Old and New Media Collide* (New York: New York University Press, 2006).

66 See Kristina Busse and Jonathan Gray, "Fan Cultures and Fan Communities," in Virginia Nightingale (ed.), *The Blackwell Companion to Audiences* (Malden, MA: Wiley-Blackwell, 2011), pp. 425–43; Derek Johnson, "Fantagonism: Factions, Institutions, and Constitutive Hegemonies of Fandom," in Jonathan Gray, Cornel Sandvoss, and C. Lee Harrington (eds), *Fandom: Identities and Communities in a Mediated World* (New York: New York University Press, 2007), pp. 285–300.

67 Axel Bruns, *Blogs, Wikipedia, Second Life, and Beyond: From Production to Produsage* (New York: Peter Lang, 2008).

68 Ien Ang, *Desperately Seeking the Audience* (New York: Routledge, 1991); Eileen R. Meehan, "Why We Don't Count: The Commodity Audience," in Patricia Mellencamp (ed.), *Logics of Television: Essays in Cultural Criticism* (London: BFI, 1990), pp. 117–37.

69 Philip M. Napoli, *Audience Economics: Media Institutions and the Audience Marketplace* (New York: Columbia University Press, 2003), p. 5.

70 See Todd Gitlin, *Inside Prime Time* (New York: Pantheon, 1985).

71 See Ang, *Watching Dallas*; Katz and Liebes, *The Export of Meaning*.

72 George Ritzer, *The McDonaldization of Society: An Investigation into the Changing Characters of Contemporary Social Life* (Newbury Park, CA: Pine Forge Press, 1995).

73 Toby Miller, Nitin Govil, John McMurria, Richard Maxwell, and Ting Wang, *Global Hollywood 2* (London: BFI, 2008).

74 Francis L. F. Lee and Li Cui, "Becoming Extra-Ordinary: Negotiation of Media Power in *Super Girls' Voice* in China," and Aswin Punathambekar, "Reality TV and Participatory Culture: *Indian Idol* and the Emergence of Mobile Publics," both in *Popular Communication: The International Journal of Media and Culture* 8(4) (November 2010): 256–72 and 241–55.

75 Divya McMillin, *International Media Studies* (Malden, MA: Wiley-Blackwell, 2007).

76 Homi K. Bhabha, *The Location of Culture* (New York: Routledge, 2004).

77 See David Morley and Kevin Robins, *Spaces of Identity: Global Media, Electronic Landscapes and Cultural Boundaries* (New York: Routledge, 1995); David Morley, *Home Territories: Media, Mobility and Identity* (New York: Routledge, 2000); Myria Georgiou, *Diaspora, Identity and the Media: Diasporic Transnationalism and Mediated Spatialities* (Cresskill, NJ: Hampton, 2006).

78 See particularly Roger Silverstone, *The Message of Television: Myth and Narrative in Contemporary Culture* (London: Heinemann, 1981), *Television and Everyday Life* (New York: Routledge, 1994), *Why Study Media?* (London: Sage, 1999).

79 Silverstone, *Television and Everyday Life*, p. 3.

80 Anthony Giddens, *The Consequences of Modernity* (Palo Alto, CA: Stanford University Press, 1991).

81 Silverstone, *Television and Everyday Life*, p. 40.

82 See Morley, *Home Territories*; Morley and Robins, *Spaces of Identity*.

83 D. W. Winnicott, *Playing and Reality* (New York: Routledge, 2005).

84 Matt Hills, *Fan Cultures* (New York: Routledge, 2002).

85 Cornel Sandvoss, *Fans: The Mirror of Consumption* (London: Polity, 2005).
86 For some other examples of recent television or television-related fan studies work not already cited in this chapter, see C. Lee Harrington and Denise Bielby, *Soap Fans: Pursuing Pleasure and Making Meaning in Everyday Life* (Philadelphia: Temple University Press, 1995); Lyn Thomas, *Fans, Feminisms, and "Quality" Media* (New York: Routledge, 2002); Christine Scodari, *Serial Monogamy: Soap Opera, Lifespan, and the Gendered Politics of Fantasy* (Cresskill, NJ: Hampton, 2004); Kristina Busse and Karen Hellekson (eds), *Fan Fiction and Fan Communities in the Age of the Internet* (Jefferson, NC: McFarland, 2006); Paul Booth, *Digital Fandom: New Media Studies* (New York: Peter Lang, 2010).
87 Jonathan Gray, Cornel Sandvoss, and C. Lee Harrington, "Why Study Fans?" in Gray, Sandvoss, and Harrington (eds), *Fandom: Identities and Communities in a Mediated World* (New York: New York University Press, 2007), p. 10.
88 Nick Couldry, *The Place of Media Power: Pilgrims and Witnesses of the Media Age* (New York: Routledge, 2000).
89 Nick Couldry, *Media Rituals* (New York: Routledge, 2003), p. 2.
90 Roger Silverstone, *Media and Morality: On the Rise of the Mediapolis* (London: Polity, 2006); Nick Couldry, *Listening Beyond the Echoes: Media, Ethics, and Agency in an Uncertain World* (Herndon, VA: Paradigm, 2006).
91 John Hartley, *The Uses of Entertainment* (New York: Routledge, 1999).
92 See also John Hartley, *Tele-ology: Studies in Television* (New York: Routledge, 1992), *Popular Reality: Journalism, Modernity, Popular Culture* (London: Hodder Arnold, 1996), *Television Truths: Forms of Knowledge in Popular Culture* (Malden, MA: Wiley-Blackwell, 2008).
93 Diane F. Alters, "'We Hardly Watch That Rude, Crude Show': Class and Taste in *The Simpsons*," in Carol A. Stabile and Mark T. Harrison (eds), *Prime Time Animation: Television Animation and American Culture* (New York: Routledge, 2003), pp. 165–84, and "The Other Side of Fandom: Anti-Fans, Non-Fans, and the Hurts of History," in Jonathan Gray, Cornel Sandvoss, and C. Lee Harrington (eds), *Fandom: Identities and Communities in a Mediated World* (New York: New York University Press, 2007), pp. 344–56.
94 Aniko Bodroghkozy, "'Is This What You Mean by Color TV?' Race, Gender, and Contested Meanings in NBC's *Julia*," in Lynn Spigel and Denise Mann (eds), *Private Screenings: Television and the Female Consumer* (Minneapolis: University of Minnesota Press, 1992), pp. 143–68.
95 Melissa A. Click, "Untidy: Fan Response to the Soiling of Martha Stewart's Spotless Image," in Jonathan Gray, Cornel Sandvoss, and C. Lee Harrington (eds), *Fandom: Identities and Communities in a Mediated World* (New York: New York University Press, 2007), pp. 301–15.
96 Martin Barker, Jane Arthurs, and Ramaswami Harindranath, *The Crash Controversy: Censorship Campaigns and Film Reception* (London: Wallflower, 2001).
97 Liesbet van Zoonen, *Entertaining the Citizen: When Politics and Popular Culture Converge* (Lanham, MD: Rowman and Littlefield, 2004).

98 See Jonathan Gray, "The News: You Gotta Love It," in Jonathan Gray, Cornel Sandvoss, and C. Lee Harrington (eds), *Fandom: Identities and Communities in a Mediated World* (New York: New York University Press, 2007), pp. 75–87; Cornel Sandvoss, "Liquid Stars, Liquid Identities: Political Discourse in Transnational Media Sport," in Cornel Sandvoss, Alina Bernstein, and Michael Real (eds), *Bodies of Discourse: Sports Stars, Mass Media, and the Global Public* (Cresskill, NJ: Hampton, in press); Jenkins, *Convergence Culture*, ch. 6; John Corner and Dick Pels (eds), *Media and the Restyling of Politics: Consumerism, Celebrity and Cynicism* (London: Sage, 2003).

99 See Jeffrey P. Jones, *Entertaining Politics: Satiric Television and Political Engagement* (Lanham, MD: Rowman and Littlefield, 2009); Jonathan Gray, Jeffrey P. Jones, and Ethan Thompson, *Satire TV: Politics and Comedy in the Post-Network Era* (New York: New York University Press, 2009).

Chapter 3   Institutions

1 Some in the humanities tradition of film studies do indeed consider institutions quite carefully. This barb is directed more toward those in English and philosophy departments who write textual analyses that completely divorce texts from their conditions of creation.

2 Jennifer Holt and Alisa Perren (eds), *Media Industries: History, Theory, and Method* (Malden, MA: Wiley-Blackwell, 2009).

3 Robert E. Babe (quoting Lazarsfeld); Babe, *Cultural Studies and Political Economy: Toward a New Integration* (Lanham, MD: Rowman and Littlefield, 2009), p. 17. Also see Paddy Scannell's analysis of Lazarsfeld's role in the development of administrative research in *Media and Communication* (London: Sage, 2007), pp. 11–21.

4 Lynn Spigel, "The Making of a TV Literate Elite," in Christine Geraghty and David Lusted (eds), *The Television Studies Book* (London: Arnold, 1998), pp. 63–94.

5 Elihu Katz, *Social Research on Broadcasting: Proposals for Further Development* (London: BBC, 1977), p. 37.

6 Theodor Adorno and Max Horkheimer, "The Culture Industry: Enlightenment as Mass Deception," in *Dialectic of Enlightenment* (New York: Herder and Herder, 1972).

7 Adorno and Horkheimer, "The Culture Industry," p. 121.

8 David Hesmondhalgh, "Media Industry Studies, Media Production Studies," in James Curran (ed.), *Media and Society* (London: Bloomsbury Academic, 2010), pp. 145–63 (p. 147).

9 Douglas Kellner, "Media Industries, Political Economy, and Media/Cultural Studies," in Jennifer Holt and Alisa Perren (eds), *Media Industries: History, Theory, and Method* (Malden, MA: Wiley-Blackwell, 2009), pp. 95–107 (p. 101).

10 Vincent Mosco, *The Political Economy of Communication*, 2nd edn (Los Angeles: Sage, 2009), p. 2.

11 Ben Bagdikian, *The New Media Monopoly*, 2nd rev. edn (New York: Beacon Press, 2004).
12 There really isn't a body of political economy research devoted specifically to television.
13 Mosco, *The Political Economy*, p. 69.
14 John Tomlinson, *Cultural Imperialism: A Critical Introduction* (Baltimore: Johns Hopkins University Press, 1991).
15 Robert McChesney, *The Problem of the Media: US Communication Politics in the 21st Century* (New York: Monthly Review of Books, 2004) and Bagdikian, *The New Media Monopoly*.
16 Many political economists move effortlessly among media such as broadcast and print. Given our focus on television studies, we do not attend to the research of those studying the political economy of newspapers, magazines, or film.
17 Phillip Lodge, "Towards an Institutional and Intellectual History of British Communication Studies," paper presented at the 2008 International Communication Association Conference, Montreal, Quebec, p. 11.
18 Lodge, "Towards an Institutional and Intellectual History," p. 14.
19 Lodge, "Towards an Institutional and Intellectual History," p. 20.
20 Lodge, "Towards an Institutional and Intellectual History," p. 20 (Golding cited in Mosco, *The Political Economy*, 1st edn (London: Sage, 1996), p. 99). Academic institutionalization is also important in terms of what types of departments and units tended to house those studying media industries. Just as early researchers emerged from various disciplines in the US, no single unit housed British scholars; however, the field of sociology proves far more central in the British case (where "communication" departments continue to be rare) than in the US.
21 Graham Murdock, "Large Corporations and the Control of the Communications Industries," in Michael Gurevitch, Tony Bennett, James Curran and Janet Woollacott (eds), *Culture, Society and the Media* (London: Methuen, 1982), pp. 114–27.
22 James Curran, "The Rise of the Westminster School," in Andrew Calabrese and Colin Sparks (eds), *Toward a Political Economy of Culture* (Lanham, MD: Rowman & Littlefield, 2004), pp. 13–40 (pp. 15–16).
23 Raymond Williams, *Television: Technology and Cultural Form* (New York: Schocken Books, 1974); Richard Hoggart, *The Uses of Literacy: Changing Patterns in English Mass Culture* (Fair Lawn, NJ: Essential Books, 1957); Stuart Hall, "Encoding/Decoding," in Stuart Hall et al. (eds), *Culture, Media, Language: Working Papers in Cultural Studies, 1972–1979* (London: Routledge, 1991), pp. 107–16; Paul du Gay, Stuart Hall, Linda Janes, and Hugh Mackay, *Doing Cultural Studies: The Story of the Sony Walkman* (London: Sage, 1997); Richard Johnson, "What is Cultural Studies Anyway?" *Social Text* 16 (1986): 38–80; Angela McRobbie, *British Fashion Design: Rag Trade or Image Industry?* (London: Routledge, 1998).
24 Glasgow University Media Group, *Bad News*, Vol. 1 (London: Routledge and Kegan Paul, 1976).

25 Tom Burns, *The BBC: Public Institution and Private World* (London: Palgrave Macmillan, 1977).

26 Glasgow University Media Group, *Bad News* (London: Routledge and Keegan Paul, 1976).

27 Gaye Tuchman, *Making News: A Study in the Construction of Reality* (New York: Free Press, 1978).

28 Philip Schlesinger, *Putting "Reality" Together: BBC News* (London: Constable, 1978).

29 Herbert Gans, *Deciding What's News: A Study of* CBS Evening News, NBC Nightly News, Newsweek, *and* Time (New York: Pantheon Books, 1979); Jeremy Turnstall, *Journalists at Work: Specialist Correspondents, Their News Organizations, News-sources and Competitor-colleagues* (London: Constable, 1976) or essays in Stan Cohen and Jock Young, *The Manufacture of News: A Reader* (Thousand Oaks: Sage, 1973).

30 Philip Elliott, *The Making of a Television Series* (London: Constable, 1972).

31 Manuel Alvarado and Edward Buscombe, *Hazell: The Making of a TV Series* (London: BFI, 1978); John Tulloch and Manuel Alvarado, *Doctor Who: The Unfolding Text* (London: Macmillan, 1983). Tulloch and Alvarado's book is mostly textual analysis but includes some interviews with production staff; however, Tulloch and Moran provide a deep examination of the making of and industrial practices surrounding the most popular Australian serial at the time. John Tulloch and Albert Moran, *A Country Practice: "Quality Soap"* (Sydney: Currency Press, 1986).

32 Muriel G. Cantor, *The Hollywood TV Producer: His Work and His Audience* (New York: Basic Books, 1972).

33 Horace Newcomb and Robert S. Alley, *The Producer's Medium: Conversations with Creators of American TV* (New York: Oxford University Press, 1983).

34 Les Brown, *Televi$ion: The Business Behind the Box* (New York: Harcourt Brace, 1971); Sally Bedell, *Up the Tube: Prime Time TV and the Silverman Years* (New York: The Viking Press, 1981); Ken Auletta, *Three Blind Mice: How the TV Networks Lost Their Way* (New York: Random House, 1991); Bill Carter, *Desperate Networks* (New York: Doubleday, 2006).

35 Todd Gitlin, *Inside Prime Time* (New York: Pantheon Books, 1983); Todd Gitlin, "Prime Time Ideology: The Hegemonic Process in Television Entertainment," *Social Problems* 26(3) (1979): 251–66. For more on Gitlin's contribution to media industry study, see Amanda D. Lotz, "Industry-Level Studies and the Contributions of Gitlin's *Inside Prime Time*," in Vicki Mayer, Miranda J. Banks, and John Thornton Caldwell (eds), *Production Studies: Cultural Studies of Media Industries* (New York: Routledge, 2009), pp. 25–38.

36 Todd Gitlin, *The Whole World is Watching: Mass Media and the Unmaking of the American New Left* (Berkeley: University of California Press, 1980).

37 Julie D'Acci, "Cultural Studies, Television Studies, and the Crisis in the Humanities," in Lynn Spigel and Jan Olsson (eds), *Television After TV: Essays on a Medium in Transition* (Durham: Duke University Press, 2004), pp. 418–46 (pp. 420–1). D'Acci cites Charlotte Brunsdon and David Morley,

Everyday Television: "Nationwide" (London: British Film Institute, 1978); John Fiske and John Hartley, *Reading Television* (London: Methuen, 1978) and Stuart Hall et al. (eds), *Culture, Media, Language: Working Papers in Cultural Studies, 1972–1979.*

38 D'Acci, "Cultural Studies," p. 421, referencing James Curran, Michael Gurevitch, and Janet Woollacott (eds), *Mass Communication and Society* (Beverly Hills: Sage, 1979). The regular updating of this volume, particularly an essay on political economy by Murdock and Golding, provides an insightful history of the field.

39 Joli Jensen, "An Interpretive Approach to Culture Production," in William Rowland and Bruce Watkins (eds), *Interpreting Television: Current Perspectives* (Beverly Hills: Sage, 1984).

40 D'Acci, "Cultural Studies," p. 441, n. 12.

41 Christopher Anderson, *Hollywood TV: The Studio System in the Fifties* (Austin: University of Texas Press, 1994); William Boddy, *Fifties Television: The Industry and Its Critics* (Champaign: University of Illinois Press, 1993); Michael Curtin, *Redeeming the Wasteland: Television Documentary and Cold War Politics* (New Brunswick: Rutgers University Press, 1995); Michele Hilmes, *Hollywood and Broadcasting: From Radio to Cable* (Urbana: University of Illinois Press, 1990); Julie D'Acci, *Defining Women: Television and the Case of Cagney & Lacey* (Chapel Hill: University of North Carolina Press, 1994); and Lynn Spigel, *Make Room for TV: Television and the Family Ideal in Postwar America* (Chicago: University of Chicago Press, 1992). Robert C. Allen, *Speaking of Soap Operas* (Chapel Hill: University of North Carolina Press, 1985) can be considered an important precursor.

42 Robert E. Babe, *Cultural Studies and Political Economy: Toward a New Integration* (Lanham, MD: Rowman & Littlefield, 2009).

43 Personal interview with Jonathan Gray, July 10, 2010.

44 Marjorie Ferguson and Peter Golding (eds), *Cultural Studies in Question* (London: Sage, 1997); James Curran, David Morley, and Valerie Walkerdine (eds), *Cultural Studies and Communications* (London: Arnold, 1996).

45 In general, neo-Marxist work is broader in its assessment of power and considers axes of power other than the class-based ones focused on in traditional Marxist thought. Foucauldian approaches to power conceptualize an even more diffuse spectrum for the operation of power and breaks away from the "top-down" or one-way models of power.

46 Stuart Cunningham and Elizabeth Jacka, *Australian Television and International Mediascapes* (Cambridge: Cambridge University Press, 1997), p. 4. Also John Sinclair, Elizabeth Jacka, and Stuart Cunningham (eds), *New Patterns in Global Television: Peripheral Vision* (Oxford: Oxford University Press, 1996); John Sinclair, *Latin American Television: A Global View* (Oxford: Oxford University Press, 1999). Tom O'Regan, "The International, the Regional, and the Local: Hollywood's New and Declining Audiences," in Elizabeth Jacka (ed.), *Continental Shift: Globalization and Culture* (Double Bay, N.S.W.: Local Consumption, 1992), pp. 75–98; Tom O'Regan, "Too Popular by Far: On Hollywood's International Popularity," *Continuum: The Australian Journal of Media and Culture* 5(2) (1990): 302–51.

47 Timothy Havens, Amanda D. Lotz, and Serra Tinic, "Critical Media Industry Studies: A Research Approach," *Communication, Culture and Critique* 2 (2009): 234–53.
48 Holt and Perren (eds), *Media Industry Studies*.
49 Chad Raphael, "The Political Economic Origins of Reali-TV," in Susan Murray and Laurie Ouellette (eds), *Reality TV: Remaking Television Culture* (New York: New York University Press, 2004), pp. 119–36.
50 Ron Becker, *Gay TV and Straight America* (New Brunswick, NJ: Rutgers University Press, 2006).
51 Amanda D. Lotz, *Redesigning Women: Television after the Network Era* (Urbana: University of Illinois Press, 2006).
52 Timothy Havens, "'It's Still a White World Out There': The Interplay of Culture and Economics in International Television Trade," *Critical Studies in Media Communication* 19(4) (2002): 377–97; Timothy Havens, *Black Television Travels: Media Globalization and Contemporary Racial Discourse* (New York: New York University Press, forthcoming).
53 Albert Moran, *Copycat Television: Globalisation, Program Formats, and Cultural Identity* (Luton: University of Luton Press, 1998); Albert Moran, *New Flows in Global TV* (Bristol: Intellect, 2009); Silvio Waisbord, "McTV: Understanding the Global Popularity of Television Formats," *Television & New Media* 5(4) (2004): 359–83; Tasha Oren and Sharon Shahaf (eds), *Global Television Formats: Circulating Culture, Producing Identity* (New York: Routledge, 2011).
54 Yeidy Rivero, *Tuning Out Blackness: Race and Nation in the History of Puerto Rican Television* (Durham: Duke University Press, 2005).
55 Marwan Kraidy, *Reality Television and Arab Politics: Contention in Public Life* (Cambridge: Cambridge University Press, 2010).
56 Aswin Punathambekar, "Reality TV and Participatory Culture: *Indian Idol* and the Emergence of Mobile Publics," in *Popular Communication: The International Journal of Media and Culture* 8(4) (November 2010): 241–55; Shanti Kumar, *Gandhi Meets Primetime: Globalization and Nationalism in Indian Television* (Urbana: University of Illinois Press, 2005).
57 Serra Tinic, *On Location: Canada's Television Industry in a Global Market* (Toronto: University of Toronto Press, 2005).
58 See Tinic, *On Location*; Janet Wasko and Mary Erickson (eds), *Cross-Border Cultural Production: Economic Runaway or Globalization?* (Amherst, NY: Cambria, 2008); Greg Elmer, *Contracting Out Hollywood: Runaway Productions and Foreign Location Shooting* (Lanham, MD: Rowman and Littlefield, 2005).
59 Toby Miller, Nitin Govil, John McMurria, Richard Maxwell, and Ting Wang, *Global Hollywood 2* (London: BFI, 2008).
60 See Timothy Havens, *Global Television Marketplace* (London: BFI, 2008); Denise Bielby and C. Lee Harrington, *Global TV: Exporting Television and Culture in the World Market* (New York: New York University Press, 2008).
61 Barbara Selznick, *Global Television: Co-Producing Culture* (Philadelphia: Temple University Press, 2008).

62 Jeanette Steemers, *Selling Television: British Television in the Global Marketplace* (London: British Film Institute, 2008); Michele Hilmes, *Network Nations: A Transnational History of American and British Broadcasting* (forthcoming).
63 Peter Iosifides, Jeanette Steemers, and Mark Wheeler, *European Television Industries* (London: British Film Institute, 2005).
64 Amanda D. Lotz, *The Television Will Be Revolutionized* (New York: New York University Press, 2007).
65 Graeme Turner and Jinna Tay (eds), *Television Studies after TV: Understanding Television in the Post-Broadcast Era* (New York: Routledge, 2009); Lynn Spigel and Jan Olsson (eds), *Television after TV: Essays on a Medium in Transition* (Durham: Duke University Press, 2004).
66 Amanda D. Lotz, *Beyond Prime Time: Television Programming in the Post-Network Era* (New York: Routledge, 2009).
67 John Thornton Caldwell, "Cultural Studies in Media Production: Critical Industry Practices," in Mimi White and James Schwoch (eds), *Questions of Method in Cultural Studies* (Malden, MA: Blackwell, 2006), pp. 109–53; *Production Culture: Industrial Reflexivity and Critical Practice in Film and Television* (Durham: Duke University Press, 2008); *Televisuality: Style, Crisis, and Authority in American Television* (New Brunswick: Rutgers University Press, 1995).
68 Laura Grindstaff, *The Money Shot: Trash, Class, and the Making of TV Talk Shows* (Chicago: University of Chicago Press, 2002).
69 Laura Grindstaff, "Self-Serve Celebrity: The Production of Ordinariness and the Ordinariness of Production in Reality Television," in Vicki Mayer, Miranda J. Banks, and John Thornton Caldwell (eds), *Production Studies: Cultural Studies of Media Industries* (New York: Routledge, 2009), pp. 71–86.
70 Vicki Mayer, "Bringing the Social Back In: Studies of Production Cultures and Social Theory," in Vicki Mayer, Miranda J. Banks, and John Thornton Caldwell (eds), *Production Studies: Cultural Studies of Media Industries* (New York: Routledge, 2009), pp. 15–24.
71 Carolina Acosta-Alzuru, "'I'm Not a Feminist . . . I Only Defend Women as Human Beings': The Production, Representation and Consumption of Feminism in a Telenovela," *Critical Studies in Media Communication* 20(3) (2003): 269–94.
72 Georgina Born, *Uncertain Vision: Birt, Dyke and the Reinvention of the BBC* (London: Random House UK, 2005).
73 Tony Bennett, "Putting Policy into Cultural Studies," in Lawrence Grossberg, Cary Nelson, and Paula Treichler (eds), *Cultural Studies* (New York: Routledge, 1991), pp. 23–33.
74 Boddy, *Fifties Television*.
75 Hilmes, *Hollywood and Broadcasting*.
76 Thomas Streeter, *Selling the Air: A Critique of the Policy of Commercial Broadcasting in the United States* (Chicago: University of Chicago Press, 1996); Laurie Ouellette, *Viewers Like You? How Public TV Failed the People* (New York: Columbia University Press, 2002); Megan Mullen, *The Rise of*

Cable Programming in the United States: Revolution or Evolution? (Austin: University of Texas Press, 2003).

77 Jennifer Holt, "Vertical Vision: Deregulation, Industrial Economy and Prime-time Design," in Mark Jancovich and James Lyons (eds), *Quality Popular Television: Cult TV, the Industry and Fans* (London: British Film Institute, 2003), pp. 11–31; and John McMurria, "Long-format TV: Globalisation and Network Branding in a Multi-Channel Era," in Mark Jancovich and James Lyons (eds), *Quality Popular Television: Cult TV, the Industry and Fans* (London: British Film Institute, 2003), pp. 65–87.

78 Vicki Mayer, "Soft-Core in TV Time: A Political Economy of a Cultural Trend," *Critical Studies in Media Communication* 22(4) (2005): 302–20.

79 David Hesmondhalgh and Sarah Baker, " 'A Very Complicated Version of Freedom': Conditions and Experiences of Creative Labour in Three Cultural Industries," *Poetics: Journal of Empirical Research on Culture, the Media and the Arts* 38(1) (2010): 4–20; David Lee, "Networks, Cultural Capital and Creative Labour in the British Independent Television Industry," paper presented at CRESC: The Future of Cultural Work, London, June 7, 2010; Gillian Doyle and Richard Paterson, "Public Policy and Independent Television Production in the UK," *Journal of Media Business Studies* 5(3) (2008): 17–33; Anna Zoellner, "Professional Ideology and Programme Conventions: Documentary Development in Independent British Television Production," *Mass Communication and Society* 12(4) (2010): 503–36.

80 Des Freedman, *Television Policies of the Labour Party, 1951–2001* (London: Frank Cass, 2003), *The Politics of Media Policy* (London: Polity, 2008); Aeron Davis, *The Mediation of Power: A Critical Introduction* (New York: Routledge, 2007).

81 See, among others, John Hartley, "Creative Industries" in John Hartley (ed.), *Creative Industries* (Malden, MA: Blackwell, 2005), pp. 1–40; Terry Flew and Stuart Cunningham, "Creative Industries After the First Decade of Debate," *The Information Society* 26(2) (2010): 1–11.

82 We also must acknowledge the stake one of your authors has as a voice in attempting to chart a way forward here.

83 Vicki Mayer, *Below the Line: Producers and Production Studies in the New Television Economy* (Durham: Duke University Press, 2011).

Chapter 4   Contexts

1 See Marshall McLuhan, *Understanding Media: The Extensions of Man* (Cambridge, MA: MIT Press, 1994 [1964]).

2 Raymond Williams, *Television: Technology and Cultural Form* (London: Fontana/Collins, 1974).

3 Harold Innis, *Empire and Communications* (Oxford: Clarendon Press, 1950) and *The Bias of Communication* (Toronto: University of Toronto Press, 1951).

4 Walter Ong, *Orality and Literacy: The Technologizing of the Word* (New York: Routledge, 2002 [1982]).

5 Eric McLuhan and Frank Zingrone (eds), *The Essential McLuhan* (New York: Basic Books, 1995), pp. 233–69.
6 McLuhan, *Understanding Media*, p. 335.
7 McLuhan, *Understanding Media*, p. 309.
8 Neil Postman, *Amusing Ourselves to Death: Public Discourse in the Age of Show Business* (New York: Penguin, 1985), p. 70.
9 Postman, *Amusing Ourselves*, p. 77.
10 McLuhan, *Understanding Media*, p. 318.
11 Michael Schudson, *The Good Citizen: A History of American Civil Life* (Cambridge, MA: Harvard University Press, 1999).
12 Postman, *Amusing Ourselves*, p. 90.
13 Erik Barnouw, *A History of Broadcasting in the United States*, vols 1–3 (Oxford: Oxford University Press, 1966).
14 James Curran and Jean Seaton, *Power Without Responsibility: Press, Broadcasting and the Internet in Britain* (London: Routledge, 2009).
15 Paddy Scannell and David Cardiff, *A Social History of British Broadcasting: 1922–1939: Serving the Nation* (Oxford: Wiley-Blackwell, 1991); Paddy Scannell, *Radio, Television, and Modern Life: A Phenomenological Approach* (Oxford: Blackwell, 1996).
16 Michele Hilmes, *Hollywood and Broadcasting: From Radio to Cable* (Urbana: University of Illinois Press, 1990); *Radio Voices: American Broadcasting 1922–1952* (Minneapolis: University of Minnesota Press, 1997; Susan J. Douglas, *Inventing American Broadcasting: 1899–1922* (Baltimore: Johns Hopkins University Press, 1987).
17 Lynn Spigel, *Make Room for TV: Television and the Family Ideal in Postwar America* (Chicago: University of Chicago Press, 1992); William Boddy, *Fifties Television: The Industry and Its Critics* (Champaign, IL: University of Illinois Press, 1993); Christopher Anderson, *Hollywood TV: The Studio System in the Fifties* (Austin: University of Texas Press, 1994); Michael Curtin, *Redeeming the Wasteland: Television Documentary and Cold War Politics* (New Brunswick, NJ: Rutgers University Press, 1995).
18 Notably, although Spigel takes domestic applications as her focus, other researchers have considered television's many extra-domestic applications. See Anna McCarthy, *Ambient Television: Visual Culture and Public Space* (Durham: Duke University Press, 2001).
19 Mary Beth Haralovich, "Sit-coms and Suburbs: Positioning the 1950s Homemaker," in Lynn Spigel and Denise Mann (eds), *Private Screenings: Television and the Female Consumer*, (Minneapolis: University of Minnesota Press, 1992), pp. 111–41.
20 Aniko Bodroghkozy, *Groove Tube: Sixties Television and the Youth Rebellion* (Durham: Duke University Press, 2001).
21 Elana Levine, *Wallowing in Sex: The New Sexual Culture of 1970s American Television* (Durham: Duke University Press, 2007).
22 Jason Mittell, *Genre and Television: From Cop Shows to Cartoons in American Culture* (New York: Routledge, 2004).
23 Lynn Spigel and Michael Curtin (eds), *The Television Wasn't Revolutionized: Sixties Television and Social Conflict* (New York: Routledge, 1997); and

Mary Beth Haralovich and Lauren Rabinovitz (eds), *Television, History and American Culture: Feminist Critical Essays* (Durham: Duke University Press, 1999).

24 Mittell, *Genre and Television*, pp. 54–89.

25 Derek Kompare, *Rerun Nation: How Repeats Invented American Television* (New York: Routledge, 2004).

26 John Thornton Caldwell, *Televisuality: Style, Crisis and Authority in American Television* (New Brunswick: Rutgers University Press, 1995).

27 Amanda Lotz, *The Television Will Be Revolutionized* (New York: New York University Press, 2007).

28 James Bennett and Tom Brown (eds), *Film and Television After DVD* (London: Routledge, 2009); James Bennett and Niki Strange (eds), *Television as Digital Media* (Durham, NC: Duke University Press, 2011).

29 Derek Johnson, *Creative License: Media Franchising, Shared Content, and the Collaborative Production of Culture* (New York: New York University Press, 2011).

30 Laurie Ouellette and James Hay, *Better Living Through Reality TV: Television and Post-Welfare Citizenship* (Malden, MA: Wiley-Blackwell, 2008), p. 3.

31 Ouellette and Hay, *Better Living Through Reality TV*, p. 2.

32 Ouellette and Hay, *Better Living Through Reality TV*, pp. 32–3.

33 Ouellette and Hay, *Better Living Through Reality TV*, p. 140.

34 Mark Andrejevic, *Reality TV: The Work of Being Watched* (Lanham, MD: Rowman and Littlefield, 2003).

35 Derek Kompare, "Extraordinarily Ordinary: *The Osbournes* as 'An American Family,'" in Susan Murray and Laurie Ouellette (eds), *Reality TV: Remaking American Culture* (New York: New York University Press, 2008), 2nd edn, pp. 100–22.

36 David Marc, *Comic Visions: Television Comedy and American Culture* (Malden, MA: Blackwell, 1997), 2nd edn; Michael Tueth, *Laughter in the Living Room: Television Comedy and the American Home Audience* (New York: Peter Lang, 2004); Ella Taylor, *Prime-Time Families: Television Culture in Post-War America* (Berkeley: University of California Press, 1991); Brett Mills, *Television Sitcom* (London: BFI, 2008); Gerard Jones, *Honey, I'm Home! Sitcoms: Selling the American Dream* (New York: St Martin's Press, 1993).

37 Catherine Johnson, *Telefantasy* (London: BFI, 2008); Glen Creeber, *Serial Television: Big Drama on the Small Screen* (London: BFI, 2008); Elayne Rapping, *Law and Justice as Seen on TV* (New York: New York University Press, 2003); Robert C. Allen, *Speaking of Soap Operas* (Chapel Hill, NC: University of North Carolina Press, 1985) and Robert C. Allen (ed.), *To Be Continued . . . Soap Operas Around the World* (New York: Routledge, 1995); Kevin Glynn, *Tabloid Culture: Trash Taste, Popular Power, and the Transformation of American Television* (Durham, NC: Duke University Press, 2000); Jonathan Gray, Jeffrey P. Jones, and Ethan Thompson (eds), *Satire TV: Politics and Comedy in the Post-Network Era* (New York: New York University Press, 2009); Susan Murray and Laurie Ouellette, (eds),

Reality TV: Remaking American Culture (New York: New York University Press, 2008), 2nd edn; Glyn Davis and Kay Dickinson (eds), *Teen TV: Genre, Consumption and Identity* (London: BFI, 2008); Sharon Marie Ross and Louisa Stein, *Teen Television: Essays on Programming and Fandom* (Jefferson, NC: McFarland, 2008).

38 Amanda Lotz (ed.), *Beyond Prime Time: Television Programming in the Post-Network Era* (New York: Routledge, 2009).

39 Mittell, *Genre and Television*, p. xii.

40 Williams, *Television*, p. 90.

41 Williams, *Television*, pp. 95, 87.

42 Horace Newcomb's project exploring the "viewing strip" at the University of Texas at Austin in the early 1980s is an exception. This study, supported by the Markle Foundation, involved analysts exploring various paths ("strip analysis") through a week's recordings of all that was on television. Some of the data is reported in Horace Newcomb, "One Night of Prime Time: An Analysis of Television's Multiple Voices," in James Carey (ed.), *Media, Myths, and Narratives: Television and the Press* (Newbury Park, CA: Sage, 1988), pp. 88–112 but, more significantly, the project supported the thinking in Horace Newcomb and Paul M. Hirsch, "Television as a Cultural Forum," *Quarterly Review of Film Studies* 8(3) (1983): 561–73. To some degree, Nick Browne's efforts to consider the political economy of "television" as a "supertext" inclusive of advertising and interstitials also used an understanding of television cognizant of flow. Nick Browne, "The Political Economy of the Television (Super) Text," in Horace Newcomb (ed.), *Television: The Critical View*, 4th edn (New York: Oxford University Press, 1987), pp. 585–99.

43 Catherine Johnson, *Branding TV* (New York: Routledge, 2011); see also Jonathan Gray, " 'Coming Up Next': Promos in the Future of Television and Television Studies," *Journal of Popular Film and Television* 38(2) (April–June 2010): 54–7.

44 Jonathan Gray, *Watching with* The Simpsons: *Television, Parody, and Intertextuality* (London: Routledge, 2006).

45 Mikhail Mikhailovich Bakhtin, *Speech Genres and Other Late Essays*, trans. Vern W. McGee, ed. Caryl Emerson and Michael Holquist (Austin: University of Texas Press, 1986), p. 69.

46 Julia Kristeva, "Word, Dialogue, Novel," in *Desire in Language: A Semiotic Approach to Literature and Art* (Oxford: Basil Blackwell, 1980), p. 66; see also Roland Barthes, *S/Z*, trans. Richard Miller (Oxford: Basil Blackwell, 1990); and Jacques Derrida, *Of Grammatology*, trans. Gayatri Chakravorty Spivak (Baltimore: Johns Hopkins University Press, 1998).

47 See in particular Susan Murray, *Hitch Your Antenna to the Stars: Early Television and Broadcast Stardom* (New York: Routledge, 2005); Mary Beltrán, *Latina/o Stars in US Eyes: The Making and Meanings of Film and TV Stardom* (Champaign: University of Illinois Press, 2009); James Bennett, "The Television Personality System: Televisual Stardom Revisited After Film Theory," *Screen* 49(1) (Spring 2009): 32–50.

48 Gérard Genette, *Paratexts: The Thresholds of Interpretation*, trans. Jane E. Lewin (Cambridge: Cambridge University Press, 1997).

49 Jonathan Gray, *Show Sold Separately: Promos, Spoilers, and Other Media Paratexts* (New York: New York University Press, 2010).

50 Will Brooker, "Living on Dawson's Creek: Teen Viewers, Cultural Convergence, and Television Overflow," *International Journal of Cultural Studies* 4(4) (December 2001): 456–72.

51 Marc Serasini, *24: The House Special Subcommittee's Findings at CTU* (New York: It Books, 2003); for commentary, see Derek Johnson, *Creative License: Media Franchising, Shared Content, and the Collaborative Production of Culture* (New York: New York University Press, 2011).

52 Henry Jenkins, *Convergence Culture: When Old and New Media Collide* (New York: New York University Press, 2006).

53 See Sharon Marie Ross, *Beyond the Box: Television and the Internet* (Malden, MA: Wiley-Blackwell, 2008); Jennifer Gillan, *Television and New Media: Must-Click TV* (New York: Routledge, 2010); Denise Mann (ed.), *Wired TV* (New Brunswick, NJ: Rutgers University Press, 2011).

54 Brian Larkin, *Signal and Noise: Media, Infrastructure, and Urban Culture in Nigeria* (Durham, NC: Duke University Press, 2008); Katrien Pype, "Of Fools and False Pastors: Tricksters in Kinshasa's Television Fiction," *Visual Anthropology* 23(2) (March 2010): 115–35, "'We Need to Open Up the Country': Development and the Christian Key Scenario in the Social Space of Kinshasa's Teleserials," *Journal of African Media Studies* 1(1) (May 2009): 101–16. See also Lila Abu-Lughod, *Dramas of Nationhood: The Politics of Television in Egypt* (Chicago: University of Chicago Press, 2005); Roxanne Varzi, *Warring Souls: Youth, Media, and Martyrdom in Post-Revolution Iran* (Durham, NC: Duke University Press, 2006); Faye D. Ginsburg, Lila Abu-Lughod, and Brian Larkin (eds), *Media Worlds: Anthropology on New Terrain* (Berkeley: University of California Press, 2002).

55 Divya McMillin, *International Media Studies* (Malden, MA: Wiley-Blackwell, 2007).

56 Ien Ang, *Desperately Seeking the Audience* (London: Routledge, 1991); Michele Hilmes, *Network Nations: A Transnational History of American and British Broadcasting* (New York: Routledge, 2011).

57 Larkin, *Signal and Noise*; Moradewun Adejunmobi, "English and the Audience of an African Popular Culture: The Case of Nigerian Video Film," *Cultural Critique* 50 (Winter 2002).

58 Lisa Parks, *Cultures in Orbit: Satellites and the Televisual* (Durham, NC: Duke University Press, 2005); Charlotte Brunsdon, "Satellite Dishes and the Landscape of Taste," in *Screen Tastes: Soap Operas and Satellite Dishes* (New York: Routledge, 1997).

59 On home theaters, see Barbara Klinger, *Beyond the Multiplex: Cinema, New Technologies, and the Home* (Berkeley: University of California Press, 2006).

60 Daniel Chamberlain, "Television Interfaces," *Journal of Popular Film and Television* 38(2) (Summer 2010): 84–8; see also Will Brooker, "Television Out of Time: Watching Cult Shows on Download," in Roberta Pearson (ed.), *Reading Lost: Perspectives on a Hit Television Show* (London: IB Tauris, 2008), pp. 53–78.

61 Max Dawson, "Television Between Analog and Digital," *Journal of Popular Film and Television* 38(2) (Summer 2010): 95–100.
62 Janet Staiger and Sabine Hake, *Convergence Media History* (New York: Routledge, 2009); Avi Santo, "*Batman* versus *The Green Hornet*: The Merchandisable TV Text and the Paradox of Licensing in the Classical Network Era," *Cinema Journal* 49(2) (Winter 2010): 63–85; Avi Santo, *Selling the Silver Bullett: Cross-Media IP Management 1933–2008* (Austin: University of Texas Press, 2012).

Conclusion

1 Horace Newcomb (ed.), *Television: The Critical View* (New York: Oxford University Press, 1976). Subsequent (and largely revised editions) were published in 1979, 1982, 1987, 1994, 2000, and 2007; James Curran, Michael Gurevitch, and Janet Woollacott (eds), *Mass Communication and Society* (Beverly Hills: Sage, 1979); then as James Curran and Michael Gurevitch, *Mass Media and Society* (London: Hodder Arnold) in 1991, 1996, 2000, 2005; and James Curran, *Media and Society* (London: Bloomsbury, 2011).
2 Julie D'Acci, *Defining Women: Television and the Case of* Cagney & Lacey (Chapel Hill: University of North Carolina Press, 1994).

Index